Adios, Strunk and White

Second Edition

Gary & Glynis Hoffman

VERVE PRESS

Adios, Strunk & White, second edition by Gary and Glynis Hoffman

ISBN 0-937363-15-4
Library of Congress Catalog Card Number: 98-61518
Printed in the United States of America
Publish by Verve Press, P.O. Box 1997, Huntington Beach, California, 92647

Printing: KNI
First Edition Printing 1997
Second Edition Printing 1999

Cover Design: Gary Hoffman
Graphic Designs: Gary Hoffman
Graphic Enhancement: Neil Hong & Signe Johnson
Page Layout: Darby's Type & Design, Inc.

Library of Congress Cataloguing-in-Publication Data
Hoffman, Gary
    Adios, strunk & white / Gary & Glynis Hoffman,—2nd ed.
      p.   cm.
    ISBN 0-937363-15-4
        1. English language — Style
        2. English language — Composition and exercises
        3. English language — Rhetoric
        4. English language — Grammar
        5. Critical Thinking   I. Hoffman,
Glynis   II. Title
PE 1408 .H46576 1999   98-61518
808.042   CIP

ACKNOWLEDGEMENTS
Our Personal Netting

Thanks for giving us our daily baguette from the La Brea Bakery; also our bread and butter, the O.C.C. English Department, and therein especially the unleavened proof-reading by the language-yeasting Donna Barnard (who was double acting), the grammar-kneader Robert Dees, and the word-sifter Geoffrey Bellah, who put his signed-by-E.B.-White *Elements of Style* aside; thanks to the U.C.Berkeley school of architecture's Bauhaus approach to learning the writing-kitchen manifest in Gary's *Writeful,* but thanks for Glynis's muse for wanting to remix and braid that book's batter lest we heap up phrases as the teachers do; thanks to "Too Hot Tamales," Mary Sue and Susan, whom we sought, asked for bread, and received a shared-third-person-point-of-view tortilla; thanks to the editors of many major publishing houses who told us to cast our bread upon the water so that it would come back to us with *Adios;* thanks be to language sandwiches—Strunk & White, Scholes & Comely, Freeman now & Freeman then; and the most thanks to the essayists in Robert Atwan and Houghton-Mifflin's *Best Essays* collections, the seek-and-you-will-find writers of *Harper's Magazine,* and great language enhancers such as Henry James, Elvis Costello, Billy Faulkner, Erich Rohmer—all of whom we take, eat, for this is the body.

CONTENTS

INTRODUCTION
The Grammar School Correction
Learning to Write Before Learning to Read
Neither a Trade Book nor Text Book Be
A Disclaimer

The Grammar School Correction

When Gary was growing up in the 1950's and early 60's, composition instruction meant pinching content into strictly defined formats, a dry, scaly burden resulting in dead papers. There was little difference between learning writing and learning trigonometry: A student persevered through blind faith that someday the worth of both would be revealed. In the early 1970's Gary began teaching, joining the academic revolution which sought to bury the scaly, dry writing beast. This revolution recognized that many good writers broke rhetorical modes and that grammatical rules were vulnerable, fractured with regional and cultural dialects. More importantly, writing was thought to be at its best when it was inspired, mostly politically inspired, and not when wrangled into ideas of correctness. As teachers understood this, they minimized rules, so that by the mid-seventies student Glynis witnessed the unraveling of writing into a free-for-all grope of touchy-feely journals, free-writing cluster balloons, and group-talk overflows. The revolution had over-compensated for the past, so that by the 1980's writing teachers had sprouted a skills-starved beanstalk. In a panic, they chopped down subjectivity and fee-fi-fo-fummed to a "back-to-basics" tune. The dry, scaly beast was back.

By the early 1990's, graduate schools, armed with deconstruction swords, began slaying the formulaic beast all over again, this time replacing the fallen creature with "process writing," a euphemism for a form-evolves-from-necessity approach to college writing. This method relied on teachers' faith that by adhering to process, students would stumble onto the usefulness of stylistic and rhetorical modes. This faith assumed students would enthusiastically truffle-up writing skills on their own time. Playing hide-and-go-seek with established writing techniques meant leaving students little time to discover and put into action the vast potential of writing techniques. Process writing became tantamount to putting a medical student in an operating room and hoping he or she would be inventive enough to learn cutting and stitching techniques before the patient bled to death: Writing is a complicated adventure, even when a person knows helpful tools.

We think it is time that teachers get off the rules-no-rules teeter-totter and start asking themselves why, for over fifty years, students have enjoyed learning in automotive, art, music, culinary, fashion design, and physical education classes but not in writing classes. For us, the reason is clear. First, students need to be taught the tools which professional writers have tested for decades, not the ones teachers have turned into painful dogma. Also, student writers cannot be asked to accept these tools on faith but must be presented the tools in ways that are immediately accessible, appealing simultaneously to both the rational and imaginative parts of the mind. This means two things must always happen: Every tool must be presented as if it were an intriguing magic wand, appearing powerful in its own right; and when the tool is tried out, students must immediately see its ability to be a language cruncher, a solution to a stylistic or organizational problem which dramatically revives a written piece. This treatment of tools and techniques is what makes art and cooking classes so energized. Students in those disciplines are never asked to accept skills on faith or defer usefulness into the distant future.

Learning to Write Before Learning to Read

Before taking our classes, many of our students had become entangled in the stylistic and organizational complexities of strong essays when they tried to read them. Our students become better readers of professional writers because the students have learned to recognize their tools when used by others. Learning how to use style enables students to comprehend the music and rhythms of writing, an exciting connection, a nexus similar to that made by an art student who has learned to use a palette knife in order to flutter millions of leaves, and thereafter can recognize when a great painter has used one as well. It is extremely difficult to even recognize what an artist or crafts person is doing if one has not tried it beforehand, and it is virtually impossible to appreciate the excellence with which a stylistic device or strategic form is used if a person has never attempted using it. A person who has tried to hit a golf ball appreciates a pro's swing more than someone who has never played golf. This means that writing comes before reading every bit as much as the standard English teacher's notion that reading comes before writing.

Selecting great writers as examples for students presents another problem. The process-writing proponents of the 1990's were inherently hypocritical in that, while they placed a gag order on form and structure in favor of endless brainstorming, revising, and cluster sniffing, these same instructors, well marinated in political correctness, felt compelled to force-feed students with socio-politically correct topics, as if only these would nourish inspired writing. Too often they rejected writers who were not topical, who did not neatly lock into an easily defined category of writing, or who had a strong personal voice. The late twentieth century has been an exciting time for the essay genre which experienced a revitalization in 1986 when Houghton Mifflin began publishing a yearly selection of expository pieces in *The Best American Essays*. Professional writers started reexamining the genre and many noted fiction writers such as Jamaica Kincaid and poets like Josephine Foo became attracted to expository writing for the richness and flexibility of the genre.

What makes these essays exciting is not whether they are topical (they usually are) or that the writers are from under-represented groups, but that the writing is energized. Shelby Steele, for instance, challenges the notion of entitlements for marginalized groups by tossing out a traditional college-textbook management of the issue, instead allowing his personal experiences, voice, and a blend of rhetorical devices, some even associated with fiction, to articulate his ideas. The result is neither strictly personal nor universal, neither sociological nor literary. It is all of these. This is the kind of writer that students should be reading. A few exist in every college reader, but we call these types of essayists the Best-American-Essay writer in honor of Houghton Mifflin's efforts to promote the idea of an essay being more than something written for and read in college courses.

Neither a Trade Book Nor a Text Book Be

Our book was conceived with teachers, students, and free-lance writers in mind. It does not pretend to fit a narrowly defined target market: It is neither a committee-toned textbook nor a personalized trade book, but something in between. Many of the approaches here will appeal to elementary school teachers, others to graduate seminar professors. This pleases us because we believe that the use of this book should be a function of the teacher's personality. The idea of an instructor's manual that tries to tell teachers how to use an instructional book makes us ill.

We never cover all of the material here in our own classes. The section on Critical Thought is usually the focus of only one or two papers in our first semester college freshman composition course, although ideally it should be the central process for every paper. We do use it as a constant focus in our second semester, critical thinking course. Both of us are thorough with the Style unit, holding off on introducing only a few of the style devices until we reach an especially relevant organizational strategy. As far as the Form unit itself goes, Glynis spends more time on a few of the strategies; Gary covers more and then allows students to drop some after working up rough drafts on them. The order in which the Forms are introduced varies to complement whatever types of essays the class is reading.

In 1919 William Strunk Jr. self-published his own textbook at Cornell entitled *The Elements of Style*, which he copyrighted in 1935. E .B. White was a student in that class, and in 1975, after Strunk died, White was asked by Macmillan to revise the book for both the college and general trade market. He did and kept updating the text until 1979, with reprints into the 1990's. For most of the twentieth century, Strunk and White's *The Elements of Style* has been the touchstone for professional writers, teachers, and students. White always admired the brevity of the book and also Strunk's "kindly lash" that made the book a series of sharp commands. Strunk and White attempted to capture the most essential elements of writing in a tightly wrapped, useful book. We like to think our book pays homage to that spirit. In other, more ideologically significant ways, we have departed from Strunk and White. Writing has too. In the last part of the twentieth century, written expression has expanded further than either Strunk or White could have dreamt of in their instructional philosophies. The rules for the twenty-first century need to be recreated and they demand new explanations, especially for a more visual-oriented, computer-literate, cyberspace-writing generation. In order to best prepare essayists for this world, we have no choice—Adios, Strunk and White.

A Disclaimer

Any of the advice in *Adios, Strunk & White* can be abused, misused, or followed without complete understanding. Strong writers always take calculated risks. Any writer who uses the advice in this book must practice it over and over again, constantly revising initial drafts and also being mature enough to know when to apply certain writing devices presented in this book and when not to. All writers are responsible for anything they write, no matter what advice they have received or whether they have clearly articulated their intentions. We take only partial credit or blame for the brilliance or gibberish which results from using this book.

1
STYLE

FLOW
PAUSE
FUSION
OPT
SCRUB

Style Before Organization

This text begins with instruction in style techniques, the small parts of writing having to do with words and sentences. Style is usually reserved for creative writing courses or discussions about literature, yet the strongest essays must be rich with style. In some ways, sentences and individual words make more difference to a piece of writing than overall organization and the general idea. Often, when we read magazine articles, newspaper columns, short stories, letters, or memos, our memories pin the overall idea or thesis onto one or two well-turned sentences and crumble away the skeletal structure of the work we have just read. Other times, we simply remember the tone of the writer's voice, created by his or her style, and that reminds us of everything we thought was important about the piece. Style is an essay's soul.

For instance, in Joy Williams' essay "The Killing Game," the writer uses style to create a sarcastic voice by using prostitution metaphors and short sentences packed with incredulity, then juxtaposing her own voice against the italicized, pro-hunting style of actual quotes Williams has lifted from hunting publications. The contrast of pro/con voices renders the pro-hunting rhetoric absurd and helps to justify William's anti-hunting arguments. Williams knows that voice and style reflect one's position. On the surface of her essay, Williams makes good points and provides support for why hunting is an appalling excuse to kill, but these examples would die if not underscored by her style.

Style creates a subtext, the mysterious under-language world that informs indirectly, and since it is indirect, writing instructors have hesitated to explore style. English teachers have always taught that essays have a major point and that such a point must be supported with examples. True, but it has been misleading to pretend that writers can travel from their introduction to a conclusion only by grafting one supporting example to another. The surface of any essay appears to be doing only this, but all the content of the essay is filtered through the writer's voice or style, and when writers neglect style, the essay is reduced to a stretched skin where all the seams show. Artificiality scars conviction and meaning. Sincerity, passion, and drama vanish.

Since style creates a writer's voice, many feel that style cannot be taught and that the distinctive styles of essayists such as Jonathan Swift, H. L. Mencken, Annie Dillard, and so many others come from these writers' DNA. Just as when we use our talking voice and body language to make our points effective, written style is largely determined by a writer's passion, understanding, and sincerity about the subject at hand; but a written piece is a crafted work, not a spontaneous outburst, and writers can refine and develop one or more styles to capture the uniqueness of their vision.

It is now feasible and necessary to teach style in composition courses. First, word processors have made stylistic revisions much easier. Also, students no longer need to spend hours planning essays: They can go straight to writing and then rewriting, devoting much more time to gradually shaping organization and spending much more time refining style. Secondly, academic writing has changed. The idea of a single, correct academic style has become passé. Colleges and universities are now populated by students and professors from diverse cultural backgrounds who bring their own style and sensibility to composition, so a writer such as Amy Tan might include a whole page of her mother's "broken English" in her essay "Mother Tongue." Also, during the last half of the twentieth century, many scholars have devoted serious thought and work to "popular culture." Not only are pop, media, and consumer cultures now subjects for serious academic discourse, writers such as Camille Paglia and William Gass blend words and images from these cultures with the priestly voice of academia, thereby depicting reality with the strengths of both literary allusions and pop imagery. In short, the distinction between learning to write essays for college and learning to write to communicate has blurred.

Style does not appear automatically when one writes. Regardless of the passion driving a writer's content, without using language principles, even the most noble thoughts and feelings can dissolve when they hit paper. The problem for most writing students is that the traditional grammatical rules for creating style can be overwhelming, and even when they are memorized, students are not encouraged to think of rules in terms of their emotional or psychological purposes. Students choke on rules that are not meaningful so we have done something never tried before. The style unit in this book boils many grammatical rules down, simplifies them, and melts them into concepts that are accessible to the playful and expressive parts of the mind. All writers, whether they are great fiction writers, business correspondents, scientific explorers, journalists, or restaurant critics, use these concepts. What writers do with them is governed by individual purposes and DNA, but all writers are using the same notes and color wheels we define in this unit to create their sounds and hues. Writing style depends on five major writing activities that together are the language of style: flow, pause, fusion, opt, and scrub. The five forces constantly combine and recombine in surprising ways to create a writer's unique voice.

FLOW:
Ways to Speed and Smooth

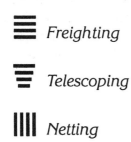 *Freighting*

Telescoping

Netting

Before we get to preschool we know how to say, "He throws the ball," and by the time we get out of first grade we can write, maybe with misspellings, "He throws the ball." But by first grade we can say so much more than we can write: "Bill, the guy who is always getting me in trouble and never listens to the teacher—but she always says 'He's trying,'—and John, the guy who fed the rat to Kurt, the python at school, both got sick and started throwing up all over the floor, the desks, and Mr. Skumawitz, the new principal everyone calls Skoomie." In his early years of teaching, Gary realized that even as adults we are afraid to write such long sentences and that until students were able to, they would never have the control and language scope available to professional writers. We both know that length-stunting stems from years of students being taught to shorten their sentences by English teachers weary from correcting length-related entanglements. Out of painful necessity, length-stunting became part of English instruction dogma.

The truth is, the sentence about Bill and John needs to be long. We make it long when we speak because we know that the characters, actions, and sub-thoughts work together to create a reality that is as exhausting and fraught with sideshows as the actual event was when it happened. The sentence's length smooths reality's flow, allowing the sentence to capture the intertwined mini experiences that together create an elongated reality. If the sentence were to be shattered into smaller sentences, the reality of the experience would be compromised, if not totally lost.

Following are three methods that smooth the flow: Freighting, Telescoping, and Netting. Strong writers use all these methods to different degrees, and you will finally combine all of them to create infinite varieties of flow, resulting in different voices that serve a multitude of purposes.

Freighting

Freighting involves thinking of the parts of a simple sentence as flat-bed freight cars, each one capable of having more similar material piled vertically on top of it. This material is then snapped onto the top of its appropriate freight load with commas. For instance, in the simple sentence "Bill chewed a red apple," there are essentially four freight cars: "Bill," "chewed," "red," and "apple." Freighting requires the writer to take a more careful look at the reality the sentence describes and decide what other details belong in the sentence's flow.

Loading.
For example, one needs to ask whether anyone other than Bill chewed the apple. If so, they are snapped on top of the "Bill" car:

> Bill, my aunt Tina, and all their cronies chewed a red apple.

Next, one looks closely at reality and decides if the apple was only chewed or whether it met another fate at the characters' hands. These actions get snapped onto the "chew" freight car:

> Bill, my aunt Tina, and all their cronies, chopped, chewed,and pulverized the red apple.

Never stop observing. Maybe the apples were not just red, and maybe more than apples filled the food trough. Using commas, snap more material on top of the "red" and "apple" cars. The final freight train could look like this:

> Bill, my aunt Tina, and all their cronies, chopped, chewed, and

utterly pulverized the red, hard, juicy, candied apple, and the mud-brown, crumbling cookies, scatter-shot with chocolate chips.

Phrases attached to the main sentence may also be viewed as freight cars. For example, if the sentence above read "While opening the door, Bill chewed a red apple," it might eventually read like this:

> While opening the door, tip-toeing across the threshold, and throwing himself at his boss's mercy, Bill chewed a red apple.

Realize too, that your piled up items do not need to be one word entries but can be phrases, adding even more information to the flow. For instance, "Bill, my aunt Tina, and all their cronies" may weigh in as,

> Bill, who you can count on to sniff out the best groceries, my aunt Tina, who is a freeloader,and all their cronies, who show up only when the larder is full . . . .

Kinks.

We have found that flow gets kinked when students forget which freight-car is getting stacked. Freighting is not an excuse to language scribble in a million directions. Remember, all the items on the subject car must stay together and then together share all the words on the verb car. If items from different cars are spread all over the flow, each subject taking its own verb off the freight car, there is a risk of creating *run-on sentences* or *comma splices*: "Bill chewed the apple, Aunt Tina pulverized the red apple." Bill and Aunt Tina must both stay together and share the freight car while "chewed" and "pulverized" stay together on theirs: "Bill and Aunt Tina chewed and pulverized the red apple."

Connecting.

Much more can be added to all the above "apple" sentences. Sentence trains can be switched onto a second track which has its own train and, if the two tracks are closely related in idea, they can be bolted together with connecting words such as "and," "but," "or," "besides," "because," and many others, including the semi-colon (;) that can be used with or replace some of these connectors. (See the Pause unit on Hieroglyphics.) The final result could read like the following:

> While opening the door, tip-toeing across the threshold, and throwing themselves at their boss's mercy, Bill, who you can

count on to sniff out the best groceries, my aunt Tina who is a freeloader, and all their cronies, who show up only when the larder is full, chopped, chewed, and utterly pulverized the red, hard, juicy, candied apple, and the mud brown, crumbling cookies, scatter-shot with chocolate chips, but this apple event is not worth developing any further, even if it makes for a telling, graphic example of a point that could result in my writing a sentence that goes on for a page but says absolutely nothing of crucial importance.

English teacherese.

If an academician questions your freighting sentence or if you need a grammar-proof description to dazzle your English teacher, here is an answer: You have written a complex sentence that many English teachers consider to be too long, complicated, and difficult to grade but that strong writers use all the time. The sentences are grammatically correct, containing multiple subjects, and/or verbs, and/or objects (direct or indirect), where each of the multiple subjects or objects is expanded with either a relative adverb clause (where, when, why) or relative pronoun clause (who, whose, whom, that, which), participle phrase (the boy *eating* butter), and/or prepositional phrase (*in, under, above* the house), and/or the verbs are expanded with an adverbial clause(*after* dinner). The sentences sometimes use either a subordinating conjunction—usually adverbial (where,when, because)—or a coordinating conjunction (and, but, or, so) to connect with another independent clause that could be expanded like the first part of the sentence.

Scope.

The taxi went up the hill, passed the light square, then on into the dark, still climbing, then leveled out onto a dark street behind St. Etienne du Mont, went smoothly down the asphalt, passed the tree and standing bus at the Place de la Contrascarpe, then turned onto the cobbles of the Rue Mouffetard. (Ernest Hemingway, *The Sun Also Rises*)

So with this reader [my mother] in mind—and in fact she did read my early drafts—I began to write stories using all the Englishes I grew up with: the English I spoke to my mother, which for lack of a better term might be described as "simple"; the English she used with me, which for lack of a better term might be described as "broken"; my translation of her Chinese, which could certainly be described as "watered down"; and what I imagined to be her translation of her Chinese if she could speak in perfect English, her internal language, and for that I sought to preserve the essence, but neither an English nor a Chinese structure. I wanted to capture what language ability tests can never reveal: her intent, her passion, her imagery, the rhythms of her speech and the nature of her thoughts. (Amy Tan, "Mother Tongue," *The Threepenny Review*)

Now, suddenly, we were in the hands of Man; that is, in the hands of Mom and Dad, proud in their new possession, proud because they have fulfilled their function, happy because they are supposed to be happy, cooing their first coos, which will be our first words—*coup de coude, coup de bec, coup de tête, coup de main, coup d'état, coup de grâce* —while we wonder why we are wet and where the next suck is coming from, or why there is so much noise when we bawl, why we are slapped and shaken, why we are expected to run on empty and not scream when stuck or cry when chafed, not shit so much, and not want what we want when we want it. (William Gass, "Exile," *Salmagundi*)

The petals spill and spill into the aisle, and a child goes past this couple who have just come from their wedding—goes past them and past them, going always to the toilet but really just going past them; and the child could be a horse or she could be the police and they'd not notice her any more than they do, which is not at all—the man's hands high up the woman's legs, her skirt up, her stocking and garters, the petals and finally all the flowers spilling out into the aisle and his mouth open on her. My mother. My father. I am conceived near Dallas in the dark while a child passes, a young girl who knows and doesn't know, who witnesses, in glimpses, the creation of the universe, who feels an odd hurt as her mother, fat and empty, snores with her mouth open, her false teeth slipping down, snores and snores just two seats behind the Creators. (Judy Ruiz, "Oranges and Sweet Sister Boy," *Iowa Woman*)

Some [new flower varieties from one hundred million years ago] were pale unearthly night flowers intended to lure moths in the evening twilight, some among the orchids even took the shape of female spiders in order to attract wandering males, some flamed redly in the light of noon or twinkled modestly in the meadow grasses. (Loren Eisley, "How Flowers Changed the World," *The Immense Journey*)

I fought migraine then, ignored the warnings it sent, went to school and after to work in spite of it, sat through lectures in Middle English and presentations to advertisers with involuntary tears running down the right side of my face, threw up in washrooms, stumbled home by instinct, emptied ice trays onto my bed and tried to freeze the pain in my right temple, wished only for a neurosurgeon who would do a lobotomy on house call, and cursed my imagination. (Joan Didion, *The White Album*)

So descended the Lem, weird unwieldy flying machine, vehicle on stilts and never before landed, craft with a range of shifting velocities more than comparable to the difference from a racing car down to an amphibious duck, a vehicle with huge variations in speed and handling as it slowed, a vehicle to be flown for the first time in the rapidly changing field of gravity, and one-sixth gravity had never been experienced before in anything but the crudest simulations, and mascons beneath, their location unknown, their effect on moon gravity considerable, angles of vision altering all the time and never near to perfect, the weight of the vehicle reducing drastically as the fuel was consumed, and with it all, the computer guiding them, allowing them to feel all the confidence a one-eyed man can put in a blind man going down a dark alley, and when, at the moment they would take over themselves to fly it manually, a range of choices already tried in simulation but never in reality would be open between full manual and full computer. (Norman Mailer, *Of a Fire on the Moon*)

Thomas Jefferson is definitely the most interesting person to ever set forth on this earth, completing what would seem impossible for one man to do in a lifetime, including abolishing slave trade in Virginia; advocating the decimal monetary system; organizing the Northwest Territory; purchasing the Louisiana territory; officiating as the First Secretary of the State, Second Vice President, and the President of the American Philosophical Society; designing the Virginia State Capitol, University of Virginia, part of the design for Washington D.C., and his home Monticello; however, the three achievements that he himself valued most highly, which he directed to be inscribed on his tombstone, stand out the most: Author of the Declaration of America Independence, author of the Statue of Virginia Religious Freedom, and Father of the University of Virginia. (Bill Singer, student)

Then she looked around the Salon and made the encompassing shrug-and-pout-and-flex-your-hands-from-the-wrist French gesture that in that context meant that the apparent absurdity of the act of fanning yourself in the cold is no more absurd than the whole enterprise of traveling to Paris to look at clothes that you will never wear, displayed on models to whom you bear no resemblance, in order to help a designer get people who will never attend shows like this to someday buy a perfume or a scarf that will give them the consoling illusion that they have a vague association with the kind of people who do attend shows like this — even though the people who attend shows like this are the kind who fan themselves against July heat that happens not to exist. (Adam Gopnik, "Couture Shock," *The New Yorker*)

Workout.

Write ten flow sentences, using the freighting technique, each one about a different aspect of your life: one about foods you enjoy, one about films or books that mean much to you, one about your family or work. They should each be six typed lines long and numbered; do not worry about putting them in an essay. As with the sample sentences, some freight cars should be stacked high with weighty material, other cars may be left with one item, and if you need to, use a connecting word (a conjunction) only one time per sentence to attach a related sentence train to your first train in order to sustain a longer flow.

Telescoping

Telescoping is another flow technique that demands that the writer view reality more closely. Although Gary devised this flow method especially for film and visual arts students to carefully examine a visual scene, Telescoping is also a structure for zooming through the intricacies of an intellectual concept. Telescoping differs from Freighting in that there is no vertical piling up of material. The initial observation in the form of a sentence is left alone. The period at the end of that sentence is replaced by a comma which acts like a zoom lens to start the telescoping. Instead of imagining freight cars, your mind's eye acts as if it were a camera with an attached telephoto lens.

Zooming.
Consider the following simple sentence about an architectural experience we both enjoyed:

> We toured the Hollyhock house.

Instead of adding more cargo to the sentence's freight cars, the sentence is left alone—no more people are added to the subject "we," no more actions are added to the verb "tour," and no more objects were toured beside the "Hollyhock house." Next the writer replaces the period after "house" with a comma, the comma representing a telephoto lens zooming up closer to any detail on any of the items in the original sentence, which could be "we," "tour," or the "Hollyhock house." If the writer decides to zoom up to the house itself, the sentence could now read:

> We toured the Hollyhock house, the walls composed of many prefabricated, cement blocks.

The period at the end of this two-part sentence may also be replaced with a comma, but now the writer may only zoom onto one of the last phrases details—"walls," "composed," "prefabricated," "cement," or "blocks"— because now these details are all that remain in the "camera's" frame. Since the sentence has zoomed onto the wall, the writer cannot zoom up to any details in the we-toured-Hollyhock-house part of the sentence (or other-

21

wise the sentence might have a *dangling modifier*.)

Now, for a second zoom, the writer can zoom up closer to the wall by focusing on the detail "blocks." The writer then ends up with the following sentence:

> We toured the Hollyhock house, the walls of the house com-
> posed of many prefabricated blocks, the blocks' abstract de-
> sign cast as a hollyhock flower, hollyhocks being the house's
> dominant motif.

The psychology behind building this sentence works like this: "We toured the Hollyhock house," (zoom up closer to the house) "the walls composed of many prefabricated blocks," (zoom up closer to the blocks), "the blocks' abstract design cast as a hol-lyhock flower," (zoom up closer to the flower to make a closing assessment) "hollyhocks being the house's dominant motif."

Panning.

At this point the writer could use a fourth comma to zoom onto a detail in the last phrase; however, most writers find little occasion to zoom more than once or twice. Instead, the writer would prob-ably now use a comma and a connecting word ("and," "but," "while," "since"), to "pan" over or "pull back" to another detail, or another idea, outside of the details from the last phrase. Pan-ning connects two sentences into one called a *compound* sen-tence. After the connecting word, this new "shot" would start over as a new sentence with its own complete verb and telescop-ing clauses. For instance, using "and" to connect, the sentence above could read,

> We toured the Hollyhock house, the walls composed of many
> prefabricated blocks, the abstract design of a hollyhock flower
> cast as the blocks' dominant motif, and the boldness of the
> blocks helped to emphasize the horizontal weight of the house,
> a weight reminiscent of Mayan government architecture.

Telescoping sentences do not have to be about physical realities; they can also describe conceptual realities. For instance, con-sider the sentence "Jesse decided to challenge Joseph Campbell's ideas." Replacing the period with a comma, the writer could "zoom" up on a more detailed description or analysis of this chal-lenge. Of course, these sentences can also expand with a con-necting word, such as "since." The final result might be,

> Jesse decided to challenge Joseph Campbell's ideas, Jesse

shuddering at Campbell's equating Buddha at rest under a tree with Jesus suffering on the crucifixion 'tree,' since the Buddha image represented contentment with the cycle of life, the productive tree creating a sharp contrast to the punishing cross, an eternal symbol of betrayal.

Kinks.

Telescoping sentences can trap you. If the zoomed focuses are described with complete verbs, then the sentence becomes a *comma splice*, an error created by splicing together complete sentences with commas instead of separating with periods, semicolons, or connecting words. To avoid comma splices, make sure only one part of the sentence has a complete verb and all the phrases that zoom up have incomplete verbs. In the Jesse sentence above, the complete verb is "decided," and then the zoom up on Jesse uses the incomplete verb "shuddering" instead of "shudders" or "shuddered" or "was shuddering," which are all verbs that would turn the "Jesse shuddering at Campbell equating Buddha at rest . . ." section into a complete sentence, breaking the flow by requiring a period instead of a comma after the word "ideas." On the other hand, when using a connecting word such as "since," you must add a new complete verb. Without the connecting word "since," and with only a comma to tie the flow together, the compete verb "represent" would have to become incomplete, "representing."

Closure.

Glynis realized that by having a complete phrase, followed by incomplete phrases, and therefore finally ending on one of those incomplete phrases, a rhythm takes over that gradually dissipates the impact of the sentence. This very focused detail, coupled with the incomplete phrase, sometimes destroys psychological closure. There are other options for ending telescoping sentences. One is to try moving the complete phrase to the end of the sentence. For instance, instead of writing

> We toured the house, our shoes scuffing the wooden floors, each shoe mark creating an architectural sacrilege,

one might write

> Our shoes scuffing the wooden floors, each heel mark creating an architectural sacrilege, we toured the house.

A second approach is to end with a phrase beginning with a connecting word such as "which" or "that" and a complete verb:

> We toured the house, our shoes scuffing the wooden floors, scuffs that became architectural sacrileges.

A third approach is to compound the last incomplete phrase with a complete thought— a connecting word and complete verb. For instance,

> We toured the house, our shoes scuffing the wooden floors, each shoe mark creating an architectural sacrilege, but we knew to take off our shoes the next time we visited.

If the connection is "for," "and," "nor," "but", "or," "yet," "so," then consider using a semi-colon (;) instead, which can replace any of these connectors if there are complete sentences on both sides of the semi-colon. We find students' fear of semi-colons irrational. Semi-colons can't hurt you. (See Hieroglyphics in the Pause section for more explanation.)

English teacherese.

If you start feeling guilty that you do not know the grammar behind telescoping sentences, or if your favorite editor gets insecure about what the hell you think you are doing, know this: You are crafting complex sentences discouraged by English teachers because they are too long, complicated, and difficult to grade. However they are grammatically correct because they contain an independent clause (a structure that contains both a subject and predicate that can stand as a complete sentence) and several dependent clauses (structures containing both a subject and predicate that are unable to stand independently as sentences) and/or nominative absolutes (a modifier with a nonfinite verb, a verb form lacking a necessary auxiliary to denote tense, usually a participle, which is a verb form using -ing or -en, or past participle, a verb form using -en or -ed), and that the sentence connects these dependent clauses or nominative absolutes so as not to create misplaced or dangling modifiers. Some of the sentences use a subordinating conjunction—usually adverbial (where, when, because)—or a coordinating conjunction (and, but, or, so) to connect with another independent clause and dependent clauses constructed the same way as the first part of the sentence.

Scope.
Cathy Smith was waiting at home for her date, reading the new *Seventeen Magazine*, the article about love and romance still simmering in her mind when the doorbell rang. (Michelle Larson, student)

The minimalist tendency to offer the anguished facts and allow the seeker to supply the emotional caption is culminated in a stark and dark modern monument, the Vietnam Veterans Memorial, a black wall furnished with no rhetoric, simply the names and dates, row on row, achieving, below ground level, the monitory and pathetic impact of that archaic epitaph on a Greek cliff top: *When my ship sank, the others sailed on.* (Mary Hood, "Why Stop?," *The Gettysburg Review*)

When the ants are massed together, all touching, exchanging bits of information held in their jaws like memoranda, they become a single animal. (Lewis Thomas, *The Medusa and the Snail: More Notes on a Biology Watcher*)

Many of the Brothers Grimm fairy tales contain violent images, a darker side to life that is usually edited out in Disney versions, resulting in sappy stories with unambiguous views towards good and evil; I would like to see a new animator redo the stories, blending Disney cuddliness with the Grimms' original gruesomeness, Cinderella dancing with her Prince while cutsey mice dance around the mutilated, bleeding feet of the stepsisters, bitchy girls desperate enough to chop off their toes to make the shoe fit, a demand made by their mother in the original. (Cynthia Brown, student)

People sidle toward [suicidal] death, intent upon outwitting their own bodies' defenses, or they may dramatize the chance to make one last, unambiguous, irrevocable decision, like a captain scuttling his ship—death before dishonor—leaping toward oblivion through a curtain of pain, like a frog going down the throat of a snake. (Edward Hoagland, "Heaven and Nature," *Harper's Magazine*)

So to Ged, who had never been down from the heights of the mountain, the port of Gont was an awesome and marvelous place, the great houses and towers of cut stone and waterfront of piers and docks and basins and moorages, the seaport where half a hundred boats and galleys rocked at quayside or lay hauled up and overturned for repairs or stood out at anchor in the road-stead with furled sails and closed oarports, the sailors shouting in strange dialects and the longshoremen running heavy-laden amongst barrels and boxes ad coils of rope and stacks of oars, the bearded merchants in furred robes conversing quietly as they picked their way along the slimy stones above the water, the fish-ermen unloading their catch, coopers pounding and shipmakers hammering, the clam sellers singing and shipmasters bellowing, and beyond all, the silent, shining bay. (Ursula LeGuin, *A Wizard of Earthsea*)

Seeing the radiating minerals is a beautiful visual experience, which is even more fascinating when integrated with your knowl-edge of nature's submicroscopic happenings, high-energy ultra-violet photons impinging on the surface of the minerals, causing the excitation of atoms in the mineral structure; and then the radiation of light frequencies corresponding exactly to the tiny energy-level spacings, and every excited atom emitting its char-acteristic frequency, with no two different minerals giving off ex-actly the same color light. (Paul G. Hewitt, *Conceptual Physics*)

Is man at heart any different from the spider, I wonder: man thoughts, as limited as spider thoughts, contemplating now the nearest star with the threat of bringing with him the fungus rot from earth, wars, violence, the burden of a population he refuses to control, cherishing again his dream of the Adamic Eden he had pursued and lost in the green forests of America. (Loren Eisely, "The Hidden Teacher," *The Unexpected Universe*)

Chuck Close's forty-by-forty-foot portrait painting of "Bob" is a titanic, bespectacled monument, Bob's face composed of wide, sparkling eyes and relaxed, ready-to-smile lips in an expression of moderate surprise and amusement, both eyes and lips be-coming acute, photo-realistic campgrounds for the eye, their normally minute lights and shadows of wrinkles, folds, and pores exaggerated to create whimsical forms: slopes, canyons, peaks, craters, lakes, summits, and fault lines. (Gina Smith, student)

Workout.
Usually writers never telescope more than once before they end the sentence or "pan" to another object for the remainder of the sentence. However, in this work out, you will gain more confidence and control by forcing yourself to telescope on a telescope, even if you rarely telescope more than once per sentence in your essays. Pick a comfortable environment such as a landscape, restaurant, or social event and observe details of the people and physical setting. Write ten telescoping sentences, zooming at least twice onto specific details in each sentence before you pan using a connecting word. Have a few of your sentences describe intellectual or emotional thoughts about the setting you are observing. Your sentences should be at least six typed lines long, but you can sometimes use connecting words.

Netting

||||

Glynis uncovered another important flow technique used by all writers. We call it Netting. In our everyday lives we create simple lists to trap our thoughts: grocery lists, things-to-do lists, accounting of bills, guests lists, movies to see, pro-con lists, but we forget to take advantage of listing when we write essays. Great essayists do not forget.

Netting can occur inside a Freighting or Telescoping sentence or on its own; it can be a series of clauses joined together with commas and semi-colons, or long sentences combined with short, incomplete sentences. Netting can be a catalog of situations, a litany of complaints or commands, or a drawer of intriguing images. Netting works by tenacity, wherein the build-up of items or images, by sheer number, combine to create a gestalt that is a multi-layered composite of reality. Rap songs are netted lists. Lists can be helpful in essays as a way of defining or exemplifying a particular abstract concept since all the items in the Netting are knotted together with a common denominator. In his essay "Burls," Bernard Cooper makes use of a short list to emphasize a point about an important personal realization:

> Like most children, I once thought it possible to divide the world into male and female columns. Blue/Pink. Rooster/ Hens. Trousers/Skirts. Such division were easy, not to mention comforting for they simplified matter into compatible pairs. But there also existed a vast range of things that didn't fit neatly into either camp: clocks, milk, telephones, grass.

Cooper gives a short list of things which cannot be easily sexed or paired. The essayist's list is brief, this brevity giving his idea some very-short-sentence punch. But when lists become extended —longer than one line, taking up whole paragraphs in an essay—then writers must arrange ideas and images in an ordering rhythm which takes advantage of the Netting's ability to capture, sustain, and reinforce an idea. Sometimes the rhythmic patterns can be so distinct that the Netting musically scores it's own piece within the larger composition of the essay. This super-netted concentration results in a non-fiction mini-performance: An expository aria. When writers purposefully craft lists, they take advantage of three weaving concepts—specificity, sizing, and juxtaposition.

Specificity.

All effective Nettings are composed of specific details. Comedy writers know the advantage of using a specific word or detail to help create rich humor. During one monologue, comedian Jerry Seinfeld satirizes and exaggerates the situation of friends who tell us to use them as referrals when going to their doctor: "Be sure you tell Dr. Smith I sent you." Unlike a salesperson, an ethical doctor would not give preferential treatment because of who a patient knows. Seinfeld satirizes such a mentality, role-playing the doctor's response: "Oh, Joe sent you. We'll give you the real pills; everybody else we've just been giving Tic-Tacs." Seinfeld knows there is an advantage in naming a specific, capsule-shaped candy whose brand name is easily recognized and associated with silly gimmickry. If he used "candy" or "fake pills" instead of

"Tic-Tacs," the comic charge would have been lost.

Using specificity means using richly detailed and non-general language to fill out reality. For instance, if you were creating a list of "things that are green" as a way of defining the abstract concept of greenness, you might include "trees" on your list, but reality becomes more sharply edged if you name a particular kind of tree—a Douglas Fir. Getting even more specific, you could narrow down to a function for Douglas Firs such as Christmas trees, especially if you wanted to evoke a happy holiday association with the color green. The more you close in on reality, the more specific Christmas trees become. There are white or flocked Christmas trees; so inserting a specific adjective can keep the tree green: "Christmas trees" becomes "unflocked Christmas trees." Or you can use a metaphoric adjective, which Gary calls Line-Ups (see the Fusion section), and your list of things that are green can include a "naive Christmas tree," which metaphorically captures the idea of fresh green and an ominous sense that the Christmas holiday may be vulnerable to unsuspected human tensions.

Sizing.

Creating specificity does not mean reducing items to single word entries. Professional writers know that the length of entries inside a Netting should be varied. This variation adds depth to the list while opening the opportunity for the rhythms. Lists which are longer than two lines but have only one word entries can get boring. A list of single words separated only by commas knots the Netting with a plodding pace. Consider the following Netting on gluttony:

> Gluttony: Gobble, gulping, gorging, gross, greedy, hungry, indulge, feasting, fat, obese, overeating, piggy, hefty, large, stuff, surplus, saturation, voracious, rapacious.

Even though there is specificity, by the time the reader gets to the second line the list has worn the reader out—there are no open spaces to relieve with surprise or insight. Compare the above to another Netting defining gluttony crafted by student writer Vanessa Schueler:

> Thanksgiving dinner or a New Year's eve party: overindulgent, guzzling, swinish belly-worship, binge drinking—praying to the

29

porcelain god. Preferring shots to mixed drinks; intoxication, inebriety, unrestrained addiction a la Robert Downy, Jr., Timothy Leary, the summer of love, oversexed, lush, lust, nymphomaniacal, wild, wolfish appetite for destruction, The Vampire Lestat, omnivorous, wasteful, untempered, spendthrift, shopoholic, sin. Gluttony is an emotional escape; a sign something is eating you: depression, austerity, spareness, sobriety.

Although the second Netting is more than twice as long as the first list on Gluttony, Schueler takes advantage of the different sizes of her entries to make the Netting more complex and informative.

Juxtaposition.

Aside from being a favorite cheese-and-wine-party word for English teachers, juxtaposition is an important concept when Netting. Once specificity is obtained, arrangement becomes crucial. Juxtaposition is simply the concept of placing two items or images next to each other. Juxtaposed items create meaningful strands, ultimately bringing order to a random sack of groceries. When Glynis's mother used to make out grocery lists, she would arrange items according to their sections in the supermarket: all produce bundled in a list, dairy products wired together, canned goods stacked together.

In Vanessa Schueler's Netting, longer statements are juxtaposed with single word entries which function as examples, associations, or reiteration of larger concepts. Schueler also uses *alliteration* (the repetition of sounds in close proximity such as Vanessa's "s" and "sh" sounds) in some places as a stitching tool. In Glynis's things-that-are-green list, she begins by choosing categories, twist-tying all the green food items into a cohesive string, groving all green plants near each other, and finally colonizing the green bugs and insects. In order to weave these strings together into a larger strand, some green items function as interesting transitions. Therefore, to seamlessly stitch the food list to the plants list, Glynis uses an item that can go both ways, such as "parsley," a leafy plant that can be eaten. Or since burrito was the last item in the food string, why not use "cilantro," then "parsley," and then "poison ivy" before moving on to larger plants? All three items together create a smooth, transitional tie.

If the writer wants to capture an experience that is real but seems imagined or a dream that seems real (sometimes referred to as *magic realism*) then Juxtaposition works magic. For instance, in *The Diaries of Anais Nin,* Nin discovers Fez, Morocco, "a city which is an image of one's inner cities," having "the layers and secrecies of the inner life." Her Netting centers on in-out imagery in order to dissipate the line between the conscious and subconscious mind: houses are "intricately interwoven" by bridges and passageways and by shadows from lattice work "that seem to be crossing within a house." Sometimes Nin's mosaic shock-cuts the concrete with the irrational:

> Mosques run into a merchant's home, shops into mosques, now you are under a trellised roof covered with rose vines, now walking in utter darkness through a tunnel, behind a donkey raw and bleeding from being beaten, and now you are on a bridge built by the Portuguese.

In describing another excursion, this time in Puerto Vallarta, Mexico, Nin even nets adjectives, describing birds' sounds by listing musical instruments that sound like birds, blending the real and unreal:

> Then the birds, vivid, loud, vigorous, talkative, whistles, cries, gossip, clarinets, and flutes.

Other nets collapse the general world into the intimate:

> Passive drinking in of color, the cafes, the shops, people; and the thrill of looking into open homes, open windows, open doors. An old lady in a rocking chair. Photographs on the walls. Palm leaves from last year's ritual Easter.

Scope.

A Netting of what it means to be alive: To see the golden sun and the azure sky, the out-stretched ocean, to walk upon the green earth, and to be lord of a thousand creatures, to look down giddy precipices or over distant flowery vales, to see the world spread out under one's finger in a map, to bring the stars near, to view the smallest insects in a microscope, to read history, and witness the revolutions of empires and the succession of generations, to hear the glory of Sidon and Tyre, of Babylon and Susa, as of a faded pageant, and to say all these were, and are now nothing, to think that we exist in such a point of time, and in such a corner of space, to be at once spectators and a part of the moving scene, to watch the return of the seasons, of spring and autumn. . . to traverse desert wildernesses, to listen to the midnight choir, to visit lighted halls, or plunge into the dungeon's gloom, or sit in crowded theaters and see life itself mocked, to feel heat and cold, pleasure and pain, right and wrong, truth and falsehood, to study the works of art and refine the sense of beauty to agony, to worship fame and to dream of immortality, to have read Shakespeare and belong to the same species as Sir Isaac Newton; to be and to do all this, and then in a moment to be nothing, to have it all snatched from one like a juggler's ball or a phantasmagoria; there is something revolting and incredible to sense in the transition, and no wonder that, aided by youth and warm blood, and the flush of enthusiasm, the mind contrives for a long time to reject it with disdain and loathing as a monstrous and improbable fiction, like a monkey on a house-top, that is loath, amidst its fine discoveries and specious antics, to be tumbled head-long into the street, and crushed to atoms, the sport and laughter of the multitude! (William Hazlitt, "On the Feeling of Immortality in Youth")

A Netting of things that are English: And they [the English] ate so much food, violating another of those rules they taught me: do not indulge in gluttony. And the foods they ate actually: if only sometime I could eat cold cuts after theater, cold cuts of lamb and mint sauce, and Yorkshire pudding and scones, and clotted cream, and sausages that came from upcountry (imagine, "upcounty"). And having troubling thoughts at twilight, a good time to have troubling thoughts, apparently; and servants who stole and left in the middle of a crisis, who were born with a limp or some other kind of deformity, not nourished properly in their mother's womb (that last part I figured out for myself; the point was, oh to have an untrustworthy servant): and wonderful cobbled streets onto which solid front doors opened; and people whose eyes were blue and who had fair skins and who smelled only of lavender, or sometimes sweet pea or primrose. And those flowers with those names: delphiniums, foxgloves, tulips, daffodils, floribunda, peonies; in bloom, a striking display, being cut and placed in large glass bowls, crystal, decorating rooms so large twenty families the size of mine could fit in comfortably but used only for passing through. And the weather was so remarkable because the rain fell gently always, only occasionally in deep gusts, and it colored the air various shades of gray, each an appealing shade for a dress to be worn when a portrait was being painted; and when it rained at twilight, wonderful things happened: people bumped into each other unexpectedly and that would lead to all sort of turns of events — a plot, the mere weather caused plots. (Jamaica Kincaid, *On Seeing England for the First Time*)

Two Nettings of reasons for suicide: People not only lose faith in their talents and their dreams or values; some simply tire of them. Grow tired, too, of the smell of fried-chicken grease, once such a delight, and the cold glutinosity of ice cream, the boredom of beer, the stop-go of travel, the hiccups of laughter, and of two rush hours a day, then the languor of weekends, of athletes as well as accountants, and even the frantic birdsong of spring— red-eyed vireos that have been clocked singing twenty-two thou- sand times in a day. . . I'm tired of weathermen and sportscasters on the screen. Of being patient and also of impatience. I'm tired of the president, whoever the president happens to be, and sleep- ing badly, with forty-eight half-hours in the day—of breaking two eggs every morning and putting sugar on something. I'm tired of the drone of my own voice, but also of us jabbering like parrots at each other—of all our stumpy ways of doing everything. (Ed- ward Hoagland, "Heaven and Nature," *Harper's Magazine*)

A Netting of ways a husband tries to educate his wife: How had he attempted to remedy this state of comparative ignorance [in his wife]? Variously. By leaving in a conspicuous place a certain book open at a certain page: by assuming in her, when alluding explanatorily, latent knowledge: by open ridicule in her presence of some absent other's ignorant lapse. With what success had he attempted direct instruction? She followed not all, a part of the whole, gave attention with interest, comprehended with surprise, with care repeated, with greater difficulty remembered, forgot with ease, with misgiving reremembered, rerepeated with error. What system had proved more effective? Indirect suggestion implicat- ing self-interest. (James Joyce, "Ithaca," *Ulysses*)

A Netting of things we wait for: Of course, we do not just wait for love; we wait for money, we wait for the weather to get warmer, colder, we wait for the plumber to come and fix the washing ma- chine (he doesn't), we wait for a friend to give us the name of another plumber (she doesn't), we wait for our hair to grow, we wait for our children outside of school, we wait for their exam results, we wait for the letter that will undo all desolation, we wait for Sunday, when we sleep in or have the extra piece of toast, we wait for the crocuses to come up, then the daffodils, we wait for the estranged friend to ring or write and say, "I have forgiven you," we wait for our parents to love us even though they may be long since dead, we wait for the result of this or that medical test, we wait for the pain in the shoulder to ease, we wait for that sense of excitement that has gone underground but is not quite quenched, we wait for the novel that enthralls the way it happened when we first read *Jane Eyre* or *War and Peace,* we wait for the invitation to the country, and often when we are there, we wait for the bus or the car that will ferry us home to the city and our props, our own chairs, our own bed, our own habits. We wait for the parties we once gave that somehow had a luster that parties we now give completely lack. We wait (at least I do) for new potatoes, failing to concede that there are new potatoes all the time, but the ones I am waiting for were the ones dug on the twenty-ninth of June in Ireland that tasted (or was it imagination?) like no others. We wait to go to sleep and maybe fog ourselves with pills or soothing tapes to lull us thither. We wait for dreams, then we wait to be hauled out of our dreams and wait for dawn, the postman, tea, coffee, the first ring of the telephone, the advancing day. (Edna O'Brien, "Waiting")

Workout.

In order to practice crafting a list and using the concept of specificity, sizing and juxtaposition, make a list of everything suggested by an abstract term such as one of the seven deadly sins—pride, envy, wrath, sloth, avarice, gluttony, and lust. Writers will want to include not only synonyms for the term but associations—foods, television shows, and people (celebrities and intimacies), habits, mentalities, and shocking items. Try to write for ten minutes without stopping. You can work on specificity now and later.

Another consideration is how to start or end the list. Writers generally choose a pertinent image to begin and end a Netting. William Hazlitt's Netting of what it means to be alive begins with an image of dawn, ". . . the golden sun an azure sky." In ending a Netting, a writer might offer some final, punctuated thought as closure. Vanessa Schueler's Netting ends on a possible antonym of gluttony: Sobriety. A writer can underscore a sense of closure at the end of the netting by slowing the pace of the list as he or she winds down toward the period.

Once items are ordered into strands, the Netting needs the finishing stitches of Pause and Flow to control pace. Commas are the punctuation marks most commonly associated with linking items in a list; however, entries in a Netting can be joined and separated with colons, semi-colons, and dashes to modulate the relationship between juxtaposed items. (See the next unit on Pause.) The drama and emphasis created by specificity and juxtaposition, works best when used in tandem with Pause—melted-together words, very short sentences, and hieroglyphics— to communicate punch.

Cool down.

Working with a partner, try to combine lists using juxtaposition, arranging the items on both lists in such a way as to create drama. Also start matching up items that go together because they are related in concept, create a rhythm, or perhaps all begin with a certain sound. As you create strings, you will also be using specificity again to help details from both lists go together.

PAUSE:
Ways to Slow and Emphasize

△ *Very Short Sentence*

△ *Melted-together Words*

△ *Hieroglyphics*

△ *Super-literalism*

Being able to flow, to smooth together details and thoughts which belong together to accurately depict reality is just as important as being able to stop this flow, to create pause in order to emphasize or dramatize special thoughts that otherwise would blend into larger language clusters. Pause sometimes occurs after flow, sometimes in the middle of flow. Pause tools seem easier to learn than flow techniques, but making them work is best appreciated after flow has been mastered because flow gives pause its context. There are many ways to create pause. The following four essential pause techniques all possess an important visual dimension and all have the ability to quickly heighten a reader's understanding or consciousness. All strong writers, whether they are business, scientific, fiction, or media writers, use the Very Short Sentence, Melted-together Words, Hieroglyphics, and Super-literalism for a multitude of effects.

Very Short Sentence

The two to five word sentence is something we learn to write in the first grade. Later, we vaporize it. Maybe we abandon it because as we get older we associate longer sentences with having important, complicated ideas to write about, or perhaps by college we feel too much pressure to get all thoughts down quickly, running together masses of details from textbooks and reams of pushed-together lecture notes. In this mental environment, the short sentence is squashed. When it appears in essays, it is a surprise. It makes us stop.

Depending on its context, the very short sentence has different potentials. It can be climactic, create finality, or give emphasis to a previously mentioned item. Without the very short sentence, a writer cannot create expectation, sarcasm, certitude, hopefulness, reversals, or edginess. In the midst of many flowing sentences, depending on its content, the very short sentence has the power to shock or sting. The very short sentence also can help underscore material that is describing something fast, terse, or tense.

Scope.

Feel the ball, turn it over in your hand; hold it across the seam or the other way, with the seam just to the side of your middle finger. Speculation stirs. You want to get outdoors and throw this spare and sensual object to somebody or, at the very least, watch somebody else throw it. The game has begun. (Roger Angell, *Five Seasons, a Baseball Companion*)

In the Koran, Allah asks, "The heaven and the earth and all in between, thinkest thou I made them in jest?" It's a good question. (Annie Dillard, *Pilgrim at Tinker Creek*)

Camouflaged toilet paper is a must for the modern hunter, along with his Bronco and his beer. Too many hunters taking a dump in the woods with their roll of Charmin beside them were mistaken for white-tailed deer and shot. Hunters get excited. (Joy Williams, "The Killing Game," *Esquire*)

All the same, if a cure were found, would I take it? In a minute. I may be a cripple, but I'm only occasionally a loony and never a saint. Anyway, in my brand of theology God doesn't give bonus points for a limp. I'd take a cure; I just don't need one. A friend who also has MS startled me once by asking, "Do you ever say to yourself, 'Why me, Lord?'" "No, Michael, I don't," I told him, "because whenever I try, the only response I can think of is 'Why not?'" If I could make a cosmic deal, who would I put in my place? What in my life would I give up in exchange for sound limbs and a thrilling rush of energy? No one. Nothing. I might as well do the job myself. Now that I'm getting the hang of it. (Nancy Mairs, "On Being a Cripple," *Plaintext: Deciphering a Woman's Life*)

So what is sent away when we are forced out of our homeland? Words. It is to get rid of our words that we are gotten rid of, since speech is not a piece of property which can be confiscated . . . but is the center of the self itself. (William Gass, "Exile," *Salmagundi*)

It was easy to read the message in [Snowden the gunner's] entrails. Man was matter, that was Snowden's secret. Drop him out a window and he'll fall. Set fire to him and he'll burn. Bury him and he'll rot like other kinds of garbage. The spirit gone, man is garbage. That was Snowden's secret. Ripeness was all. (Joseph Heller, *Catch 22*)

And they [white brothers] have come to realize that their freedom is inextricably bound to our freedom. We cannot walk alone. And as we walk, we must make the pledge that we shall always march ahead. We cannot turn back. (Martin Luther King, "I Have a Dream")

For though I am a wholly vicious man/ Don't think I can't tell moral tales. I can! (Geoffrey Chaucer, "The Pardoner's Prologue," *The Canterbury Tales*)

I have neither heard nor read that a Santa Ana [wind] is due, but I know it, and almost everyone I have seen today knows it too. We know it because we feel it. The baby frets. The maid sulks. I rekindle a waning argument with the telephone company, then cut my losses and lie down, given over to whatever it is in the air. (Joan Didion, *Slouching Towards Bethlehem*)

Your time of decay may be distant, but it will surely come, for even the White Man whose God walked and talked with him as friend with friend, cannot be exempt from the common destiny. We may be brothers after all. We will see. (Chief Seattle, "Reply to Governor Steven")

Melted-together Words

Many English words are made by melting together other words with hyphens. For instance, the words "blue" and "green" mean two different colors, but when they are melted with a hyphen into a third word, "blue-green," they are now both part of a new word and a whole new color. Years ago, Gary noticed students were never taught that strong writers often create new words, melting together words never joined together before. These words can be created as long as they function as a single word in the structure of the sentence, typically as a single word adjective, less often as a noun.

Melted-together Words, because of their uniqueness, their cleverness, and heavy content load, slow sentence flow and focus attention on their content. We always enjoy the wit these fresh words offer. The packed material of original hyphenated words transforms simple sentences into show-stoppers, the melted-together word focusing attention on material that might otherwise be blended away, usually by being split into two sentences. For instance, the following would normally be relegated to two sentences:

> Nadia attempted two flips just before entering the water. The flips seemed real easy, but they turned out to be nightmares.

If a writer wished to create more pause by focusing attention on material in the second sentence, then that sentence or phrases from it may be melted together and used as single word adjectives in the first sentence. The result could be the following:

> Nadia attempted two, seemed-real-easy, turned-out-to-be-nightmare flips before entering the water.

Kinks.

Melted-together words may never be melted to each other or to other words that work alone, as adjectives in the examples above, in the structure of the sentence. For instance, notice that there are no hyphens between the three adjectives "two," "seemed-real-easy," or "turned-out-to-be-nightmare," nor is there a hyphen between "nightmare" and the noun "flips," the word that all these new melted-together-words are modifying.

Some writers melt together words by using quotation marks around them. For us, using these marks becomes a guilt-ridden, I-know-this-word-does-not-really-exist signal from the writer to the reader. Unless the writer is using quotation marks to suggest their Melted-together Word is a cliché, overused phrase that is not new or a melted together word created from a quotable line, quotation marks should be saved for quotes. Also, always avoid using prefabricated Melted-together Words such as "do-it-yourself" or "in-your-face." Phrases that have already been established as cliché phrases are too recognizable, speeding the reader up since the brain chews them up and spits them out without giving them any consideration.

Scope.

The experience of being the lone black in a group of whites was so familiar to me that I thought nothing of it as our trip began. But then halfway through the trip the professor casually turned to me and, in an isn't-the-world-funny sort of tone, said that he had just refused to rent an apartment in a house he owned to a "very nice" black couple because their color would "offend" the white couple who lived downstairs. (Shelby Steele, "On Being Black and Middle Class," *Commentary*)

I've seen this flavor of happiness before . . . friends returning from half-years spent in Europe—faces showing relief at being able to indulge in big cars, fluffy white towels, and California produce once more, but faces also gearing up for the inevitable "what-am-I-going-to-do-with-my-life?" semiclinical depression that almost always bookends European pilgrimage. (Douglas Coupland, *Generation X)*

(Dickerson, a black woman, Harvard law graduate, and widely published writer, describing the person who shot her nephew for no apparent reason) . . . a brother did it. A non-job-having, middle-of-the-day malt-liquor-drinking, crotch-clutching, loud-talking brother with many neglected children born of many forgotten women. (Debra Dickerson, "Who Shot Johnny?," *The New Republic.)*

She couldn't recall the precise moment she began to feel resentful of the hand-shake-only good night, of the moist, cold, kiss-on-the-forehead routine, but she suddenly found herself unable to think of anything but how she could seduce him. (Olga Bloom, student)

Essentially this is a movie about Jessica Lange's spirit-of-the-prairie face. (Pauline Kael, *The New Yorker*)

In the internship year, we came very close to a divorce. Your basic doctor-in-training-meets-gorgeous-nurse-and-wants-to-leave-his-wife-and-small-baby story. (Louise De Salvo, "A Portrait of the Puttana as a Middle-Aged Woolf Scholar," *Between Women*)

This is not to say that all penises are, according to Pound's dictum, moral. Indeed, a gratuitously shocking penis, an extraneous-to-our-story penis, a hey-look-at-me-for-the-sake-of-nothing-but-me penis, however imposing, is literally immoral (that is, incompetent), because by jarring the reader from the narrative or argumentative flow into a mood of "What's this stupid penis doing here?" the author has undermined the greatest truth of his

41

tale: i.e. our ability to immerse ourselves in it. (David Duncan, "Toxins in the Mother Tongue," *The Los Angeles Times Magazine*)

Hieroglyphics

How much of a pause the reader should take and whether it creates emphasis or establishes a complex relationship between ideas depends on visual codes called punctuation. Commas slow writing with soft, slightly breath-catching pauses; the period is an abrupt, long rest. In between the comma and period there are four more hieroglyphics: the *colon* (:) and/or *single dash* (— or —); *semi-colon* (;), and the *dash skewer* (—XXX—). Whenever we introduce these in class, students balk, letting out a since-this-has-to-do-with-rules-I'll-pass-on-it groan. Professional writers are dependent on these hieroglyphics, not because they want to demonstrate their command over English grammar, but because these marks act as signs, helping the reader know how to interpret the writer's music. In fact, learning to read a colon, single dash, semi-colon, and dash skewer in a professional essay is as important as learning to use them in your own writing.

Semi-colon.
There are many rules of usage for the semi-colon, colon, dash, and dash skewer; here we are just concerned with using these hieroglyphics for the pause that gives writing its drama. A good place for semi-colons (;) is to replace a connecting word such as but, or, yet, so, for, and, nor. Remember the words with the letters BOYS FAN. Here is an example: "I made a special trip to the store to buy eggs, but all the eggs were broken." "But" can be replaced by a semicolon if you want to create dramatic pause, in this case one suggesting a gasp of incredulity: "I made a special trip to the store to buy eggs; all the eggs were broken." Using a semi-colon to replace BOYS FAN is a judgment call: Always

know how it is adding a specific tone, voice, or attitude to your writing.

Semi-colons are also useful when you are freighting and you have a long list of items which are loaded with modifying information set off by commas:

> Today, I received several packages from mail order companies: a hundred rolls of recycled, non-bleached toilet paper from Seventh Generation, an environmentally sensitive retailer; a raspberry beret to go with my navy wool suit from Tweeds in Roanoke, Virginia; a two-pound box of assorted chocolates, all soft centers, no nuts, including the scotch mallow, a dark chocolate candy filled with a layer of butterscotch and a layer of marshmallow, from See's Candies.

The semicolons here are useful for keeping the mail-order items separate from the details given about each of the packages.

Kinks.
One rule to remember: Unless connecting a list of items, the semi-colon can replace BOYS FAN only when there is a complete sentence on either side of the semi-colon. In a sentence which reads "I went to the mall and bought underwear," the "and" cannot be replaced with a semi-colon. But, the semi-colon works here: "I went to the mall; I bought some sexy lingerie." Also there is not a reason for the semi-colon in the first sentence; in the second one, the semi-colon creates a pause that is almost a seductive glance. What starts out as an ordinary sentence becomes an enticement.

Colon & Single Dash.
The colon (:) and the single dash (—) are used to indicate that an example, restatement, summation or elaboration of the first part of the sentence will immediately follow in the next part of the sentence. When using a colon or single dash, the writer drops transitional words (like, such as) or verbs to connect the first part of the sentence with the second sentence or clause. The colon and single dash are therefore used at the end of a complete thought where a period would be allowed; then a list of examples or a restatement follows immediately and abruptly. For instance, "Verna is the kind of employee who feeds off her coworkers' mistakes and disappointments to nourish her own career: A workplace vulture." or "Verna is the kind of employee who feeds off

43

her coworkers' mistakes and disappointments to nourish her own career—A workplace vulture."

When using a colon or single dash, the material that appears before the colon is usually a complete clause and the material after the mark is sometimes a complete clause and sometimes not. The clause following the colon, whether complete or incomplete, should be poetic, pithy commentary. This characteristic of the colon and single dash—that a complete or incomplete clause can follow either hieroglyphic—also distinguishes the single dash and colon from their cousin, the semi-colon.

The use of the colon or single dash, instead of a period or transitional words and phrases, gives both halves of the sentence fresh emphasis. For instance, one could write,

> The colon and single dash are magical hieroglyphics which connect the world of generalities with the world of specifics: the barnyard with chickens, cows and pigs; criminals with pickpockets, thieves, and killers; language with instruction manuals, student essays, and great prose.

The colon or single dash here replaces the transitional phrases "such as" or "for example," phrases that cannot be replaced with a semi-colon. The pause created by the colon or single dash does two things: It gives emphasis to the general statement about colons so that the statement does not get lost in the rest of the long sentence, and it makes the list of examples seem special in their own right rather than subservient to the general statement they support. After the colon, the listed examples can be read the way they would be spoken during a roll call — abruptly, almost out of nowhere. In deciding which to use, the colon or the single dash, consider this: Generally, colons are considered more formal and give writing polish; dashes are casual and make writing more conversational.

Dash Skewer.
A dash skewer—two dashes used to enclose a parenthetical statement or modifying clause— has become a popular and versatile hieroglyphic. With the post-modern preoccupation for subtext—ideas that are implied below the surface of the texts—and with the impulse to pay closer attention to information that was once

considered mundane, beside the point, or non-crucial, writers need to signal readers they are entering a parallel level of reality without totally exiting the surface one. In this sense, a dash skewer transports readers to worlds sometimes considered parenthetical but now actually held in high esteem. Parentheses ( ) shut items up in a closet, almost whispering to the reader that the information being divulged is meant as an aside or is relatively unimportant: "Sue (the girl who keeps coughing) was the last to leave the party." However, a set of commas signal that the information within should be read and considered with equal importance to the surrounding text: "Sue, the girl who keeps coughing, was the last to leave the party." Compared to a set of commas or parentheses, a dash skewer is very strong—raising the information within quickly and forcefully to the surface: "Sue—the girl who keeps coughing—was the last to leave the party." Parentheses, commas, and a pair of dash skewers all signal volume control: A dash skewer screams.

Scope.

Audubon saw that the behavior of birds, their instinctual code of greetings and seductions, could be recorded as affectations: the heron's dainty, bent-wristed greeting to its fellows; the red-necked grebe sapiently lecturing its child; the great horned owls staring down their accusers. Mated birds in Audubon are not slaves of instinct but married couples; they are always in cahoots. Or else his birds stand alone in fancy dress and become worldly types: the senatorial pelican, the demagogic shrike, the seigneurial blue heron, the outlaw vulture. (Adam Gopnik, "Audubon's Passion," *The New Yorker*)

Our previous definition of the human—that we reason; that we reflect upon ourselves; that we make tools; we speak—is in the shop for microchip repairs. We are really, when you count performance and tabulate behavior, not super computers, but a lot like locusts, little chafing dishes maybe, small woks, modest ovens, simple furnaces, barbecue pits and picnic grills: we consume. (William Gass, "Exile")

It might be argued that America's fascination with sports—if "fascination" is not too weak a word for such frenzied devotion, weekend after weekend, season after season, in the lives of the majority of men—has to do not only with the power of taboo to violate, or transcend, or render obsolete conventional categories of morality, but with the dark, denied, muted, eclipsed, and wholly unarticulated underside of America's religion of success. Sports is only partly about winning; it is also about losing. Failure, hurt, ignominy, disgrace, physical injury, sometimes even death— these are facts of life, perhaps the very bedrock of lives, which the sports-actor, or athlete, must dramatize in the flesh; and always against his will. (Joyce Carol Oates, "Blood, Neon, and Failure in the Desert," *The Profane Art*)

I have a dream that one day down in Alabama—with its vicious racists, with its Governor having his lips dripping with the words of interposition and nullification—one day right there in Alabama, little black boys and black girls will be able to join hands with little white boys and white girls as sisters and brothers. (Martin Luther King Jr., "I Have a Dream")

Whatever my romantic notions were about the ideal forms of American Indian wisdom—closeness to the land, respect for other living creatures, a sense of harmony with natural cycles, a way of walking lightly in the world, a manner of living that could make the ordinary and profane into the sacred—I learned that on the reservation I was inhabiting a world that was contrary to all these values. (Diana Hume George, "Wounded Chevy at Wounded Knee," *The Mississippi Review*)

Lanegrin's equation for motion therefore has its roots in two worlds: the macroscopic world represented by the diagonal force and the microscopic world represented by the fluctuating, or Brownian force. (Bernard Lavends, *Scientific America*)

In the world of canned dog food, a smooth consistency is a sign of low quality—lots of cereal. A lumpy, frightening, bloody, stringy horror is a sign of high quality—lots of meat. (Ann Hodgman, "No Wonder They Call Me a Bitch," *Spy*)

Some books are to be tasted, others to be swallowed, and some few to be chewed and digested: that is, some books are to be read only in parts; others to be read, but not curiously [with great care]; and some few to be read wholly and with diligence and attention. (Francis Bacon, "Of Studies")

Life's but a walking shadow, a poor player/ That struts and frets his hour upon the stage/ And then is heard no more: it is a tale/ Told by an idiot, full of sound and fury,/ Signifying nothing. (William Shakespeare, *Macbeth*)

Super-literalism

A powerful way to bring pause to a piece of writing is to reduce words or phrases to their most basic, taken-for-granted elements. This requires treating a simple word like "apple" as if it were abstract terminology, then reducing that word to an even simpler, down-to-earth reality. Super-literalism slaps euphemisms in the face (see the Scrub unit). Notice that in the following sentence, apple gets no more attentive pause than any of the other fruits: "I bought grapes, oranges, bananas, and apples." When Super-literalism is used as a reducing agent, notice how the apple now receives stunning attention: "I bought grapes, oranges, bananas, and *shiny red seed pods.*" "Shiny red seed pods" is a more truthful, graphic phrase than "apples," more truthful because "shiny red seed pods" reduces "apple" to characteristics we have taken for granted.

Super-literalism is not metaphor: It does not compare unlike things. Describing spaghetti as slimy worms is metaphoric; describing it as *dry sticks of crushed grass seed and chicken embryo* is Super-literal. Super-literalism is always a shock. It reminds us that we and the world are a bit more vulnerable, animalistic, or manufactured than numb, common words allow us to believe. Super-literalism is conscious-raising because it is a complacency shaker. The more abstract, intellectual, or sophisticated the tone of the ongoing flow in a piece of writing, the more abruptly the injection of Super-literalism forces the reader's nose down into reality.

Gary has always been impressed by philosopher Alan Watt's use of Super-literalism in his book *Does It Matter?* For instance, imagine an ecology or biology teacher talking about food chains, a hierarchy of predators that live by eating animals lower on a prey list. Typically, the professor would refer to this as a food web or maybe symbiotic relationships. Watt stops the reader cold though when he reduces this phenomenon to its most graphic, taken-for-granted version: ". . . almost all the substance of this maze [of life], aside from water, was once other living bodies — the bodies of animals and plant—and that I had to obtain it by *murder* . . . I exist solely through membership in this perfectly weird arrangement of beings that flourish by *chewing each other up.*" "Murder," and especially "chewing each other up," reduce "food web" to an explanation a small child could understand. "Food web" or "food chain" protects the reader, distancing the reader from reality by being more abstract. "Chewing each other up" shocks us into remembering our animal selves. We cannot help but take pause. Super-literalism punches the wind out of euphemism and makes us reconsider what we have read even more than most short sentences can.

Many so-called primitive or aboriginal tribes use language that is graphic Super-literalism. This type of language has powerful identifying capabilities that later vanishes in industrial, scientific societies, trapped by the need to categorize or label to keep track of fine distinctions. Ruth Bebe Hill lived for over thirty years with the Lakota native Americans to learn their language before writing her novel *Hanta Yo* . Looking through the glossary of Bebe's novel is revealing. *"Long-claws"* is a much more descriptive name for an animal than grizzly bear. *"Lump-raiser"* is a name that describes a physical interaction that is taken for granted with the label "mosquito." *"Bird-that-vexes-air"* captures more about the relationship between the bird and its amazing manner of flight than "hummingbird."

Super-literalism has magic that turns a reader's head. It is a powerful stun tool; it needs to be used sparingly to be effective. When a writer is aware of the possibilities of Super-literalism, all language comes under playful scrutiny and so over-all expression becomes clearer. In some ways, no other pause tool adds as much clarity, honesty, irony, and sometimes humor, to all kinds of writing— scientific, philosophical, or business— as Super-literalism does.

Scope.

We have italicized the Super-literal language. Some might argue that a few of these are metaphors, but given their context, we think everything here is Super-literal.

There is no question that there is an unseen world. The problem is, *how far is it from midtown* and *how late is it open*? (Woody Allen, "Examining Psychic Phenomena," *The New Yorker*. For a literal-minded person, who does not see spirituality in metaphorical terms, Allen's question is literal, and therefore humorous to those who are not literal-minded.)

Gerber dismisses the Stages line as a copy of its own color-coded system, which differentiates the *mush* from the *chunks* but does not organize the food according to the baby's age. (Jaclyn Fierman, *Fortune Magazine*. Normally these foods would be referred to as strained and natural; here they are what they really look and feel like.)

I said there was a society of men among us, bred up from their youth in the art of proving by words multiplied for the purpose, that white is black and black is white, according as they are paid. To this society all the rest of the people are slaves. For example, if my neighbor hath a mind to my cow, he hires a lawyer to prove that he ought to have my cow from me. I must then hire another to defend my right, it being against all rules of law that any man should be allowed to speak for himself. . . . It is likewise to be observed that this society hath a peculiar cant and jargon of their own, that no other mortal can understand, and wherein all their laws are written, which they take special care to multiply; whereby they have wholly confounded the very essence of truth and falsehood, of right and wrong; so that it will take thirty years to decide whether the field, left me by my ancestors for six generations, belong to me or to a stranger three hundred miles off. (Jonathan

49

Swift, "Voyage to the Houyhnhums," *Gulliver's Travels.* Maybe the whole passage should be italicized.)

In World War I [engineers] made a machine that would *throw five hundred pounds of steel fifty miles.* (Andy Rooney, "An Essay on War,"*Literary Calvacade.* Super-literalism here reminds us of the gravitational limitations an artillery canon must overcome.)

In the Amazon, on the other hand, should you have had too much to drink, say, and inadvertently urinate as you swim, any home-less candiru, attracted by the smell, will take you for a big fish and swim *excitedly* up your stream of uric acid, enter your ure-thra like a worm into its burrow, and, raising its gill cover, stick out a set of retrose spines. Nothing can be done. The pain, ap-parently, is *spectacular.* (Redmond O'Hanlon, "Amazon Adven-ture," *Granta.* Normally these words would be used as hyperbole or exaggeration; here they are almost understatements.)

Jones is next wheeled into the appointed slumber room where a few touches may be added — his favorite pipe placed in his hand or, if he was a great reader, a book propped into position. . . . Here he will *hold open house* for a few days, visiting hours 10 A.M. to 9 P.M. (Jessica Mitford, *The American Way of Death.* No corpse, no open house. It really is the dead's last party.)

I am an *invisible* man. No, I am not a spook like those who haunted Edgar Alan Poe. . . . I am invisible, understand, simply because people refuse to see me. (Ralph Ellison, *Invisible Man.* For the Afro-American persona that speaks here, white people literally do not see him, in the same way a student sitting in a hallway is perceived as part of the walls by a professor who car-ries on a personal conversation within that student's listening range.)

As Aristotle put it, the beginning of philosophy is wonder. I am simply amazed to find myself living on a *ball of rock* that swings around an immense *spherical fire* . . . (Alan Watt, "Murder in the Kitchen," *Does It Matter?* We do live on a ball of rock that can crack, crumble, and get slammed into by other rocks. The word "earth" is a grand, more comforting term.)

I'm sick of peering at the world through false eyelashes, so everything I see is mixed with a shadow of *bought hairs*; I'm sick of weighting my head with a *dead mane*, unable to move my neck freely, terrified of rain, or wind, of dancing too vigorously in case I sweat into my *lacquered* curls. (Germaine Greer, *The Female Eunuch*. Check the ingredients for hair spray.)

Although the two [eternities of darkness before and after life] are identical twins, man as a rule, views the prenatal abyss with more calm than the one he is heading for (at some *forty-five hundred heartbeats an hour*). (Vladimir Nabokov, *Speak, Memory*. "Living" is reduced to its mechanics. We forget wear and tear is at the essence of our bodies.)

Workout.

To practice all the pause techniques, write an essay about a subject that you feel especially passionate about. Consider writing about a political, personal, artistic, business, legal, psychological, sports, educational, or any other issue that makes you especially angry or ecstatic. Several dramatic pauses, interrupting flows of details, will become especially appropriate in order to capture the ideas and details you want to stress.

Do not worry about a formal introduction or organization. Write your rough draft so that you cover as many details and related issues as you can. Refer to books or visual material, personal experiences, or discussions you have had that relate to your issue. Make sure every opinion you bring up has some detailed support.

On the final draft, continue to consider introductions and conclusions optional. The important thing is to practice combining opinions and details by using the flow tools and then decide which of these opinions or details you want to have special emphasis. Decide where pause effectively helps to create your voice and reflects your attitude towards the subject. Within two double-spaced typed pages you should have about five very short sentences, a few colons and dashes, a few semi-colons, four invented melted-together-words, and five super-literal expressions. Of course, the point is not always to maintain these quotas; they are here artificially to practice these techniques.

FUSION:
Ways to Spark and Compress

✗ *Recyclables*

♟ *Line-ups*

✗ *Break-ups*

✗ *Mix-masters*

Essentially there are two kinds of language systems that we all use—literal and metaphoric. Literal language is straight-forward, dictionary-defined language that is essential to living and survival. If we were in a burning theater and someone warned us by shouting "the evil gods have farted" or "a liquid sun tumbles over us," we would want to cut that person's tongue out and curse language forever. In an emergency, we want a literal signal: "Fire!" The other, more ambiguous warnings are from the world of metaphor, and although they are undesirable when warning others of a fire, in many other situations metaphor has the ability to depict the complexities and subtleties of reality in a way that is impossible for literal, dictionary-defined language. Only metaphoric language flash-fuses three layers of mental involvement: its originality excites the reader's interest in the subject matter; the metaphor's associations capture the writer's attitude towards the subject; other associations quickly capture the complexity and subtly of the literal subject that is fused to the metaphor. In short, metaphor sparks interests, fine-tunes attitude, and compresses explanations or descriptions.

For instance, describing a building on fire as "the evil gods have farted" intrigues because the phrase has never been heard before, while at the same time the speaker's attitude is implied by the reference to "gods," suggesting that the writer finds the fire to be prophetic, and the word "farted" suggests that the speaker also finds the start of the fire to be capricious or comically absurd. Aside from intriguing the reader and implying something about the speaker's attitude, a description of the fire is compressed: The fact that "gods have farted" suggests that the fire is of cosmic magnitude or size and with an enormous foul, windy back draft. The other metaphor, "a liquid sun tumbles over us," creates an entirely different concept of a fire. Again it incites interest because of its originality, but the speaker seems more awe-struck than the first writer since the "sun" is a more essential, important aspect of life than a "fart." The metaphor also defines the nature of the fire differently: The idea that the intensity of the sun could liquefy makes its heat especially intense and threatening, while "tumbles over us" suggests a fire-storm that is inescapable.

Metaphors usually work on the reader quickly and intuitively. With the fire expression above, the reader or listener has an emotional and intellectual reaction where all three dimensions of the metaphor are sucked in without analyzing the metaphor the way we have done above. When metaphors are rich, we take them for granted, usually giving homage to them only through a split-second smile before reading or listening further. Because metaphors are so multidimensional, fusing literal material to them is essential to all kinds of writing: fictional, historical, journalistic, business, sociological, critical, theological, political, and scientific.

English teachers avoid teaching students to use metaphor for several reasons. First of all, rules cannot be cited to evaluate metaphors; their worth can only be discussed by analyzing them in the context of their use. Secondly, discovering original metaphors demands that the writer maintain a playful mind set and then a sense of correctness to evaluate their worth in a particular context. Most teachers avoid teaching craft that requires such paradoxical skills. Thirdly, textbooks and teachers do not always know playful methods to generate a metaphorical vocabulary. We do.

Teachers will define metaphor, but the definition sounds like an absurd riddle or mathematical corollary: "Metaphors inform by comparing something to be understood, or to be revitalized, to a second thing that in some crucial ways is like the first thing to be understood or revitalized, but in other important ways is very different from that thing." Other teachers go no further than to define different figures of speech: personification, simile, synecdoche, metonymy, and metaphor, a general term that loops together figurative language that does not fit the other categories. Teachers know that informing through both similarities and dissimilarities makes metaphor a powerful communication tool; but more important than defining metaphors, writers need to know how to generate metaphors and practice using them. We have developed several ways to generate metaphors: Recyclables, Line-ups, Break-ups, and Mix-masters. It is important to practice all the techniques, but eventually one may work better for you than the other.

Recyclables

Slang is to adolescents what the Modern Language Association is to graduate students. Adolescent slang is shock-value metaphor created in the teen years to shrink-wrap sexual embarrassment by cartooning genitalia or styrofoaming social insecurities by making fun of outsiders. Several years ago, a survey of nostalgic college students recalled metaphors such as "wrinkled-necked pigeons," "fur burgers," and "choke my chicken." Other times adolescent slang is used to over-dramatize the grotesque such as "smells like something crawled up your ass and died," "lung cookies," or "break wind." These metaphors do not measure up to everyone's literary or moral sense of decorum, but they never have; the slang created by the great medieval English writer, Geoffrey Chaucer, to make his Bible students seem more realistic, was also raw. They took pride in telling of every opportunity to "grind their corn;" at the same time, the Wife of Bath made fun of her man's "silly instrument," especially in light of her "God's plenty." However, for a youthful audience, not haunted by adult inhibitions, slang is genuine metaphor.

The difference between slang metaphor and metaphor in general is that slang is sometimes secretive and has value within only a narrow social group. For instance, Garry Trudeau, the creator of the "Doonesbury" comic strip, once made fun of movie industry metaphor, peppering his characters' dialogue with the slang of a motion picture deal: "We're looking at a package that's going to make this town weep," "When word hits the streets, the majors will break down our doors," "Then we're talking green light? You ran it up the flagpole and the money saluted?," and "The money loved it." Even though it is insider language, slang enlivens mundane material. When a waitress says, "I need a crowd on the hoof; let them walk," she makes having to say all day "I need three rare hamburgers to go" more fun and eventful.

In the gang world, devoid of material comfort and educational advantage, creative use of slang becomes a way to achieve status. Inventive language is a sign of power. When a member says he's "good from the pocket, but better from the shoulders" instead of "I can use a knife, but I am better with my fists," he not only lets his group know that he is an insider who knows the code, but that he has mental energy. In Bertolucci's masterpiece *Last Tango in Paris*, slang-creating mental energy compensates for the emotional and sexual impotency of Marlon Brando's character when he says, "I got a prostate like an Idaho potato, but I'm still pretty good stick."

Slang's ability to spark interest and fine-tune frays when subjected to a great deal of repetitive usage: popularity and overuse pound inventive slang into clichés. The same thing happens with other common metaphors, especially cliché *similes*, metaphors that use the word "like" or "as" to make a direct comparison. Typical clichés include "easy as pie," "stubborn as a mule," or "broken hearted," which is not a simile. These tiresome phrases could have been religious chant to Neanderthal man, and certainly fresh surprises five hundred years ago, but now they are prefab sound bytes, already packaged and shoplifted from the language market. A writer who serves up prefabricated text to his reader achieves the opposite effect of strong metaphor: Instead of capturing the reader's attention and forcing the reader to rethink reality, the cliché allows the reader's brain to go on a coffee break. Below we list resources for when you have used up your slang-creating brain fuel.

Simile-Reforming.

Similes call a great deal of attention to themselves and so usually taste very artificial. Use them sparingly. One way to reform a simile is to become much more specific. For instance, instead of writing "Her hand shot up like a balloon," Bernard Cooper thinks of a specific, powerful aspect of a balloon: "Before the teacher had even finished asking a question, Mary would let out a little grunt and practically levitate out of her seat as if her hand were filled with helium." A second way to recycle a cliché simile is to drop the "as" or "like," as well as the adjective. For instance, instead of writing "The test was as easy as pie," write "The test was pie." You can also reform by substituting an object that is the equivalent of pie for one of the ingredients of pie such as "The test was cake" or "The test was sugar." (Substituting a part of an object for the entire object is called *synecdoche*.) Exacting comparison is always the goal. If parts of the test were easy and others were difficult, write "The test was lemon meringue."

Antiquing.

One of Glynis's favorite flavors of recyclables is to combine Greek and Latin prefixes, suffixes, or stems with existing cliché slang. We provide our students with lists of the suffixes, bases, and prefixes. Combining English words with French, Spanish, or Italian words also works since they come with built-in Latin echoes. When our niece throws a fit, demanding her favorite donut, the kind with sprinkles on top, we say "Simone suffers from Sprinklerrhea," using the common word sprinkle and combining it with the Greek suffix "rrhea" meaning "abnormal discharge."

Soldering.

We require our students to always have on hand a *Roget's Thesaurus*, one that has a wide selection of choices, ranging from common slang to lofty language. By looking up synonyms in the thesaurus and combining them with other important words or their synonyms, you can create a cast of Fusions. This was the basis for Rich Hall and Friends who wrote a book called *Sniglets*.

Examples included "express holes," people who violate the rules for a ten-items-or-less grocery line; "cinemuck," the sticky trash on movie theater floors; "hozone," the place where one sock in every laundry load disappears. (A melt of two words to make a new word is called a *portmanteau* word.) For instance, if you were writing about the people who hang out at your local coffee house, you would simply look up "coffee" and related details ("brown," "pastries," "drink") in the thesaurus to find creative alternatives which could then be paired with synonyms you look up for "drinking." Instead of referring to the clientele as "coffee drinkers," you could then create new metaphors that best capture who the people really are: mud guzzlers, pastry spongers, or java-junkies.

Culturing.

In order to capture the essence of a particular group, person, idea, or image, try using a cultural reference point borrowed from pop culture, high or low art, technolog or anything that is well known to your reader, then attach an ending such as "esque," "ism," "ian," to form a new word. For example, in his novel *Generation X*, Douglas Coupland includes a glossary in which television shows or other pop icons are used to create slang. Coupland explains that "Bradyism" is "A multisibling sensibility derived from having grown up in large families. A rarity in those born after approximately 1965. Symptoms of Bradyism include a facility for mind games, emotional withdrawal in situations of overcrowding, and a deeply felt need for a well defined personal space." Even numbers can be used. A common cultural reference point for everyone with a college education is Introductory Psychology 101 so Coupland comes up with "101-ism" which is "the tendency to pick apart, often in minute detail, all aspects of life using half-understood pop psychology as a tool." (English teachers might refer to this cultured fusion as *metonymy*, the substitution of an object closely related to the subject being written about, such as "crown" for "king.")

Scope.

After we studied the differences between planets and moons, I told my cheese eagle that I had to leave early for an appointment with my nerve diver and his spit-sucker. (Alicia Eddy, student)

It would be years before I heard the word "transvestite," so I struggled to find a word for what I'd seen. "He-she" came to mind. . . "Burl's" [a restaurant's name] would have been perfect, like "boys" and "girls" spliced together. . . (Bernard Cooper, "Burl's," *The Los Angels Times Magazine*)

Phlegm and impatience mingle in his voice. . . He cannot see her view—the angle of his vision, the slant of her finger, makes it incomprehensible to him. His lumpy red hand plops around in the glass casing like the agitated head of a chicken outraged by the loss of its body. (Toni Morrison, *The Bluest Eye*)

The monster's face looked like a Domino's pizza that had just been run over by a semi— those pizzas don't look too pretty even in their normal state—and even if the furious tone of its voice could be put through a sound mixer, someone would not be able to sort his snort from his retort. (Jesse Hoffman, seventh grade)

Just as raging surf forces a would-be wader out of the ocean and onto the beach, the jangled polar field lines can shove cosmic rays away from the sun and back into the outer heliosphere. (Edward Smith and Richard Marsden, "Shooting the Solar Breeze," *The Sciences*)

The menu says the cinnamon bun is "legendary." Bunyanesque in size, it is a full meal and then some . . . . The big fry bread is split open like a clam shell and loaded with chunks and shreds of utterly scrumptious, deeply seasoned roast beef. . . Nonetheless, Frito pie (known among local connoisseurs as a "stomach grenade") is one of the most beloved dishes of the real people in and around Santa Fe . . . (Jane and Michael Stern, *Roadfood*)

Whenever Nathan Shapiro regarded Eleanor Parnell, it was like looking at the transparent overlay in the *World Book Encyclopedia*. In his mind he would flip back and forth from today's deep-voiced, black-haired, chain-smoking, heavy-breasted woman in a red sheath dress or tight dungarees, gracefully working the cork from another bottle of pink California wine, to the vague, large friendly woman in plaids who had fed him year after year on Cokes and deviled-ham sandwiches, whose leaves he had raked for seven autumns now, and who still lay somewhere underneath the new

Eleanor, like the skeleton of a frog beneath the bright chaos of its circulatory system. (W.S.Trow, "You Missed It," *The New Yorker*)

At the far end of Giotto's chapel, rank after rank of angels throng the skies. Today "angels" can be found on the Internet, where millions of disembodied cybernauts fly around in an idealized, immaterial realm . . . On entering net space, the frail ties of the flesh are left behind. Fat, acne, bad eyes, weedy physiques and creaky joints are jettisoned. (Margaret Wertheim, "The Medieval Consolations of Cyberspace," *The Sciences*)

Workout.

List ten words or phrases that describe items, events, problems or kinds of people associated with a given profession or endeavor. Endeavors could include being a student, a parent, a son or daughter, or any job or athletic team. Now opposite each item in the list create Recyclable slang words or phrases using the techniques listed above. Everything must be fresh, nothing cliché. Most of our students create phrases that are too long: After you create slang, always ask yourself if you can shorten the word or phrase so that it is easier to read and speak. Now write a short paper using at least eight of the slang words or phrases you created; if they do not read well, change them. Do not worry about explaining what they mean in the paper, but if they seem too obscure, give the reader more details about the situation you are describing so that the Recyclable metaphor will hit with more meat. For instance, in the first example under "Scope" above, the reader may miss the meaning and humor of the recyclable "cheese eagle" if the writer left out the opening phrase.

Line-ups

Our composition students often ask how they can expand their vocabulary, thinking that if they only knew more words, they could think of more interesting metaphors. Creating tasty metaphors is not dependent on possessing a huge vocabulary. Glynis loves the following two recipes for making metaphors because, aside from adding flavor to sentences, Line-ups and Break-ups add to the writer's vocabulary pantry by simply using "what you have" to make tastier essays. Similes are discussed in "Recyclables" as being an especially overt, attention-calling metaphor: "A chocolate brownie is like a consoling friend." The simile-forming word "like" spells out the metaphor for the reader rather than allowing the metaphor to play out in the reader's subconscious. Line-ups remove "like" or "as" from similes to create smoother metaphors. Line-ups are confident similes.

In its most basic form, a Line-up metaphor is simply a metaphoric adjective, a word that modifies a person, place, or thing. If you were describing a chair in your house, you might point out that it is a "leather chair" which gives literal information about chair. But suppose you wanted to describe more complex qualities about the chair, that the chair is uncomfortable, that everyone avoids sitting in that particular chair, and that the other chairs, in comparison, look more appealing. Your first impulse might be to use a simile. "The chair is like a jealous lover." In many instances, essays call for the subtle metaphor-making capabilities of Line-ups: A Line-up transforms the simile into "jealous chair." By assigning an adjective that would normally accompany an animate subject, such as the emotion "jealousy," to an inanimate object, such as "chair," you capture and compress new dimensions of reality that are difficult and lengthy to express with literal adjectives.

Line-ups work in the opposite direction as well: a live or animate object, such as a person, can be assigned an adjective that would normally be associated only with inanimate objects—"a metallic woman," "a nuclear friend," or "a stuccoed supervisor." The way to test your Line-ups is to ask whether your metaphor can literally be true. Can a chair really be jealous? Can a woman literally be metallic? Some potential Line-ups are too literal or can be used with both animate and inanimate nouns. Consider the phrase "stressed chair." Normally we use stress to apply to a psychological state, but stress is also frequently used to express a worn state of an object, so the Line-up has minimal metaphoric potential.

Many students worry that once they take away the simile words "like" or "as" that the reader won't understand the metaphor. Line-ups are meant to be understood intuitively; Line-ups are not intellectual puzzles to be painstakingly decoded. In the context of a particular conversation you are having or in a specific paragraph you are writing, a well-crafted metaphor is easily and instinctually understood—

Describe the rain last winter:

Demented rain/ Bashful rain/ Licentious rain.

Describe the last novel you read:

Impotent novel/ Elastic novel/ Sculptured novel.

Describe your professor's attitude:

Melted attitude/ Purple attitude/ Gnarled attitude.

Note that you can also flip-flop the adjective and noun and place a "to be" verb between them. Instead of writing "a metallic woman" a writer could write "The woman is metallic." Also realize that Line-ups can turn nouns— people, places, and, things—into adjectives: "Chris gives Heinz Ketchup lectures, while Donna expects her students to write Mop-&-Glo essays."

Scope.

A chromosome, with its snaking strands of stacked nucleotides, is a microscopic Great Wall of China. (Howard Bussey, "Chain of Being," *The Sciences* , New York Academy of Sciences)

I am firmly of the opinion that the Macintosh is Catholic and that DOS is Protestant. . . . [The Macintosh] tells the faithful how they must proceed step by step to reach—if not the Kingdom of Heaven—the moment in which their document is printed. . . .

[DOS] allows free interpretation of scripture, demands difficult personal decisions . . . (Umberto Eco, "La Bustina di Minerva," *L'Espresso*)

The "organization man" may be well fed, well amused and well oiled, yet he lacks a sense of identity because none of his feelings or his thoughts originates within himself; none is authentic. (Erich Fromm, "Our Way of Life Makes Us Miserable," *Saturday Evening Post*)

The interior decor bespeaks superb *Roadfood* : Tired wood paneling, Formica-topped tables, . . . and a Chevrolet-time clock on the wall. (Jane and Michael Stern, *Roadfood*)

Clint Eastwood is a tall, chiseled piece of lumber— a totem pole with feet. . . . he's tense and clenched, anally vigilant. (James Walcott, "Is That a Gun in Your Pocket," *Vanity Fair*)

The paintings by Robert Williams are not Tom & Jerry or Fred & Barney but more Bugs Bunny and Mighty Mouse with a bit of war-time, pin-up girls and guys that are half-human, half-Taz added here and there in an Adam-Q setting. Williams ducks in and out of boyhood dangers through the "Warriors-of-Rust" painting where a not-quite-Dennis-the-Menace kid is trying to cruise on his skateboard while avoiding life's, every-day, rusty-nailed spikes. (Marie Avila, student)

Workout.

To practice this technique, pick a particular location: your home, job, park, supermarket. List all the items in that place and label their major characteristics, then all the people in that place, labeling them with job descriptions and physical attributes, not their names. Now change all the labels to Line-ups. If you visualize a tall woman in the park, think of a Line-up replacement for the adjective "tall" that captures the woman's height and also her other, more subtle characteristics: Maybe she is a skyscraper woman, which would suggest having a very bold and erect posture as well as height. However, if the woman were tall and flamboyant, a better Line-up would be a "feathered woman"; tall and large-framed, a "glaciated woman"; tall and gawky, a "shaky-ladder lady."

Break-ups

Like Line-ups, Break-ups make use of vocabulary you already have to help formulate interesting metaphors. Break-ups work by taking items you already know, usually represented by a noun, and breaking it into all its smaller parts and associations, also represented by nouns. All of these nouns can then be instantaneously turned into metaphoric verbs and nouns using one of two methods: Verb Force or Possessive Force.

Object Force.
In picking an object to break-up, the writer simply asks "What image captures the mood of my subject, but seems very unlike my subject?" If you are describing a garden and want to bring out its threatening atmosphere, choose a military tank; if you are writing about the physical logistics of an amusement park, and wish to emphasize the efficient but inhuman qualities of the design, choose the human digestive track. In the example below, we pretend to be writing an essay about family members' social and physical qualities, and since we know they all like to cook and eat, we decided to use the kitchen to break into parts. Note that if we wanted to write on their cooking abilities, the kitchen parts would be too closely related to our subject to create good metaphors. Maybe then we would choose the decorative components of a living room. Never anticipate what you are going to do with your objects parts. You will freeze up if you do.

Verb Force.
The verb slot of any sentence is a good place for a metaphor to appear since verbs power and process the sentence's action: Verbs are a sentence's cuisinart. Take an object that somehow captures a mood or tone of your subject. In order to create metaphors about family members, a writer might Break-up the kitchen into its parts, listing all the details: saucepan, refrigerator, cupboard, oven, cereal, counter top, butcher block, microwave, oil, salt, pepper, eggs, forks, knives. By taking these ordinary nouns and using them as verbs, the writer can create interesting im-

ages. Many of the nouns will need to change form—add an "s," "ed," or "ing"—to function as verbs or verb forms missing an auxillary verb ("to be" and "to have" verbs such as "is," "was," "has," "having") used above in Telescoping sentences. The translations below demonstrate how much description and imagery are compressed into these nouns when they are turned into metaphoric verbs.

> All the people in my family deal differently with their ideas and feelings—Gary *microwaves* his ideas; Jesse prefers to *saucepan* his. Others carefully display their feelings, Leslie *countertopping* hers and Candace *butcherblocking* hers. Other members hide their thoughts: Trevor *cupboards* and Sonya *refrigerates* their ideas.

The Break-up Translation: Gary's feelings quickly rise and unable to wait, he shares them without giving all the steps he used to develop them, while Jesse's thoughts slowly develop as he waits patiently for results of people's reactions before sharing his thoughts. Leslie displays her emotions in a convenient place for everyone to see and access while Candace breaks her emotions into smaller parts before presenting them to others. Trevor holds onto his ideas, using them only when he needs them, sometimes forgetting he had ever thought of them in the first place, but Sonya's ideas remain in a protected state which allows them to keep for a long time before slowly deteriorating. (Notice that the translation is longer than the original paragraph. Metaphors are economical).

Possessive Force.
If verbs are a sentence's cuisinart, possessed nouns—ones that have an *'s* (singular) or *s'* (plural) attached—are a sentence's blender because they smooth together two items by having one belong to the other. For example, Break-up another subject, such as a pasta dinner: fettucini noodles, Parmesan cheese, garlic, oregano, basil, chianti.

> All of the men contribute to the family's character: Glenn is the family's *fettucini noodle* and Alastair is the *Parmesan cheese*. Keefe is the family's *garlic* and, in contrast, Alexander is the pinch of *oregano*.

The Break-up Translation: Glenn entangles himself into everyone's business, absorbing everything around him, while Alastair is clingy and adds sharpness to the family's opinions. Keefe has an overpowering personality which can dominate but also gives definition to the family while Alexander is sweet but distinctive and balances out the other more dominating personalities.

The most important thing to realize about these Break-ups is that, once the reader understands the context of the sentence, paragraph, or essay, the possessed noun can be dropped. For instance, in the set of sentences above, once the writer establishes for the reader that the essay is about one's role in a family, the writer might later write "Glenn is a fettucine noodle; Alastair is Parmesan cheese; Keefe is garlic." So the possessed force of a Break-up resembles a Line-up.

Finally, realize that Break-ups can be made from *proper nouns* (people's names): "Harriet is the Martha Stewart of the division, while Peggy sees herself as the department's Joan of Arc. Students think of Tom as the tweed jacket of professors."

Scope.

[In reference to Delilah,] Samson said to the Philistines, "If you had not plowed with my heifer, you would not have found out my riddle." ("Judges," Revised Standard Version of the Bible)

My mother almost shattered me once, with that instinct mothers have — blind, I think, in this case, but unerring nonetheless — for striking blows along the fault-lines of their children's hearts, by telling me, in an attack on my selfishness, "We all have to make allowances for you [who have MS], of course, because of the way you are." (Nancy Mairs, "On Being a Cripple," *Plaintext: Deciphering a Woman's Life*)

Seeing the woman as she was, made them remember the envy they had stored up from other times. So they chewed up the back parts of their minds and swallowed with relish. They made burning statements with questions, and killing tools out of laughs. It was mass cruelty. (Zora Neale Hurston, *Their Eyes Were Watching God*)

Lolita had been safely solipsized. (Vladimir Nabokov, *Lolita*)

There is no mention of jalepeño peppers in the Christian Scriptures, and neither the average child nor the average televangelist can handle them. That's no reason to legislate them clean out of our *huevos rancheros.* (David Duncan, "Toxins in the Mother Tongue," *Los Angeles Times Magazine*)

My family's a garden full of dreamers lying on their backs, staring at the sky, drunk and choking on their dreaming. (Lê Thi Diem Thüy, "The Gangster We Are All Looking For")

Spring jitterbugs inside me. (Gretel Ehrlich, "Spring,"*Antaeus*)

The history of a species, or any natural phenomenon that requires unbroken continuity in a world of trouble, works like a batting streak. All are games of a gambler playing against a house with infinite resources. The gambler must eventually go bust . . . The best of us will try to live by a few simple rules: Do justly, love mercy, walk humbly with thy God, and never draw to an inside straight. (Stephen Jay Gould, "The Streak of Streaks," *Bully for Brontosaurus: Reflections in Natural History*)

Goya took their [Madrid's court painters] pedestrian, literal attention to flesh and materials and intensified it until it became a way of representing the world as a spot lit theater of façades and scrims. The people in his pictures have no bones or muscles; they are bags of silk and flesh, puffed up with vanity or collapsed with pain. (Adam Gopnik, "Goya Today," *The New Yorker*)

Take one gruff, vulgar, immature brute and marinate in the daily, desperate, overpopulated scramble for survival among the drunk gypsy thieves and carnival con artists praying upon the road of life; saute in a cheap Chianti savored with false madonnas and forgotten virtues; roast until rigid with hostility in the oven of rejection and disapproval; and finally sprinkle with the salt of retribution born of self-hate too long a simmer. (Dick Rawe, student on *La Strada* by Fellini)

[At the dentist] It is not the local pain that causes dread, but the greater pain: the loss of speech, the pinioning, the drool tides coming and washing out, the marooning of the brain. For two hours, the brain is Robinson Crusoe alone in the bone cup of the skull, peering out at faraway chrome implements and rubber-sheathed fingers and cotton cylinders red with blood, peering out but forbidden to signal for help. (Peter Freundlich, "The Crime of the Tooth: Dentistry in the Chair," *Harper's Magazine*)

Workout.

If you are working with a piece of writing or text you have already written and you are revising for metaphors, first identify all the nouns and verbs. Think of an object that captures the inner essence of your essay. Try anything for breaking up: a computer, car, holiday, city, film, or the human body. Using items from the one broken up object will help unify the entire piece. For a longer work, or just to explore possibilities, you may want to make two or three Break-up lists.

Cool down.

Avoid the temptation to explain your metaphor. You must try different Break-ups until discovering one that is understandable in the context of the sentences in the essay in which it appears. Good metaphors should take away explanation space, not add to it, since explanatory space defeats metaphoric compression. Make sure your Break-up is not an *homonym*, a word that has the same spelling or sound as another word with a different, literal meaning. For instance, suppose you broke up "bicycle" into handlebars, spokes, wheels, gears. "The politician high-geared through the debate" works well, but "The politician spoke through the debate" does not work as a metaphor at all since "spoke" can be both a noun and a literal verb. As always, avoid clichés. Worn out wiring, such as the metaphor in "Ivy put her ideas on the back burner," does not spark interest; it short-circuits interest.

Mix Masters

One game-like way to create inventive metaphors, almost in spite of one's lack of imagination, involves mixing words into sentences through Mix Master rules. Start with at least thirty interesting words. Gary has his students come up with their own wordbank by tearing a sheet of paper into sixteen small pieces and asking the students to write thirty-two words, one on each side of the scrap pieces, each entry reduced to one word nouns (unless using a title) which represent the most important things in their lives: food items, songs, perfumes, vacation images, films and books, clothes items, work essentials, good things and bad things from past and present experiences. To help achieve variety, Gary tells students to think of equal amounts of items they associate with the senses: touch, sound, sight, smell, taste. Three of the nouns may be abstractions such as God, humor, anger, kindness. Other lists might require students to come up with thirty-two items they associate with engineering, art, politics, or philosophy. If this assignment anticipates a larger research paper, then the list could be with items associated with the subject of that project. (See the Critical Thinking & Research unit.)

Mix-masters.

Now the class gets in groups of no more than four people. One student starts the game by laying out three of his or her "cards," or pieces of paper, at random. That person, and everyone else, must write a sentence using all three words, and the sentence must make metaphorical sense. It cannot be literal. Here are the rules: (1) You can change the forms of any of the words; (2) You can add as many articles as you wish (a, an, the); (3) You may add one preposition (words than denote place, such as in, over, under, near); (4) You may add any other word whatsoever, but only one such word. The rules force you to be spontaneous in the use of all the fusion techniques listed above: turning nouns into verbs, creating unusual adjectives, inventing unheard of similes.

Here are typical examples using words from a list about the student's personal life: "The sprinklers gossiped about mowed grass," the student having used "sprinklers," a life renewing childhood image from the desert; "gossip," something important to the student's present social life; and "mowed grass," a chore that had to be cranked through every weekend while the student was a teenager. The only added word here is "about." Another student employs a melted-together, line-up metaphor, writing "The mowed-grass gossip, used the sprinkler." This sentence actually has two metaphors in it since "gossip" cannot use the sprinkler, only a person who is a gossip. The extra word is "used." A third student might write "Gossip is a sprinkler on mowed grass," "is" being the extra word, "on" being the allowed preposition, "a sprinkler on mowed grass" being the metaphor that describes what gossip is.

The first student who writes a complete "legal" sentence announces this, and everyone else has sixty seconds to finish. Everyone reads his or her sentence aloud, and then the next person puts out three "cards," and the game continues around the group several times. Sometimes the sentences become reckless, but most of the time students are amazed at what they have created. This approach to creating metaphors trains writers to play, forcing them to try different words that are important to themselves personally or to a subject they are writing about. Remember that any combination of words can become metaphorical. Mix Masters teaches you to put pressure on yourself, to be playful, to be willing to keep throwing metaphors out that do not work, and to realize that there is the potential to create metaphors out of any words.

Workout.

The game above can be the workout; however, Gary developed a follow-up workout that involves trying to understand the literal worth of what has been created by the above mixing "accidents." When you finally unravel one of these mix-mastered sentences, you will appreciate how efficient metaphors really are, how much material they actually compress.

Unraveling these sentences is a three-part process that is bootcamp training in how to analyze anything. For part one, simply

write out the sentence. Part two, decide which words are metaphors in the sentence. Sometimes you have a choice. For instance, look again at the sentence "The sprinklers gossiped about
mowed grass." If "gossiped" is the metaphor, then "sprinklers"
and "mowed grass" are literal, with the word "gossip" being a
metaphor describing what the sprinklers are doing to the "mowed
grass." However, if "gossiped" is literal, people actually gossiped;
then there are two metaphors, "sprinklers" and "mowed grass"
becoming metaphors that describe who these people are.

After you decide which will be the metaphor or metaphors, and
which part of the sentence will be considered literal, write down
each word that is a metaphor, and opposite each one write down
all the universal associations most people have when they hear
or read the literal word. Do not think of the word as being a
metaphor when you write these associations down and do not
write down associations that are only personal to you. Also, do
not anticipate step three when you do this part or you will limit
the possibilities inherent in the metaphor. For instance, if "gossip" is the metaphor, then for step two you will write "gossip:
whisper, secretive, usually about something personal that is untruthful or unkind, the information changes drastically as it is
passed along." You will not write "my mother" as this would be a
personal association, not a universal one.

Part three is the most difficult step. Now you look at both step
one and two in order to write a literal sentence that replaces all
the metaphors with as many words from the list in step two or, in
most cases, words that parallel the words in step two. Add as
many words as you need to make the list words or their parallels
work and change the structure of the sentence if you need to,
but do not change the sentence in any way that would wipe out
the original literal part of the sentence. The translated sentence
must continue to be about sprinklers doing something with mowed
grass. One thing you can count on: Your final, literal, translated
sentence will be much longer than the original metaphoric sentence. Remember, metaphors compress. In this case, the word
"gossip" is loaded with associations.

Here is a possible translation for our sentence. "When no one
could see, the faintly hissing sprinklers damaged the mowed grass,

changing its appearance." There may be other translations, but they will all be about what the sprinklers did to the mowed grass. The reasoning on this translation worked by equivocating "When no one could see" with "secretive" from step two; paralleling "faintly hissing" with "whisper" from step two (You might be tempted to use "whisper" directly in the third step, but remember, no metaphors); spinning off "damage" from "usually about something personal that is untruthful or unkind" from step two; and reducing "changing its appearance" from the larger phrase "the information changes drastically as it is passed along" from step two. You do not have to use every association from step two, but try to use most of them. They are what quickly floods the subconscious mind when someone hears the metaphor. Here is how the final exercise looks when written:

<u>step one</u>: The sprinklers gossiped about mowed grass.

<u>step two</u>: gossip: secretive, whisper, usually about something personal that is untruthful or unkind, the information changes drastically as it is passed along.

<u>step three</u>: When no one could see, the faintly hissing sprinklers damaged the mowed grass, changing its appearance.

The creator of the metaphoric sentence had no idea what the sentence implied when he or she first playfully created it. The person probably did not think about the metaphor but had a sense of whether the sound of the total fusion of metaphor with the literal made a likable, interesting sentence or not. The "accidental" sentence sounded right because metaphors always communicate very indirectly. The key to shifting from the metaphoric world to the literal one is to explore all possible associations in step two without anticipating step three, and then to be imaginative in paralleling the associations in step two to others that work within the original, literal part of the sentence. If you can analyze these sentences, you will be close to analyzing the metaphorical implications of anything.

OPT:
Ways to Wield Point of View

T *Personalizing Lens*

Ti *Humbling Lens*

iii *Distancing Lens*

The phrase "point of view" can mean two things: It can refer to the philosophical position of a person; or it can refer to the position of the writer to the reader. In the latter sense, point of view can be first person (I, we), or second person (you), or third person (he, she, it, they). In truth, all of these point of views define reality, each perspective offering a variety of advantages just as different kinds of camera lenses have different photographic advantages and limitations: Telescopic lenses allow the viewer to capture reality up close but make objects seem closer together than they really are; wide angle lenses allow the viewer to see great horizontal scope but make distances seem wider apart than they really are. Just as photographers can change optics to various advantages, strong writers can opt for different points of views in achieving particular advantages. Many English teachers believe that first person point of view is too personal, that second person point of view is too informal, that third person point of view is totally objective. They are wrong on all counts.

Personalizing Lens

By writing in the first person singular (I), the writer maintains the intimacy inherent in a speaker talking directly to a reader: "I think that. . . ," "I love you," or "I think people must realize. . ." First person plural (we) also gives a piece sincere clout, backed by real people. In the "American Declaration of Independence," Thomas Jefferson outlines the peaceful alternatives the Americans tried before finally declaring their independence: "We have warned. . . ," "We have reminded. . .," and "We have appealed. . ."

However, there are spectrums of first person that are more complicated. For instance, historical writers are usually expected to research the past thoroughly enough to be able to write about it as fact from a third person, omniscient point of view: "There were many reasons for the Civil War. *They* included ideas about Lincoln. *He* knew that. . . " But the editors of *American Heritage* magazine once encouraged authors and scholars to comment on history from a personal perspective. The magazine editors asked historians to write about the one incident in American history that they would have liked to have personally witnessed and explain why. Writing from this I-wish-I-were-there, fly-on-the-wall persona resulted in writing that made history alive, ambiguous, and complex. One of Gary's favorite entries was written by historian Walter Lord who found the Golden Spike ceremony at Promontory Point, Utah, on May 10, 1869 to celebrate the first time the nation was linked coast to coast with a railway, a moment so full of promise that Lord returned to it as a panacea to the darkness of present day realities.

Like a primitive tribesman entering a spiritual world that allows entrance only on special occasion, Lord steps into A. J. Russell's famous photograph of the celebration by using first person to be part of someone else's reality. This allows him to explore the unknown details that go beyond the obvious truths:

> I want to mix with that boisterous crowd of track layers, soldiers, dishwashers, gamblers, and strumpets. I want to listen to

the 21st infantry band thumping away. I want to watch the cowcatchers touch. I want to sample the bottle of champagne held out by the man standing on the Central Pacific's locomotive Jupiter. I want to know who the lady is in the exact center of the preliminary photograph, but who vanishes in the final, climactic shot. I want to know the identity of the one man in the picture who turned his back to the camera. Was he just inattentive, or was his likeness perhaps posted as "WANTED" in every post office in the West? I want to watch Leland Stanford swing his hammer —and miss the golden spike.

When a writer places him or herself in a different space or time period, and writes from the first person point of view, new realities get emphasis and the scene comes alive: background or low status people come forward (details of people in the crowd), noise and movement come alive (the band thumps and the cowcatchers touch), people's motivations and intentions breathe again (a lady vanishes and one man turns his back), and humor escapes time's graveyard (Leland Stanford misses the stake).

First person masquerades can become even more dramatic when used to become the object, animate or inanimate, which the writer wishes to analyze or discuss. For instance, Walter Lord could have become one of the characters in the photograph mentioned above, using what he imagined to be the character's speaking style, but staying within the limits of what can actually be seen in the photograph in order to point out its details and indirectly analyze it. Mario Vargas Llosa, in an essay called "Bacon's Man" entered a grotesque portrait by the twentieth century painter Francis Bacon entitled "Head I." Llosa casts himself as the Head to describe the portrait —

> Should I call it a nose—this immense membraneous organ which picks up all smells, even the most private one? I'm referring to the grayish lump, with white scabs, that starts out at my mouth and descends as far as my bull's neck

and to discuss the implications of the bizarre portrait—

> I am not pitiful, and I do not want others to feel sympathy for me. I am what I am and that's enough for me. To know that others are worse off is a great consolation.

On a more benign note, often in children's books, authors become plants, refrigerators, or castles in order to explain the way those objects function.

Workout.

Analyze a painting, photograph, or a historical event by placing yourself in it and writing from the first person point of view. Mention the name of the painter and the title of the painting; then let the reader know immediately if you are one of the characters in the painting or are an additional character. For instance, in Giovanni di Paolo's "Christ Carrying the Cross" painted in 1426 in Sienna, you could be outside the action looking in:

> I am thankful that a stranger presses Jesus's shoulders to brace his cross-loaded shoulders but I can tell from the steadiness of his eyes, the calmness of his mouth, and the vertical strength of his body that he can carry his burden without anyone's help.

Cover all the other postures, faces, architecture, colors, lightings in the painting so that when you are done the scene comes alive (in this case not according to any previous knowledge of the Bible but according to Giovanni di Paolo's unique perspective of the event.)

If you are describing an historical event from the first person, be sure to include details you would actually encounter if you were a witness: Not only details of political, legal, artistic, or philosophical events but perhaps rituals, clothes, newspaper headlines, interior decorations, famous paintings and books that are being discussed at the time. Aside from describing sensory details of sights and sounds, also consider smells, tastes and tactile details of texture and temperature.

Humbling Lens

In an emotionally intense conversation, we tend to raise our voices, and sometimes we even have to fight the temptation to point our forefinger at the other person's face. When making a plea in a written piece, an essayist figuratively finger-points without social-breaching by addressing the reader as "you." Using the second person, a writer establishes an up-close-and-personal relationship with the reader, pulling the reader inside of the essay, as opposed to creating a comfortable distance between writer and audience. A sentence written in first person—"I am having a private thought"—allows readers to observe something intimate about the writer's experience without the reader imagining themselves in the writer's place. A sentence written in the third person— "He and she are having private thoughts."—allows both the reader and writer to look in from the outside. Strong writers know that switching to the second person point of view—"You are having a private thought."—is an effective way of jumping off the page and pulling the reader in by the collar.

In her essay "Save the Whales, Screw the Shrimp" written for *Esquire* magazine, Joy Williams uses second person, drawing attention by finger pointing right from the start of her essay:

> I don't want to talk about *me*, of course, but it seems as though far too much attention has been lavished on *you* lately—that your greed and vanities and quest for self fulfillment have been catered to far too much. You just want and want and want.

By avoiding reference to her target in the third person "they" ("They just want and want and want.") which would allow Williams's audience to escape culpability, Williams captures hypocritical yuppies who compulsively consume yet want to think of themselves as environmentally conscientious. Williams's audience, eager to acquit themselves of any blame or wrongdoing, read on, only to find that they closely resemble the profile of Williams' "you" target.

Aside from Williams's use, there are other compelling ways to use second person. One is to use the imperative form where "you" is implied through a command, such as "Turn the knob; turn off the lights." This imperative voice is most commonly associated with instruction manuals or process essays which explain how to perform a particular task, such as baking a cake. When used for non-process forms of expository writing, the effect can be dramatic. Whereas Williams uses the second person "you" form to force the reader to take responsibility for his or her actions, another writer, Danna Schaeffer, uses the imperative "you" to help the reader have compassion for her subject, former Los Angeles county prosecutor Marcia Clark.

Aside from her infamous role as the lead O.J. Simpson prosecutor, Clark also successfully prosecuted the murderer of actress Rebecca Schaeffer, Danna Schaeffer's daughter. Danna Schaeffer wrote an essay entitled "How to Be Marcia Clark" for *Mirabella* magazine, using the "you" voice to capture Clark's complicated persona. Schaeffer begins like this:

> Yell when you are born. Don't grow up rich. Learn to work hard and crave victory. Do well in school. Develop an Old Testament sense of justice. Turn into a beautiful woman but don't think of yourself as sexy. Marry someone who's not right for you. Go to law school and discover your fabulous memory stands you in perfect stead. Finish law school. Divorce. Marry again. Take a job with a criminal-defense firm.

Schaeffer knows many of her female readers who watched the trial disapprove of Clark. Anticipating her audience's unwillingness to "relate to" the sharp-edged prosecutor, Schaeffer chose finger-pointing to dress a non-Clark-fan reader in Clark's clothes, forcing the reader to try on Clark's persona by stationing the reader's point of view behind the attorney's unlikable characteristics. The imperative voice, in tandem with the intimate and poignant details of Clark's personal and professional life, help to create a more sympathetic portrait of Clark. On the other hand, the imperative voice gives readers already sympathetic to Clark the privilege to participate in Marcia-Clark Day: the essay, for Clark supporters, serves as an homage to the prosecutor. Finger Point commands often become a list, so it may be helpful to review "Netting" in the flow section of the Style unit.

Prophets and preachers make more philosophical commands with implied second person point of view, some of the most poetic and meaningful being ascribed to Jesus in Matthew, 5:1-7:28:

> You cannot serve God and mammon . . . Do not throw your pearls before swine, lest they trample them under foot and turn to attack you . . . Enter by the narrow gate; for the gate is wide and the way is easy that leads to destruction, and those who enter by it are many. For the gate is narrow and the way is hard, that leads to life, and those who find it are few.

Prophetic second person is poignantly used in Squamish Indian Chief Seattle's "Reply to Washington Territory Governor Isaac Stevens" in 1854, after the sale of two million acres to the federal government and before the great Indian relocations and massacres of the 1860's. The letter starts in first person then shifts to second person: "You wander far from the graves of your ancestors and seemingly without regret. Your religion was written upon tables of stone by the iron finger of your God so that you not forget" as opposed to the Native Americans whose religion is found in the dreams of old men in"solemn hours."

As with Chief Seattle's letter, often finger point enters a piece unexpectedly. "The Art of Teaching Science" by Lewis Thomas for *New York Times* was written while he was chancellor of the Sloan-Kettering Cancer Center. Thomas's speech also starts in first person and then shifts to second in order to stress what needs to be done to teach science effectively:

> You cannot possibly teach quantum mechanics without mathematics, to be sure, but you can describe the strangeness of the world opened up by quantum theory . . . that there are deep mysteries and profound paradoxes . . . Do not teach that biology is a useful perhaps profitable science; that can come later. . . Teach ecology early on. Let it be understood that the earth's life is a system . . . held in an almost unbelievably improbable state of regulated balance.

Thomas' lines remain prophetic.

Workout.

Write about an important personality in the second person the way Danna Schaeffer writes about Marcia Clark. Consider politicians, artists, philosophers, scientist, or writers. For instance, an analysis of Sherwood Anderson, who wrote a collection of short stories entitled *Winesburg, Ohio*, might start something like this:

> Your name is Sherwood Anderson and you know that life in a small town is not as tranquil and simple as most people suppose it to be. You decide that very short stories about all the people who live in a town called Winesburg will allow you to enter the private lives of people, dramatizing their secret aspirations and perverse emotional needs. These people would realistically intersect each others lives and so you realize some would have to enter each other's separate stories. This could potentially make the stories seem hectic so you decide to create George Willard, a reporter who would naturally intersect several people's lives at different times in his life. But you do not want the reader to fall into the trap of thinking that the most noticed character in either one's life or a collection of stories is necessarily the touchstone of morality or reality so you create a second character named Dr. Reefy who. . .

Distancing Lens

Third person point of view (he, she, it, they) has other advantages. Try starting a piece with "He" and never refer to who that "he" is. When writers use third person without an antecedent, English teachers get nervous. However, third person without an antecedent has advantages. For instance, in his short story entitled " A Very Short Story," Hemingway's first sentence is "One hot evening in Padua they carried him up onto the roof and he could look out over the top of the town." We never find out this person's name (and it takes a second to understand that "they" refers to other soldiers) as he goes through a humiliating affair with Luz, a nurse, who "they all liked." The affair includes a surgery where Luz takes care of him, a desperate need to get married because "they wanted every one to know about it" but they had no time for the banns, delayed letters to him on the front, Luz's demand that he get a job in the States before she join him, her affair with an Italian major, Luz's rationalizations about the affair with the original "he" as being unserious, and his contacting gonorrhea from a sales girl in a taxi. By knowing Luz's name, Hemingway empowers her and underscores her controlled manipulations, and on the other hand, by having the man's real name calloused with "he," Hemingway implies the man's value-empty, identity-robbed, stereotypic nature.

Third person singular (he, she, it) also can create a composite that turns individuals into an ugly giant. The writer assigns a long list of particulars to one single person that in reality could only be found among several people of the target group. Germain Greer does this in her landmark book *The Female Eunuch*. She wants to shatter the stereotypic self-indulged woman. When all the items that these women desire as a group are assigned to a single, indefinite "she," for a split second the reader associates all the listed items weighting on one person, this tonnage rendering the subject a grotesque composite.

79

For Greer this creates a giant, a cosmic vacuum cleaner, sucking up all that the natural world has to offer:

> She is the crown of creation, the masterpiece. The depths of the sea are ransacked for pearl and coral to deck her; the bowels of the earth are laid open that she might wear gold, sapphires, diamonds, and rubies. Baby seals are battered with staves, unborn lambs ripped from their mothers' wombs, millions of moles, muskrats, squirrels, minks, ermines, foxes, beavers, chinchillas, ocelots, lynxes, and other small and lovely creatures die untimely deaths that she might have furs.

Later the parts of many ad-page women merge into a giant plastic doll whose "glossy lips and mat complexion, her unfocused eyes and flawless fingers, her extraordinary hair all floating shining, curling and gleaming, reveal the inhuman triumph of cosmetics, lighting, focusing and printing, cropping, and composition." Such constant Netting allows a writer to build a cartoon that unravels anyone who identifies with any part of this exaggerated, third person composite.

Workout.

"Shipping Out" by David Foster for *Harper's Magazine*, created a hilarious attack on ship cruising. It never looked worse than after the lists of grotesque perspectives on recreation, food, attitude, and environment that make this lengthy article hard to put down. Smelling "suntan lotion spread over 2,100 pounds of hot flesh" is only the start of this voyage of horror. Pick your own disgusting target group: fast food gulpers, prideful athletes, pompous English teachers, hypocritical religious leaders, arrogant computer sales people, sentimental aunts and uncles. You need to create your own categories: the group's most important issues, ritual objects, clothes, dialogue for specific situations, diets, ambitions, self-images, and anything else you wish to write about concerning your target group. You will need at least ten categories. Second, list five to ten individual responses under each of your categories. For instance, if you were writing about prideful athletes, one of the categories might be dialogue you have heard individuals of the group use to flirt and hustle the opposite sex. Write down five to ten of these lines. Interview members or hang out in locker rooms and eavesdrop on conversations. For other categories, visit the library.

Finally you are ready to write your paper. Use the flow techniques to sweep together all the details under each category together into sentences so that, connected under third person, you create a third person singular ugly giant. For instance, if you were writing about prideful athletes, you will have "He says," not "They say," followed by a list of flirtatious remarks that actually come from five to ten members of the group. The third person singular point of view sucks group characteristics into one swollen vat and then pops the group's plug.

SCRUB:
Ways to Purge Pretense

 *Facial Pack*

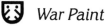 *Metal Mask*

 War Paint

Strong writers scrub euphemistic language out of their writing. *Euphemism* is agreeable or inoffensive language which replaces words that are considered offensive, unpleasant, painful, indelicate, frightful, embarrassing, or mundane but accurate. In short, euphemism's purpose is to make reality more pleasing, or more important than it really is. Some writers are paid or encouraged not to scrub. Euphemistic clogging starts in graduate school where students are encouraged to establish priestly positions by surrounding their material with insincere jargon-haze. Lawmakers, business correspondents, newscasters, and attorneys all cloud, anesthetize, or intimidate litigants, electorate, viewers, and customers with versions of euphemisms.

The best way to learn to scrub euphemism is to get behind the euphemistic mask of a person who depends on inflated language; then pop off the mask. Once you recognize euphemism and understand the tricks used by those who create it, inflated language should be purged from your writing forever, unless one of two things happen in your life: you grow so cynical that you count on subtle forms of lying to manipulate people, or you lack the energy to carefully think through ideas and articulate them. Below are three groups of euphemistic realities, some more harmful than others: Facial Pack, War Paint, and Metal Mask. To purge the evil spirits, put on each mask, and for a moment, clown with it.

Facial Pack

For the most part, facial packs are harmless attempts to make unimportant, normal-but-unappetizing realities more pleasing or important than they really are. Most of us have a few minor insecurities about facing some of the mundane realities of life. For instance, no one really cares to go into details about what pours out of their intestines or where it gets poured. That place was once euphemized as the "toilet," because a toilet was where one merely used cosmetics or shaved, in other words, a place for more pleasant, perhaps vain, activities. "Toilet" went the way of all euphemisms after a long period of time: the reality which the euphemism replaces gradually seeps back in, and a new euphemism needs to be concocted. In this case, "bathroom" became a euphemism for the "toilet," but for many, that word has begun to stink; so "little girls' room," "John," or "convenience" cover the fumes.

Sex is another animal function that most humans would rather euphemize. Again, this is usually a harmless use of language softening; it depends. For instance, if two people have a great deal of affection for one another and call sex "making love," they cover up their animal desire for sex, and highlight the emotional or spiritual attraction of sex. However, if the couple have no affection for one another, but are merely using each other as a live tissue surrogate to have orgasmic satisfaction, then to describe their sex as "making love" becomes especially euphemistic, a lie used to hide their motivations from others or to fool themselves into believing their sex is meaningful.

The term "sexual intercourse" makes the act more mechanical, because multi-syllabic, Latin or Greek stemmed words sound more important to us than monosyllabic, Anglo-Saxon words such as the word "fuck." The euphemism "sexual intercourse," by removing both the animal, passionate, or spiritual associations of sex, becomes a facial pack for medical personnel who wish to perceive the act as outside the realm of both the spiritual and the animal. Even the animal can be taken out of animals, and re-placed with Jane Austenalia, when guides at Sea World refer to animal sex as "courtship behavior." Sexual euphemism can even be extended into interior design. During the late 1800's, when the word "leg" was considered too meaty and had to be euphemized as "a limb," the legs of furniture had to be covered with fringe. In the commercial world, personal ads hide "sexual desires" with "warm imaginations" and pornographic films get facial packs of "adult" or "frank."

The human ego is also groomed by euphemizing jobs and pro-fessions. These euphemisms can inflate résumés or make job descriptions seem more attractive. People who stuffed dead bod-ies with chemicals, boxed them, and lowered them into a hole in the dirt—notice that Super-literalism kicks dirt on euphemisms—took on a face called "undertaker" until people really imagined themselves being taken under. At that point, "undertaker" changed to "mortician." Likewise, garbage collectors upgrade to "sanitation engineers," a teenage employee who opens up an ice cream shop inflates to a "manager;" "managers" to "execu-tives;" "executives" to "vice presidents."

Consumer products often get waxed with facial packs to make their appearance more pleasing. If a "used" car is referred to as being "previously owned" or "repossessed," subconsciously one can hope it was used much less than if it were a "used" car. A vomit bag on an airplane takes on a friendlier face if it is labeled only "for motion discomfort." "Small," "medium," and "large" genital athletic supports for men are almost always euphemized as "medium," "large," and "extra-large;" while the pentagon gets more Congressional support for toothpicks if they are hyped as "wood interdental stimulators."

Everyday, simple realities are facial-packed. How harmless these are always depends on the context. Do you make a "weak" de-cision and then hide it as a "compassionate" one; collect "cro-nies" who give you simplistic advice and then you hide them as "friends;" do you live or work with a group "wracked with dissen-sion" and hide it with a "healthy difference of opinion"? We find many family and work related discussions are focused on the seriousness of euphemisms. So did Leo Braudy, a member of a Dean's Search Committee at the University of Southern California, who according to *Harper's Magazine*, once warned his fellow members to be skeptical of the following euphemisms found in letters of recommendation for candidates requesting teaching positions: "charismatic" replaces "no interest in any opinion but his own"; "committed to the university" means "appears at every cocktail party"; "consults with faculty" neutralizes "indecisive"; "internationally known" hypes up "likes to go to or manage conferences"; "listens well" facial packs "has no ideas of his or her own." Facial packs can help people get through many painful days and cover for small sins, but they can also cover up serious professional, political, or moral dilemmas that require more truthful thought.

Workout.
To dramatize how much we depend on euphemisms, make a list of all your nasty habits as a student, or your flaws as a parent or child, or your shortcomings as a mate, or your inadequacies as an employee. Be sure that you list about ten or fifteen of your solidly unattractive qualities. Then for each of the flaws on your list, think of a euphemistic word or phrase which puts a prettier face on each item. For instance, if one of your student flaws is that you procrastinate, you might doll up your fault by saying you are "spontaneous" or that you have "a unique sense of time." In Molière's play "The Misanthrope," the character Eliante points out that male lovers do this assignment with their ladies: "The spindly lady has a slender grace; The fat one has a most majestic pace . . . The haughty lady has a noble mind; The mean one's witty, and the dull one's kind . . ."

Avoid creating antonyms, or terms which simply mean the exact opposite. Remember, the purpose of euphemism is to distort reality, and in the case of Facial Packs, the idea is to make real unpleasantries more pleasing; so in coming up with euphemisms for your flaws, you want to retain the basic flaw, but with willfully misleading language that makes a fault seem to be a virtue.

Cool down.
Now pretend you are working for a public relations firm and write a ten line classified advertisement trying to sell yourself to

your professors, your parents, your children, your mate, or your employer. If you feel you are among the blessed and without faults, then write a flaw list for your instructor, your parents, your children, your employer, even a famous person, and then write a Facial Pack for that person. For instance, if student Vanessa Schueler wrote a personal add that truthfully described her negative self and the cynical list of attributes her boyfriend must have to fulfill her most selfish needs, it would look like this:

> Young single mother with bitchy attitude, procrastinates, and is always late, seeks single man from early twenties to mid-late thirties, who must have stable job and not live with parents, in order to have stable relationship, good times, financial well-being, and vacations.

After Vanessa applies a Facial Pack to the personal ad, it is ready for publication:

> SWF Seeks Mr. Right: Puerile maiden well sprung with moxie, deference, and a knack for fashionable entrances, endeavoring to match with independent active professional, ranging from youthful to early middle age; welcome his attachment to indissoluble enterprise and disengagement to his begetter's domicile in order that we have a moored affiliation, merrymaking, underwriting, and furloughs.

Metal Mask

When euphemisms move from every-day world usage to describing official business, academic, governmental, social, or other professional truths and experiences, they harden into metal mask. Metal Mask is also referred to as jargon, buzz words, and official labels. Instead of making language more lively or reality more accurate as metaphoric slang can, jargon sterilizes life by protecting the reader from something complex that deserves more thought or explanation. A Metal Masked writer cuts himself or herself off from the reader and cuts the reader off from reality.

All professional, governmental, and academic endeavors have their own hypnotic language chanted by their own expert metal maskers. They believe that jargon-face is necessary because it both hypes and simplifies discussion by dissolving complexity into a single, important sounding code word. Here is a typical complexity that gets metal-masked: There are people who live in demolished buildings; whose schools are a mess and whose English is almost unrecognizable; who are resentful of people who have money, but who have little chance of ever making substantial amounts of money themselves unless they do it illegally though murder, robbery, drug sales or legitimate back breaking work; who are treated as less than human because of the pigment of their skin. A neutral-sounding, official metal mask word or phrase—"disadvantaged," "underprivileged," or "culturally deprived"—can sedate the pain of these details. This is dangerous because metal mask protects a jury member, researcher, official, or lawmaker from mentioning, and eventually from even thinking about, the details of the experience the metal mask labels.

George Orwell was one of the first to pull the disguise off jargon used to mask military atrocities. For instance, during different wars of this century, waged by different countries with different ideologies, metal masks have been used to numb the effects of war's horrors on both the soldiers that wage those wars and the public that must support them. For instance, when defenseless villages have been bombarded from the air, inhabitants driven from their homes, livestock machine-gunned, grain supplies torched, women raped, and children murdered, the official anesthesia is jargon such as "pacification" or "neutralization." When innocent people are killed as scapegoats to build unification through hate, jargon such as "elimination of unreliable elements" numbs to make it easier to kill; when troops kill their own troops, the stupidity and pain is camouflaged with "friendly fire" or "incontinent ordinance."

Metal Mask goes to war everywhere, even at entertainment centers. The war on truth takes the form of an official language-mist at places such as Sea World in Orlando, Florida, where, according to the *Orlando Sentinel* a few years ago, tour guides first were required to be guided by language-numbing manuals. The guides learned to replace realities such as "hurt" with "injured," "captured" with "acquired," "cage" with "enclosure," and "captivity" with "controlled environment." When it is time for management at an amusement park to fire employees, management puts on another metal mask. "Firing" is replaced with "right-sizing," "redundancy elimination," "career assessment and re-employment," or "involuntary separation."

All industries use jargon to hide dangerous or unpleasant realities from employees and the public. The atomic energy industry sedates us with "energetic disassembles" and "plutonium taking up residence," as if a good neighbor moved in when radiation leaks and spreads cancerous poison; the lumber industry "manages standing inventory through regeneration cutting" instead of logging live trees through clear cutting; the medical industry pulls sheets over eyes with "therapeutic misadventure" when someone dies on the surgery table; and the airlines evaporate responsibility for an airline explosion by referring to it as "involuntary conversion." Government softens tax bites by muzzling them with metal masks such as "revenue enhancement" and the Environmental Protection Agency neutralizes acid rain as "poorly buffered precipitation."

The humanities arena has its own tournaments where metal masking jousts with reality. When jargon such as "semiotic discourses," "symbolic registers," "experimental anti-myths," "formalistic breakdowns," "derivative from the deconstruction of _____ (fill in with any famous writer or artist)," or "psycholinguistic truths" trot out as weapons, two dangerous things happen. First of all, Metal Mask numbs the listener and reader and declares that, even though art is special and breaks from the ordinary, the understanding of that art can only be articulated with inflated language outside of everyday reality. Secondly, the Metal Mask labels replace the details of the art or literary work itself. For instance, if a literature course fills with metal mask, the authors' senses of humor, irony, moral dilemmas, and characters' sensibilities begin to fade and lose importance. Metal-Masking the language to talk about literature cannibalizes the literature itself. The murder of great art is not as horrifying as the murder of people, but it is still painful.

One reason teachers have stopped discussing jargon and labels is because of guilt about political correctness. Social planners, leaders of support groups, and teachers started covering realities with Metal Mask in order to mitigate the stigma associated with racial, cultural, medical, emotional, and intellectual minorities. Metal Mask created out of good intentions has the same problems with Metal Mask created out of negative intentions. For instance, in an article "The New Verbal Order," for *U.S. News & World Report*, John Leo points to teachers in Philadelphia creating a support group for disabled students, softening the word "disabled" into "special needs," only to attract a homeless person who had a "special need" for housing. Then the teachers hyped up to "disabled" to "physically challenged," only to bring in a frightened fifth-grade teacher intimidated by "physically" rowdy students.

Trying to make unpleasant problems more pleasant confuses comprehending what the problem is in the first place. In the brothers Grimm tale "Snow White and the Seven Dwarfs," the dwarfs are small adults, considered misshapen by the upper class, and so are social outsiders. Snow White's treating them as equals, even humbling herself by cleaning their house, makes her humanity credible. On the other sterile hand, Disney's Snow White cleans for goo-goo, muffin-faced, stuffed dolls with sentimental names. This cutsey clientele turns her cleaning into a doll-house, little-girl activity that has nothing to do with the humbling that builds character in the original Grimm's tale. Disney damages the moral quality of the story when he visually euphemizes dwarfs so that they look more like toys for the normal proportioned society to which Snow White belongs. Social planners wipe out the same reality when they change "Snow White and the Seven Dwarfs" to John Leo's parody, "One of the Monocultural Oppressed Womyn Confronts the Vertically Challenged."

Workout.
Not only do college courses and manuals become clogged with metal mask, this jargon begins to need its own classes to explain itself. Metal mask creates layers of meaning that take time to peel away. The price for such hyped up reality is that what could have been taught in two weeks needs to be stretched into a

semester. To purge this mentality, create your own Metal Masked course by giving instructions on a simple procedure—washing your face, throwing out the trash, giving someone a kiss—by breaking the procedure into six, numbered steps and by giving each step its own jargoned label. Create your own labels by using your thesaurus and thinking in terms of long, multi-syllabic words. Title your subject, and any of its "parts," with original Metal Mask.

For instance, J.Robertson and G.Osborne did a similar assignment for *Datamation Magazine*. They gave directions on how to use a "Postal System Input Buffer Device," in plain English, a mailbox. They broke dropping letters into a mailbox into several paragraphs of instructions, each one labeled with metal mask: "Position of Operator," "Initial Setup," "Start Operations," "Feed Cycles." These steps were sprinkled with parenthetical "notes" and "warnings" and reference to parts that were hyped into "multi-function control lever," "but gate," "box memory."

War Paint

War Paint uses a pinch of Metal Mask, stirs in a redundancy of words, and grinds up distinctions of meanings made by *Anglo-Saxon* and *Latin* or *Greek* based words. This paste covers a larger surface of writing than Metal Mask, replacing vivid, thoughtful writing with a mass of confusion that sounds impressive and intimidating. War paint is sometimes smeared over professor's lectures, legal papers, law books, business correspondence, and speeches of the self-important. As with Facial Packs, and especially Metal Mask, War Paint relies on multi-syllabic English that has Latin and Greek origins as opposed to the often simpler Anglo-Saxon based, one syllable words. The fact that English is made up from both bases makes English a rich, exacting language that can differentiate between fine shades of meaning. War Paint abuses that richness.

For instance, "said" is an Anglo-Saxon based word that means something very different from the Latin based word "indicated," a word that derives from the Latin word for "say" or "speak." Since we have both, over the centuries English has assigned a special meaning to "indicated," which implies a response that is less committed, or less direct, or more vague than "said." In fact, "indicated" can even suggest affirmation through lifted eyebrows as opposed to the directness of speech: "When we asked the instructor if homework was due tomorrow, she raised her eyebrows and grimaced, indicating that we should get it done, but she never said we must do it." Someone putting on war paint abuses this difference. For instance, if the teacher "told" the class to do their homework, it would be painting over the truth to say she "implied" that the class do their homework. That is exactly what War Paint does. It uses a closely related, multi-syllabic Greek or Latin based word in place of a more accurate monosyllabic Anglo-Saxon word in order to sound more impressive and to create confusion. In the case of the teacher example, that confusion is used to make being told to do homework ambiguous and then avoid responsibility for doing it.

Avoiding responsibility is a big part of War Paint. For instance, when an attorney or business correspondent for an automobile manufacturer must admit in a recall letter to a customer that the company's poor manufacturing might kill the customer driver, a palette of war paint is immediately applied. The admission is made, but it is crafted to sound intimidating and beyond reproach, while at the same time the reality of the dangerous situation is flattened through confusion. The result is designed to quiet the customer's outrage and also shift the blame away from the manufacturer. The War Paint could look like this: "Please bring your car in for service. A certain deficiency could adversely affect vehicle control." The multi-syllabic word "deficiency," that normally implies "a slight lacking," paints over the truth of "poor manufacturing." Meanwhile "adversely affect vehicle control" glazes over "the car could crash, killing you." Some call this war paint professional writing; it is nothing but distortion.

Every student has one time or another tried to make up for lack of knowledge through redundancy of words. Likewise, lawmakers try to please everyone by loading laws with enough chaos for people on opposite political sides to both claim victory. Here is some layering of War Paint from the *Congressional Record* : "The oil price structure should give the President a substantial measure of administrative flexibility to craft the price regulatory mechanism in a manner designed to optimize production form domestic properties subject to a statutory parameter requiring the regulatory pattern to proven prices from exceeding a maximum weighted average." A previous president of the National Council of Teachers of English scrubbed this statement to find "Congress should authorize the President to design an oil price structure. The system must encourage domestic production, but outlaw exorbitant prices."

Unfortunately, humanities professors, including English teachers, are sometimes guilty of War Paint. Here is a line from a description of a graduate literature course on a University of California campus: "If persons are answerable for the characters they construct when they as much as think about a person, writers of stories are no less answerable for their characters —the standard disclaimer about the resemblances between characters and persons being 'purely coincidental': notwithstanding." Is this saying "All people, including writers, imagine characters based on people they know, even if they claim they do not"? Alex Heard, writing for *The New Republic,* discovered the following phrases at a Modern Language Association convention, all designed to "obliterate the layman": "derivation from the deconstruction of Kantian formalism," "the shift from expressive to structured totality cannot *ground* mediation," and "History can be totalized when being reified only if it moves into the absence of the real."

Workout.
One way to demask War Paint, purging it and also being able to see through the fabrications of others who use it, is to rewrite a simple adage, nursery line, or a well known quotation into war paint so that it extends a few lines over almost a third of a page. Here are some ways to do this: First, change all simple words to more complicated ones, and use as many words for each word as you can find. Second, take simple items and actions and break

them into smaller unnecessary-to-talk-about parts, and use more words to discuss these. "The grass is always greener on the other side of the fence" becomes "The growth of minute, macilent leaves consistently and invariably exists in a more stimulating propagation, and in a higher realm of verdant hue or vibrant chlorophyll on the territory and confines antipodal to the separating barrier that is hued from heavily vegetated terrain and then fabricated for use of property definition." Notice that the word "fence" is broken down into its functions, "separating barrier" and "property definition," and where its material comes from, "heavily vegetated terrain," and how that material is obtained, "hued." All of these items are pumped up with facial pack and metal mask and expanded.

Cool down.

Aside from blown-up words and wordiness, over-use of the verb "to be," having the subject of the sentence acted upon instead of doing the action, adds to war paint. This is called the *passive voice*. For instance, if "Mary had a little lamb as white as snow" is changed to "It is known Mary had a little lamb," "It is known" makes Mary seem especially important, known to many people. Likewise, if "A little lamb was given to Mary," whereby the lamb is acted upon instead of Mary acting on or having the lamb, the little lamb puffs up into a more special item than the original lines intended. This passive voice or weakened verb, sometimes combined with it-phrases, creates subtle War Paint, adding just enough color to the mask's nose to lift it slightly higher in the air.

2
FORM

TIME WARPING
ENCIRCLING
LAYERING
BURSTING

Forming Humpty-Dumpty

Aside from knowing how to craft with style, a writer needs to design a larger form to interweave myriad details and ideas. Typically, this form might be a legal brief, a magazine article, a cookbook chapter, a business report, a history term paper. There are many alternatives to designing within any of these contexts. Sometimes style helps influence the shape of this form; sometimes the form decides the style.

Most English teachers have dictated what this form should be, reducing it to the following formula: Decide on a thesis statement. Start the paper off with that thesis statement. Cluster all similar details and their implications into three to five different paragraphs. Include enough explanation in each paragraph so that the reader understands how the details and implications in each paragraph support the thesis statement. Restate the thesis in a concluding paragraph.

This traditional organization works well for in-class essay exams because it is easy to follow and appears to be fail-safe. However, the precast bones of the essay's structure can protrude, distracting from the piece's meaningfulness. If the writer does not apply the stylistic choices to give the essay soul, the material has no flesh, dehydrating into a tedious, unreadable academic exercise. Too often the form is an English-teacher-pleaser because over the decades teachers have made the essay's bone structure a holy relic.

Strong writers never believe there is only one way to shape a large piece of writing, particularly an essay that has been crafted over several days or weeks and has undergone countless revisions. The new breed of essayists do not base their organization on the academic thesis essay described above. Designing organizational architecture for any occasion can be creative and stimulating, often evolving from the function or purpose of the piece. Whatever shape a piece takes, the notion that an ideal organization for writing exists is an illusion shattered by many learning-to-write books, beginning with the ancient Greek philosopher, Aristotle. His works on writing knocked the written world off the ancient wall; then he created new modes, never intending those modes to be cast in bronze.

We have re-examined the forms of classic and contemporary essays, knocked them off the wall, and put them back together again, some as variations of classic forms, others as new forms, but not with the idea that any should ever be ossified in stone. We think Aristotle would approve. Each form has its own purpose, strengths, and weaknesses. All can be combined with each other to form countless others for endless applications, ranging from academic purposes to personal or practical ones. Essayists typically shape in one of four ways: They narrate, define, divide, or disarm. We include discussion of the problems of each and possible design solutions under Time-Warping, Encircling, Layering, and Bursting.

TIME WARPING:
Ways to Narrate

ʻ, *Splitting the Second*

⭕ *Flashback*

↻ *Strip Tease*

Ⓐ *Raising the Dead*

Narrative essays, ones that describe a sequence of personal, scientific, business, political, or historical actions, pose interesting challenges for an essayist: In order to narrate, the essayist must story-tell, exaggerating some details to enhance, adding others to clarify, and editing out others to open the flow of the narration. To intensify any event, some of the best narratives blur the line between fact and fiction. (The opposite can happen. Many works of fiction, such as Don Delillo's "Videotape," which is half-rooted in real events, blur the line between fiction and fact.) Whatever the narrative piece, detailed organization of events in a time-frame bend material to control the reader's perception.

Time can be used and organized in countless ways, each method serving different narrative purposes. Sometimes a writer may want to slow down time, detailing an event by Splitting the Second. Other times, the essayist may need to focus on poignant events that lead up to an important revelation or conclusion, leapfrogging through stepping-stones of time, intensifying the importance of each time-step by using present tense narration. We call this Flashback. When each time-step is a revelation in itself, where time keeps resetting itself to create mini-climaxes, we see the piece as a Strip Tease. Finally, Raising the Dead allows for a blend of narration with imagination that can transcend time.

Splitting the Second

Writers must sometimes narrate brief, poignant moments of fleeting reality in which an event has lasting, significant meaning or which causes an important change in perspective. These fleeting moments present a challenging narrational task: The narrator must take an action that happens within seconds and fill out the experience with so much detail that the narration of the event takes much longer to read and savor than the actual experience took in real time. In fact, the reader can only believe in the reality of the event if the writer makes it more vivid and detailed than it actually could be perceived in real time, where the speed of the event blurs many details. Therefore, the writer stroboscopes the action in slow motion, slicing the action into separate, smaller segments —whether the action is a passionate kiss, wolfing down a bowl of chili verde, the landing of a red-shafted flicker in a tree, or a single flight stage of a newly engineered space shuttle. Consider this excerpt from N. Scott Momaday's *House Made of Dawn*:

> They were golden eagles, a male and a female, in their mating flight. They were cavorting, spinning and spiraling on the cold, clear columns of air and they were beautiful. They swooped and hovered, leaning on the air, and swung close together, feinting and screaming with delight. The female was full grown, and the span of her broad wings was greater than any man's height. There was a fine flourish to her motion; she was deceptively, incredibly fast, and her pivots and wheels were wide and full bloom. But her great weight was streamlined and perfectly controlled. She carried a rattlesnake; it hung shining from her feet, limp and curving out in the trail of her flight. Suddenly her wings and tail fanned, catching full on the wind, and for an in-

stant she was still, widespread and spectral in the blue, while her mate flared past and away, turning around in the distance to look for her. Then she began to beat upward at an angle from the rim until she was small in the sky, and she let go of the snake. It fell slowly, writhing and rolling, floating out like a bit of silver thread against the wide backdrop of the land. She held still above, buoyed up on the cold current, her crop and hackles were gleaming like copper in the sun. The male swerved and sailed. He was younger than she and a little more than half as large. He was quicker, tighter in his moves. He let the carrion drift by; then suddenly he gathered himself and stooped, sliding down in a blur of motion to the strike. He hit the snake on the head, with not the slightest deflection of his course or speed, cracking its long body like a whip. Then he rolled and swung upward in a great pendulum arc, riding out his momentum. At the top of his glide he let go of the snake in turn, but the female did not go for it. Instead she soared out over the plain, nearly out of sight like a mote receding into the haze of the far mountain. The male followed, and Abel watched them go, straining to see, saw them veer once, dip and disappear.

Splitting.

Instead of seeing the eagles' flight as a single general action—"Two eagles were flying and mating overhead"—Momaday breaks down each moment of action, harnessing subtle movements, carefully selecting details and using style to both fragment actions and flow them together. The general action "flying" is slow-motioned to see specific movements with specific verbs such as "cavorting," "spinning," "spiraling," "swerved," and "sailed." Strong writers know that every action is made up of smaller, related actions. For instance, if you were to follow a recipe which calls for a cup of chopped onion, you know you will be chopping; however, hidden beyond this seemingly simple task is a whole list of other actions: *choosing* an onion, *purchasing* it, *taking* it home, *peeling* it, and then *chopping*. The chopping itself can be broken down further: the cook *slashes* the onion in one direction, *slashes* in another, and then *slices* the onion through both cuts to create small dice.

Toning.

Detailed verbs not only establish reality, they also create an overall mood or attitude. Without ever saying directly what the mood is, Momaday confirms that the experience was majestic or awesome. The verbs "cavorting" and "spinning" suggest agile play-fulness and gracefulness, especially when looped with the speed suggested by the verbs "swerved" and "sailed." Aside from verb selection, Momaday carefully filters the scene by using color elements such as blue, silver, copper, clear, or golden, all gleaming visuals that suggest an ethereal tone as opposed to lime-green, rust, and purple—all colors which would plummet the mood earth-bound. The subject of flight may seem to inevitably create a mood of majesty, but no subject is on automatic pilot. Contrast Momaday's piece with Annie Dillard's Splitting the Second in "Stunt Pilot":

> Pitching snow filled all the windows, and shapes of dark rock. I had no notion which way was up. Everything was black or gray or white except the fatal crevasses; everything made noise and shook. I felt my face smashed sideways and saw rushing abstractions of snow in the windshield. Patches of cloud obscured the snow fleetingly. We straightened out, turned and dashed at the mountainside for another pass, which was made, apparently, on our ear, and fell away. If a commercial plane's black box, such as the FAA painstakingly recovers from crash sites, could store videotapes as well as pilots' last words, some videotapes would look like this: a mountainside coming up at the windows from all directions, ice and snow and rock filling the screen up close and screaming by . . . I saw the windshield fill with red rock. The mountain looked infernal, a dreary and sheer plane of lifeless rock. It was red and sharp; its gritty blades cut through the clouds at random. The mountain was quiet. It was in shade. Careening, we made sideways passes at these brittle peaks too steep for snow. Their rock was full of iron, somebody shouted at me then or later; the iron had rusted, so they were red. Later, when I was back on the ground, I recalled that, from a distance, the two jagged peaks called the Twin Sisters looked translucent against the sky; they were sharp, tapered and fragile as arrowheads . . . I caught a snake in the salt chuck; the snake, eighteen inches long, was swimming in the green shallows.

In this flight, danger rips grace. Dillard's verbs are unsettling—"smashed," "dashed," shouted"—and even the fact that she uses many verbs which end in an edgy, quickly-spoken "-ed," as opposed to a rolling and lilting "-ing," adds to the tension. Dillard continues to make her flight rocky by using pausing, disconcerting, short sentences which force the prose to engine-stall. Dillard also filters the flight with mood-suggesting colors—black, gray,

99

white, and red—serious colors associated with danger or oblivion.

Fusing.

Aside from verbs and colors, the metaphors and other sensory details fuse reality with mood in both pieces. For instance, both writers include details about a snake, but have different metaphorical implications: Momaday's snake flickers "like a silver thread," becoming a symbol of the sun, and is a shared object of play which unites the male and female in a mating dance; Dillard's snake "in the green shadows" is unexpected, an ominous reminder of life on the ground. Dillard fuses other details with metaphors which suggest earthy vulnerability: "fatal crevices," "the mountain looked infernal," "fragile as arrowheads."

Dillard slows the action through diversions, subconscious meanderings, such as dwelling on a video-action black box which the reader associates with plane crashes. The black box detail would mental-sputter anyone flying with a stunt pilot. Dillard also includes other sensory details, not just what she sees, but kinesthetic details that register panic, "I forced myself to hold my heavy head up against the G's, and to raise my eyelids, heavy as barbells," and nerve-rattling acoustic details, "everything made noise and shook" and "somebody shouted at me." In contrast, Momaday's silence buoys the eagles' majestic flight.

In both pieces, details filtered through style are themselves the proof of the reality of both events. Strong writers know that the careful showing of details is stronger than telling the reader what to think about reality. If Momaday merely told the reader that the mating flight was awesome, or Dillard told the reader that the stunt flight was nerve fraying, then only the reader's faith would wing reality. Reality based on complete faith is always suspect.

Scope.

For different Splitting-the-Second tastes, read almost any great fiction. For instance John Hawkes, in *Death, Sleep & The Traveler*, splits dream-sequence seconds in order to satirize Freudian clichés about dream symbols. Also many memoirs contain poignant Splits, such as *Red Azalea* by Anchee Min, which splits moments of a betrayal Min was forced to take part in when she was the leader of the Little Red Guards during the Chinese Cultural Revolution. Gretel Ehrlich's *The Solace of Open Spaces*, Splits Seconds to capture seasonal moods where rich metaphors blend her emotional journey and the landscape during "smooth-skulled" winter.

Workout.

Pick out a walking course that can be traveled within ten to twenty seconds, or focus on a simple meal which would take only a few minutes to eat, or fleeting dramatic moment of a sporting event or a famous trial. All these events would normally occur too quickly for anyone to notice their small details and subtle changes. Put the event in slow motion by breaking it into at least three smaller time slots.

Force yourself to spend an hour taking notes. Look closely at small details, taking notes on everything: stains, light reflections, insects, aromas, textures, and colors. To help you notice all the sensory details, head two or three sheets of paper with each of the five senses. During the note-taking phase, stay away from qualifying or judgmental terms or abstractions such as "beautiful," "ugly," "dirty." Write down only the details that make you think in these terms: an orange-flamed flower petal, the edge of a crumbled plastic cup, a grease smeared curb.

When you have three pages of notes, pick one of the following five moods: paranoia, ecstasy, surreal, amusement, serenity. This mood is your thesis or controlling idea and will help you to decide which details to include and which to omit. Without ever saying what your mood is, organize your draft, describing the details in a way that suggests your mood. Use Break-up and Line-up metaphors to help create a second-splitting, mood-evoking description. Since you are describing a physical experience, telescoping sentences may be especially helpful. Flow and Pause can help underscore mood: Lots of flow can be calming and circular; lots of pause can help create tension. Realities made of details speak more powerfully than abstract or judgmental statements. Avoid the phrases "the way," "kind of," and "sort of" because they sound as if they mean something but say nothing at all, gobbling up chunks of space needed to use exact words to express a complex thought or observation. We call these phrases Amoeba Vocabulae. Filter them out.

Cool Down.
Although this assignment will help build writing control and make interesting essays, Splitting the Second can also appear as a part of other larger pieces. Many times it is necessary to include a descriptive tract within larger narrations or arguments. In his "Critical Writing About the Visual Arts" course, Gary has tested students' understanding of specific artists by requiring them to analyze that artist's visual style and imagery and then invent a writing style which echoes that visual style. Instead of the moods listed above, students then use that artist's style to describe the twenty second walk above and label the essay with the name of their chosen artist.

Flashback

Replaying an experience that developed over time, finally resulting in an important revelation, can be enlivening and inspiring. Both personal and historical events are not static realities but complex, fluctuating worlds where meaning is lost and can be rediscovered very effectively through writing. Flashback starts this process by demanding that time be rewound so that the reader first experiences the seeds of the unfolding event, participates in its development, and then gradually arrives at a final, substantiated understanding of that experience's importance. To reset the clock, the writer must first create a special time-traveled rough draft. This rough draft, but not the final draft, must be written backwards, starting with the conclusion, and then working backwards in time, traveling into an unformed past, the writer having no idea where he or she is going to end up in terms of the original seeds of the experience and its revelation. Flashback is an act of discovery back into time for the writer; then it is an act of discovery forward in time for the reader. Flashbacks require Stepping

Backwards, Clocking Transitions, and Pulsing the Tense by using present tense verbs.

Stepping Backwards.

This is how the essay is designed: First the writer develops the conclusion: a carefully described summary or insight that is either personal, historical, scientific, economic—anything. This paragraph is placed at the end of the essay. For instance, the following paragraph written by Jamaica Kincaid would make for a rich concluding revelation:

> The space between the idea of something and its reality is always wide and deep and dark. The longer they are kept apart— idea of thing, reality of thing—the wider the width, the deeper the depth, the thicker and darker the darkness. This space starts out empty, there is nothing in it, but it rapidly becomes filed up with obsession or desire or hatred or love—sometimes all of these things, sometimes some of these things, sometimes only one of these things.

Only after writing such a revelation does the writer then recall and describe the event that immediately preceded, defined, and assured the validity of the insight summarized in the conclusion. This second paragraph is a snapshot of the last crucial past situation which clenched the conclusion that has already been written. This second paragraph is then placed near the end of the essay just before the conclusion.

Only after writing this second-to-last paragraph does the writer recall and discover a second situation or event, not one that supports the conclusion to the essay, but one that historically, emotionally, or intellectually carved the way for the event captured in the second-to-last snapshot. This paragraph fills the third-from-the-last slot in the essay. We require our students to time-step back at least four times from the conclusion. (*Betrayal*, a darkly humorous film scripted by the great modern playwright Harold Pinter, explores the cutthroat exchanges between two literary agents. The film is about the crucial stepping stones in an affair, but the sequence of its events is related backwards, as if it were the rough draft for this assignment: The viewer sees the affair's last fizzles first and its hyperbolic jump-start last, a strategy that sets up stunning ironies.)

Remember, these paragraphs are not necessarily examples in support of the conclusion; they are solely time stepping-stones that help the reader understand the next paragraph or slice of time that follows. The writer cannot always anticipate where hop-scotching back into time will lead: The writer never knows which event to write next until asking, "I have just discovered and described event X, but what event happened before X that prepared the emotional, intellectual, or physical way for event X to happen before it occurred? Now I need to describe that event." When the essayist is finished, the reader will have the advantage of seeing the early seeds which sow each event, each one chronologically setting down roots for the next piece of growth. (Realize that you are not always looking for events that cause the next event, but ones that provide fertile ground for the next event. To suggest that one event creates the next one runs the danger of creating the *post hoc proptor hoc* fallacy, mistaking a causal link between two events simply because one quickly follows or precedes another.)

Clocking Transitions.

Flashback is a time warp that allows for the removal of chunks of time, speeding the reader forward to the next most important event. Because of these fast-forward flashes, each paragraph must start with a time reference to help the reader know which time stepping-stone the essay has reached. George Kennan's essay referred to below uses phrases such as "Let us jump ahead now to the days, fifty-one years ago this past November," "Another change of scene," "Let us jump ahead again," "The scene shifts to Washington," and "Next picture" to open every paragraph or section of his essay. These transitions allow the writer to jump quickly to key events, leaving out anything that does not build towards the final revelation.

Pulsing the Tense.

The next issue the writer must face is what tense to use to describe the past. Usually when we discuss something that happened in the past, we use the past tense: people in the past walked, talked, ate, loved, and fought. However, sometimes life's pulse becomes much stronger when past events are narrated as if they were happening in the present time. When a writer explores past events using the present tense, we join that writer in a very special reality where details seem both unreal, haunted by a backwards movement through time possible only in dreams and also super real, outlined with a clarity obtained only when considering events in retrospect. Therefore, instead of saying, "Ten years ago I walked into my lover's house; everyone was watching," the writer writes "It is ten years ago and I am walking into my lover's house; everyone is watching."

When embarrassing or painful past events are in the past tense, the reader psychologically relaxes, knowing time has softened those events, but when an event takes place in the present, the reader is more alert, sensing that reality is still warm and can be modified. Delmore Schwartz's short story "In Dreams Begin Responsibility," from *The World is a Wedding*, is about a person dreaming that he is in a movie theater watching a movie about his parents courting each other in the past. Witnessing our parents before they are our parents has to be one of life's great embarrassments. Present tense Flashback brings alive that potent embarrassment that would usually be softened and faded away by past tense, such as finding out that the father is not yet sure that he loves the mother; the mother's father is not sure the father would make a good husband; the mother and father try extra hard to impress each other. Present tense narration gives these poignant moments pulse.

Scope.
George Kennan's article, actually titled "Flashback," for *The New Yorker*, flashbacks to his role as diplomat and American Ambassador to the Soviet Union, but first he explains why he uses the present tense to describe the past: "To stress the responsibility of these memories in speaking for themselves and to distance the young man who received the experiences from the elderly one who now recalls them" Kennan uses Flashback to underscore that we are two different, living, breathing people with different kinds of knowledge at two different times in our lives. However, Diana Hume George uses dramatic shifts between past and present tenses in "Wounded Chevy at Wounded Knee" to dramatize her growth from innocence to experience. Hume George's journey began when she married a Native American carnival worker out of personal rebellion stemming from her romantic clichés about native Americans. Her romantic image shattered as she experi-

enced real life on the reservation and found out that her husband was a rapist; then Hume George uses a long present tense anecdote to exemplify her understanding of the death of the Indian culture into which she married.

Workout.

To begin Flashback, craft your conclusion. Your conclusion is a description of yourself as a mature person, one whose previous naive view about something—religion, education, social respect, friendship—has been replaced by a more realistic, or more affirmative, or perhaps even a more cynical position. Another option is to describe a historical figure's revelation about an important issue or to describe the culmination of an important scientific, political, or legal event. This second option will require research. Depending on the length of the essay, you will need to decide how far back to go in time and what parts of the past to leap frog over in order to describe only the crucial events that lead up to the conclusion. Recently we had our students write a Flashback on an important historical trial. One way students were able to skip some early, but relevant, chunks of information from pretrial days, was to assume the persona of a jury member, attorney, or journalist and at a given present moment remember back to an earlier historical detail or legal precedent.

Assuming you are writing about yourself, avoid trite realizations such as "I no longer believe money grows on trees" or "It is very difficult to be a responsible adult." Limit this description to a specific philosophical concern rather than trying to describe your entire world-view. Formulating this section is the most difficult part of the essay, and even though it will come at the end of the essay, this conclusion will be fraught with the getting-started anxiety normally associated with composing an introduction.

Now work backwards. Once you have formed a solid conclusion, begin by going back in time to the next closest event which led to your revelation or conclusion. Describe it in detail, making sure you have given the reader enough details to understand how the incident could lead to the conclusion you have already written. Even though you are writing this section second, remember that it will not be the second section in you paper. It is the second-to-last section. To maintain intensity, keep all the verbs in the present tense. Once the second-to-the-last portion is completed, keep working backwards, asking yourself what experience must have prepared or under-prepared you (or the historical event or person you are writing about) for the second-to-last event. This experience will form the third-to-last event. Keep working back days, weeks, or years. Create too many events, and then cut back to the best ones so that you end up with about four or five incidents.

Cool Down.
Rewrite your essay so that now the essay starts with the oldest incident and ends with the conclusion you wrote first. Keep all incidents in the present tense. Make sure each section starts with a statement that lets the reader know what kind of time shift you are making. Transitions such as "The year is 1993 and I overhear my parents fighting" will provide order, while at the same time create a dream-like, time-warping, history-making sensation in which events appear to unfold moment by moment while the reader watches as if the event is happening for the first time. Play with order. As always, should you accept this mission, revise with Flow, Pause, and Metaphor. Lastly, if done with raw honesty, you will write a piece that shames the typical, event-which-changed-your-life or historical essay.

Strip Tease

As demonstrated above, Flashback links several seemingly insignificant events as they fast-forward toward one important revelation. However, other narratives (personal revelations, historical events, scientific cause and effect arguments, or economic developments) can be the result of several events that each have their own conclusion or feeling of finality. In a Strip Tease, the writer resets time in each section, narrating a new beginning and moves to a mini-climax. Each event is so climactic that readers think the end of the paragraph is the essay's conclusion. They find out otherwise. This tease creates a gasping hesitation of disbelief throughout the essay. Also, unlike with Flashback, each event is described and evaluated in the past tense, a tense better suited to underscoring each section's climactic tone.

Aside from creating an element of suspense, slowly stripping off episodes allows the reader to savor each one— the way a reader experiences subplots in works of fiction—each unit of time having equal importance to any overall conclusive ending. Just as in novels and films, this essay works especially well when writing about a subject that has many unexpected twists and turns. A good example is "A Worm from My Notebook," a chapter from Richard Selzer's *Taking the World in for Repairs*, a subtle drama from the world of parasitology involving the *dracunculus medinensis*, the Guinea worm. The first section narrates what happens while Ibrahim, a cattle herder in Zaire, drinks water infested with a microscopic crustacean Cyclops which are the "parent, pantry, and taxi" of *dracunculus*, a parasitic worm which eventually casts off its host Cyclops. This drama, already sufficiently horrifying, moves off stage to reveal even more episodes, each one seeming to be the last one in a ghastly cycle only to give way to the next, which seems ever worse: Inside Ibrahim's body the worm grows two feet; later Ibrahim feels its body ridge his abdomen; finally *dracunculus* migrates to Ibrahim's foot, senses water, and breaks through the skin. Each mini drama gets its own few paragraphs. Had enough? Ibrahim's several-days-long remedy involves twisting the worm out with a stick. But this is not even the end. This and other Strip Teases depends on two techniques, Curtain Calls and Transitional Resets.

Curtains Calls.

The Strip Tease essayist must first decide whether the different parts of the narration have enough interesting details with their own interesting results to give the smaller sections climactic clout. If so, then each will receive its own stage. For instance, consider Strip Teasing a scientific discovery such as "The Body in the Bog," by Geoffrey Bibby for *Horizon* , which starts, "My part in the story began on Monday, April 28, 1952, when I arrived at the

Prehistoric Museum of Aarhus, in mid-Denmark, to find a dead body on the floor of my office." Bibby knows that an explanation of why a male body preserved in a peat bog over 1500 years ago was killed could seem uneventful. He decides to write about each puzzle piece as a strip tease in order to give murder-mystery suspense to how he figured out the reason for the killing: In the first part a forensic specialist figures death to be from a slit throat; next botanists study grain pollens to determine how the burial took place; archaeologists of Danish prehistory clarify A.D. 310 religious beliefs on afterlife; the Roman historian Tacitus describes a mother earth goddess that demanded human sacrifice around A.D. 98; finally, food studies reveal stomach grains that place the murder in spring. Bibby makes each explanation so significant that it seems to be the last one, but there is always one more that confirms the reason for the killing was from ritualistic beliefs.

Helen Caldicott's essay "What You Must Know about Radiation" from *Redbook* has even more curtain calls in order to stress the endless problems with nuclear waste. The first curtain goes up to reveal a story on uranium mining, inhaling radon gas, and the results fifteen to thirty years later when infected cells go berserk, producing trillions of daughter cells instead of the normal two, but this incident concludes only to be replaced by a second curtain raising describing uranium tailings and how easily they become wind borne. More seemingly final scenes include discussion of the 99 percent waste that comes from uranium; the dangers of Isotope Uranium-28; melt downs; radio-active coolants; Stontium-90; and cancer-causing Plutonium, toxic for half a million years, one speck for every human lung on earth being enough to kill all of us. Each detail Caldicott discovers is described in bone-chilling detail. Enough? Caldicott still has more to go.

Transitional Resets.
A strong Strip Tease uses a refrain as a transition for each section to rewind time and start over. For instance, each section could start with the refrain "The situation became even more horrible," "Revelation number three," "But there was even a greater irony," or something more involved such as "The use of metaphor to capture a vision of family life became even more complicated in Faulkner's next novel." Marvin Kaye uses the transition refrain

"Accident number ____ " in his essay entitled "The Toy with One Moving Part," from *A Toy Is Born,* a collection of essays describing marketing success stories. In this piece, Kaye quickly lists what silly putty can do—stretch, shatter, pick up newsprint, mold, bounce—then he dramatizes the sequences of accidents that shaped Silly Putty as a marketable product. Each event or accident is written with vivid detail leading to a mini-climax so every section of the essay becomes a story in itself. In 1945, General Electric was experimenting with synthetic rubber for the war effort when an engineer happened to drop boric acid into a test tube with silicone oil. The glob bounced. Kaye declares, "Accident number one: Silly Putty is born."

With this miraculous birth of a new product, the essay seems to be at an end. Not so. Great products wither when they are are not marketed; so next comes "accident number two." This ministory picks up with the history of Peter Hodgson, a man who fails as a research consultant, is hired by a toy shop to publish a toy catalog and he decides to include toys for grown ups, including a mystery goo circulating at cocktail parties which then outsells virtually everything in the catalog. Kaye carefully describes and savors all these details in separate paragraphs so that each one seems like the essay's climax. But there is much more to come.

In fact, in the next section the chemical putty putters out. Once out of the catalog and onto the shelves, Hodgson finds that retail packaging cannot match catalog appeal. Sales tumble. Next comes "accident number three." Economically pinched, Hodgson is forced to put the putty in plastic "eggs;" orders mount from a few dozen each day to eventually five hundred a day. A writer for The *New Yorker* ends up writing about it and sales bounce all over the place. End of story? Not quite. The Korean War erupts and there is a clamp down on the materials used for Silly Putty's guts. Hodgson is thrown out of business. Finished? No, kids start buying Silly Putty. It takes ten years to solve quality control problems for kids, such as detaching it from human hair and carpets. Finally, in the 1960's Silly Putty is a $6.3 million a year winner.

Scope.
Geographical descriptions make for insightful Strip Teases. "The

City by the Sea," by Shiva Naipaul from *Beyond the Dragon's Mouth: Stories and Pieces*, is a Strip Teased description of Bombay India. The theme of this piece is that "Bombay deceives at every level," an ideal thesis for Strip Tease. Naipaul shock-cuts the whole essay right from the beginning where an unexpected international tennis tournament ends, "the spell is broken," and an unseen, dwarfish, "less-than-human crew" owns the courts with their brooms. The essay moves from nightmarish evening life to a glitzy film industry; from wealth to opium dens; from tuberculosis to plans for a New Bombay on neighboring islands; from mass migration of people to mass migration of rats; to incredible lists of what people do for work, including cleaning ears of passerbys. After each section, the reader is constantly left whispering, "You mean, there is more?"

Almost all good fictions employ some strip tease, but "Will You Please Be Quiet, Please?" by Raymond Carver, later used as a basis for a vignette by Robert Altman in his film *Short Cuts,* is an especially good example. In the story, the husband questions his wife about a past event where another man tried to hit on the wife at a party. Each of the husband's inquiries is delivered with an it-was-a-long-time-ago, it's-all-right-to-talk-about-it-now nonchalance, so that in a how-did-we-ever-get-off-on-this-subject tone, the wife gradually reveals more and more about her sexual escapade. Each section of the story, in this case represented by several paragraphs, seems like the last one: first she reveals a kiss; as the husband's shock dies a new cycle of questioning reveals a breast grope; finally, with so much already admitted, the last cycle of questioning has the wife confessing to sexual intercourse. Even this is not the final strip: Now fuming, the husband must know if the acquaintance "came" in her.

Workout.
Review an important time in your own life that was made up of several mini-events—a family problem, an athletic or dramatic event you watched, a long school or work project or conflict, a legal problem—or research an important development in a writer's, politician's, or artist's career; an historical, scientific, or political development; a philosophical or religious movement. You need to center on at least four mini-events that have their own mini-climaxes, the last one representing a final major outcome

of the whole development. Because of the suspense Strip Tease provides as an essay, by the end of it your reader will have paid strict attention to each development.

As you write your notes into each paragraphed section of your essay, keep in mind that by the time you get to the end of that particular section, you want the reader to feel that so much has happened and has come to fruition or failure that there could be no more to read. The essay appears to be finished after each section. This tease can be accomplished in two ways. At the end of each section, stress those details that create calm, quiet, utter failure, ecstatic success, satisfaction; then at the beginning of the new section, use transitions that call attention to the abruptness of the next event such as "Accident number three," "The nightmare started again," "That was only the beginning."

Raising the Dead

People think the past is dead but it can quickly be brought to life to help the living. Pretending that different points of time from the past can merge with one another in one moment of time has several advantages for the essayist. Imagine dialoguing with the past, or bringing past thinkers into the present moment to test their philosophical, economic, scientific, or theological theories on our world. Time travel and created characters are the elements of fiction, but when these characters narrate what they have witnessed and discuss its significance, fictional techniques can enliven nonfiction debates. There are essentially four ways to time travel: Converging, Back-dating, Up-dating, and Immortalizing.

Converging.

Converging involves bringing together characters from different time periods. One of the most informative time-mix narrative debates in literature happens in Fyodor Dostoyevsky's "The Grand Inquisitor," a chapter from his famous Russian novel *The Brothers Karamazov*. Ivan tells his brother Alyosha about imagining Jesus returning centuries after his death to Spain during the Church's inquisition to rid the country of heretics, but when Jesus reappears, he is thrown into jail by the Grand Inquisitor. Most of the chapter is a philosophical dialogue in which the Inquisitor talks to Jesus, narrating his view of the world's general response to Jesus, and trying to justify his rationale for arresting Him. In essence, Dostoevsky uses the incident and dialogue to pit "the exceptional, vague and enigmatic" that the Inquisitor says Jesus represents against "miracles, mystery, and authority" that the Church champions. The debate: Which makes humans happier? The argument is lengthy and carefully developed, but creating this mini-narrative drama and having Jesus Himself listen at a time when the Church was at one of its most powerful and violent moments, gives the argument both everyday-life and cosmic potency. The television comedian Steve Allen brought a more playful tone to this time travel strategy with a television panel made up of famous guests from different time periods (Freud, Shakespeare, Katherine the Great, Galileo) meeting on a panel to discuss a large range of philosophical issues.

Up-dating.

One way to spark interest in the past is to rewrite it in a modern style. Often times in literature courses we both find ourselves transforming an experience in an older work of literature into a present day situation and modern language to dramatize the older work's relevancy to our students. Without first understanding the work's situation—unencumbered by dated social customs, an unfamiliar setting, language which is archaic, unusual story telling techniques—many students will lose interest in the work before we can show them the writer's special craft. We need to keep recreating this way, always quickly bringing the students back to the unique use of language in the original work. However, the recreation of a work in a contemporary language and setting is an art form in itself.

For instance, Gary once had students create their own under-standing of Shakespeare by having them rewrite the part of act one, scene five from *Hamlet* where the ghost tells Hamlet that he was killed at his own brother's hand. The following is an excerpt from the original:

Ghost: Pity me not, but lend thy serious hearing
                 To what I shall unfold.
Hamlet: Speak. I am bound to hear.
Ghost: So art thou to revenge, when thou shalt hear.
Hamlet: What?
Ghost: I am thy father's spirit,
                 Doomed for a certain term to walk the night,
                 And for the day confined to fast in fires,
                 Till the foul crimes done in my days of nature
                 Are burnt and purged away. But that I am forbid
                 To tell the secrets of my prison house,
                 I could a tale unfold whose lightest word
                 Would harrow up thy soul, freeze thy young blood,
                 Make thy two eyes like stars start from their spheres,
                 Thy knotted and combined locks to part,
                 And each particular hair to stand an end
                 Like quills upon the fearful porpentine,
                 But this eternal blazon must not be
                 To ears of flesh and blood. List, list, O, list!
                 If thou didst over thy dear father love—
Hamlet: Oh God!
Ghost: Revenge his foul and most unnatural murder.
Hamlet: Murder?
Ghost: Murder most foul, as in the best it is,
                 But his most foul, strange, and unnatural.
Hamlet: Haste me to know't, that I, with wings as swift
                 As meditation or the thoughts of love,
                 May sweep to my revenge.

The father's ghost then explains it was his brother who killed him and "won to his shameful lust/ The will of my most seeming-virtuous queen." Knowing he must vanish by morning, the ghost hurries, explaining the details of the poison his brother poured in his ears that "Holds such an enmity with blood of man/ That swift as quicksilver it courses through/ The natural gates and alleys of the body,/ And with a sudden vigor it doth posset/ And curd, like eager droppings into milk,/ The thin and wholesome blood." Death came so quickly that there was no time to confess. The father's ghost tells Hamlet to "Leave [his mother] to heaven/

And to those thorns that in her bosom lodge/ To prick and sting her." The ghost exits and asks Hamlet to "Remember me."

Everyday language might have worked, but extremes work better because they create even more of contrast with the past, emphatically emphasizing the up-dating. Therefore the students were asked to rewrite the scene using the lively, but not so decorous, vernacular of different gang members. Following is a composite Gary made from a few of the entries:

Ghost: I don't have much time before I must make like a duck and get the flock out of here, but listen up cuz I got some serious shit to lay on you.

Hamlet: It's cool. Spill your guts.

Ghost: You are going to kick some heavy duty ass when you comprehend, man.

Hamlet: Say what?

Ghost: I'm your blood bro and old man's ectoplasm, the leader of the sharks. I'm supposed to cruise this ditch at night; in the day I barbecue in the Big Man's basement and I can't get upstairs until the mother fucker who did these bad ass crimes eats shit. What I am about to say will make you crap your insides out.

Hamlet: Holy shit!

Ghost: Your old man was dusted and you must splatter the slease's brains for my unnatural biting the big one.

Hamlet: Waste him?

Ghost: You got it. We're talking about putting his asshole where his mouth is now.

Hamlet: Just tell me who the geek is and it will be signed, sealed, and delivered.

Ghost: Now you're talking. Some say I was dusted by a snake in the orchard but this is a crock of shit. My own bro offed me.

Hamlet: I can't take it. Our main man Bubba?

Ghost: You got that shit right. Now he's plugging my bitch every night. I can't believe she'd hang out with a freak who'd snuff a guy just 'cause he was born first. I was the perfect stud to my main squeeze but now that a-hole has her. Oh well, Christ. I can catch a whiff of the morning air. Short but sweet I'll lay it out for you: Like, I was crashing in the orchard one day, burned-out as usual, and my brother slides up and pours this poison-shit in my ear. This stuff courses through me like Montezuma's revenge of the blood, man. I break out in blisters all over like I had a bad case of syph or something. Then he starts stabbing me as if I was Mr. Bill. This guy cuts me short before I can get off even one Hail Mary for all the bad karma I bought before. This bunk man. Bunk! Whatever you do to this guy, don't mess with your old lady. Her guilt trip will do her righteously anyhow. The damn firebug is pooping out so morning is almost here. Stay tuned to my vibes. Later days!

Moving to another extreme, student Joe Jacob went past cute to pretending Dr. Seuss could do a children's version Joe called "Green Eggs and Hamlet." Here is an excerpt:

Ghost: Pity me not, nor eat mold,
              but hear the story I shall unfold.
Hamlet: Talk to me, talk with me, with me you will talk,
              and I will listen as we walk.
Ghost: Avenge must you when I tell who.
Hamlet: Well apples and cheese and a jelly bean,
              Tell me Mr. Ghost, what do you mean?
Ghost: A spirit am I, but please don't be shy
              I'm your father's spirit, and yes I can fly.
Hamlet: Oh heavens me, oh heavens my,
              I did not know that spirits could fly.
Ghost: Yes I can fly, but never mind that.
              You must avenge a murther, and take off that hat.
Hamlet: Murther or murder, which did you say?
              I have never seen murder spelled that way.

With both examples, the past work gets a new muse, parts of the past work come alive so that curiosity about the older work is restored, and a new work is created so that the reader sees the issues of the original in a different context. Sometimes an old form can be updated with more of a philosophical purpose in mind. For instance, in 1900 the Woman's Suffrage Movement wrote a "Declaration of Sentiments" modeled precisely on the "Declaration of Independence," effectively updating the spirit of the original document by having it apply directly to their own cause.

Back-Dating.

Another method of mixing time travel is for the writer to take part in the past by imagining being there. Earlier we discussed an issue of *American Heritage* magazine, where the editors put together an essay titled "I Wish I'd Been There," a compilation of entries by such great writers and scholars as Stephen Jay Gould, Noel Perrin, Annie Dillard, Alfred Kazin, John Kenneth Galbraith, and others. (See Intimacy Focus under Opt.) Each writer was asked to narrate one scene or incident in American history that he or she would have liked to witness by "being a fly on the wall." By placing their psyches back in time, imagining being in the midst of a past event, the writers unlocked historical details that revived that event's original breath, something almost impossible to do when looking at an event as an outsider from a temporal distance.

For instance Oliver Jensen, one of the founders of the magazine, writes:

> I would like to have been at Lexington Green on the morning of the nineteenth of April, 1775. It might be possible to discern who actually fired first, a question argued ever since, but what interests me much more is the spirit of the moment, the attitude of the British officer, Major Pitcairn; of John Parker, the militia captain; of the disciplined but ignorant Redcoats, of the farmers, and of onlookers . . . All over quickly, they say, whereupon the drums pick up the beat and the fifes play and the files parade off to Concord. . . Tum-ta-ta-tum, and we march. Maybe the drums are a bigger menace than the weapons.

Even though Jensen has more questions than answers, by imagining himself there and having a list of wonderments, the reader is forced to see the event in real-life, emotional terms. History professor Robert Johannsen does more speculation about Lee's surrender to Grant at Appomattox in 1865 with "Lee riding among the remnants of his army, comforting, reassuring, speaking to the men from horseback":

> Men wept, not, I suspect, because of the failure of their cause—for long before that day the cause, if it was understood at all, had ceased to evoke the dedication it once inspired. Rather I think it was because the hardship and sacrifice was suddenly over, because the shedding of blood had ended, and because the memories of all those thousand who didn't make it to the final day came rushing to the fore. They might also have wept. . . for a world and a time that was now lost forever. . . [The nation] left its formative period and entered into a maturity in which the romantic ideals, aspirations, and yearnings of that earlier time would no longer have any place.

Much of this entry might have been written in any historical essay looking back, but simply by framing the interpretation with a desire to have been there, and noticing some physical details that existed at that moment, the interpretation takes on an added emotional intensity.

Another taste of Returning was "A New Year's Meal of Their Dreams" by Laurie Ochoa and Ruth Reichl in *The Los Angeles Times*, a stew of responses by Los Angeles's most well-known chefs who were asked to describe the New Year's meal of their dreams. Some thought of meals from their past, some thought of famous people who cooked well, such as Thomas Jefferson and Archestratus, others thought about when the first meals from foreign countries entered the United States. The articles's total impact recreated the complex dimensions of food culture and history.

Immortalizing.
There is one more version of Raising the Dead which does not necessarily have to do with time travel, but it does have to do with using fictional or real characters to narrate incidents and breathe life into an argument that might expire if written in straight prose. The writer immortalizes the present moment by establishing a straight man, or insignificant minor character who the main philosophizer bounces off his or her dialogue. The ancient Greek philosopher Plato's *The Republic* is one of the earliest examples. Plato develops all his arguments by having his friend and teacher, Socrates, present allegorical stories and arguments to an agreeable student who responds positively to Socrates's probing questions. For instance, in the section known as "The Allegory of the Cave," a short narration about men who see shadows instead of reality and are threatened by anyone who has, Socrates adds that "in the world of knowledge the idea of good appears last of all, and is seen only with an effort." The pupil cordially struggles through with, "I agree. . . as far as I am able to understand you." This response adds little to the argument, but it is enough of a response to remind us that there is a thinking, feeling, speaking person behind the ideas, and that we are in the company of other minor, humble characters who are grappling with understanding those ideas. Dialogue dissolves book pages that otherwise could trap and mummify ideas.

This same spirit Raises the Dead in the witty dialogue of James

Boswell's biography *The Life of Samuel Johnson*. Johnson is the eighteenth-century moralist reported on by his much younger, best friend, Boswell, who primarily dramatizes the dialogue between the two. Boswell sets items up for argument by dragging Johnson on an arduous journey in the Hebrides, arranging for him to dine with notorious, unlikable people, and then asking Johnson a range of questions having to do with the sacred and the profane. Boswell himself plays the straight man for his friend.

Boswell: I asked him what he thought was best to teach children first.

Johnson: Sir, it is no matter what you teach them first, any more than what leg you shall put into your breeches first. Sir, you may stand disputing which is best to put in first, but in the mean time your breech is bare. Sir, while you are considering which of two things you should teach your child first, another boy has learnt them both.

You will find more modern witty-dialogue-as-philosophical-track in . . . *And Then I Told the President: The Secret Papers of Art Buchwald* by Buchwald, a compilation of his syndicated columns, essays almost always done as make-believe dialogues that are disguised, satiric comments on everything from politics to fashions to psychological mentalities. Chit-chatters include correspondents hiding out from Presidents in gym lockers, opposing political figures trapped together in a rescue boat, children using school prayer to do better on the school tests, a husband and wife having an affair with each other only to return home to boring selves, and Pilgrims who decide growing beautiful lawns is more important than growing produce.

In the same spirit as Buchwald's characters, cartoon characters by artists such as Linda Barry, Matt Groenig, Charles Schulz, and Garry Trudeau are actually two dimensional dialogue prompts before they are visual entities. At their very best, even the characters' settings are visual killers, focusing steady attention on philosophical discourse: there is very little movement of body positions between frames, little dramatic lighting, and virtually no shifts in perspectives common to super-hero and romance comic strips. Instead the emphasis is on dialogue, often being bounced off a straight person.

119

Workout.

To practice Converging, have someone from the past reappear and confront someone from another time period, including the present. The possibilities are endless: A present day rock singer discussing music with a classical composer; Einstein correcting a present day scientist's use of physics; a talk show host refereeing a panel of philosophers from different time periods; a well known writer asking for advice from Shakespeare; an historian getting spit at by an ancient king. Use the event to define, evaluate, or propose ideas. Keep past personalities in character by researching and being clear on their perspective about related issues. Also, if you can study anything they wrote, analyze their writing style and imitate it for their dialogue style. In 1988 when Glynis enrolled in Gary's "Humor in Literature" course, she wrote a paper discussing important attitudes that shape male and female relationships by having Dr. Ruth, who hosted a popular television show giving frank sexual advice, argue with the Wife of Bath, a passionate, scheming life-force from Geoffrey Chaucer's medieval *Canterbury Tales.*

For Updating, take a famous literary work or political tract from the past and change its style to that of a typical modern group's vernacular: teenager's, educator's, politician's, a specific poet's. For Back-dating find a manuscript, letter, painting, dialogue, photograph, or story and imagine yourself taking part in it as another character. Use this opportunity to imagine details that help give the reader a clearer idea of what was being argued or depicted in the work that would normally not be thought about. You may need to research the context or setting of the work.

For Immortalizing, try reconstructing a dialogue between famous fictional characters, famous writers, or philosophers and a straight person (maybe you, your instructor, or a minor fictional character.) Use the dialogue to create an argument. One way to do this is to imagine this dialogue taking place in fifty cartoon frames and then heightening each part by cropping the argument into chunks of four to five frame strips each, one published each day in a newspaper. If you have visual talent, you could draw the frames; otherwise, use stick figures. Use good writing style in the language balloons since your dialogue must be as rich and detailed as if you wrote it in a paper.

ENCIRCLING:
Ways to Define

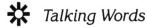 *Talking Words*

Blood Flow

Animation

Strong definition forges belief. Most English teachers discuss definitions in terms of denotation (dictionary meaning) and connotation (implied associations). We have added some other ways to explore meaning in Talking Words. Definition goes beyond defining single words: it includes defining sweeping events, omnipresent forces, complex problems and their intricate solutions. Blood Flow and Animation offer strategies for encircling these hard-to-define realities.

Talking Words

Unless a writer carefully defines important abstract words (concepts that can only be understood through the intellect and not the senses) such as "love," "purity," "coolness," sensitivity," the writer's argument risks becoming unclear, misunderstood, or powerless. Without careful definition, those words become *empty*

abstractions. To assume that abstract concepts mean the same to everyone is a fallacy. For instance, if someone writes an essay on political action that tells people to do something with moderation, the essayist must first pin down a definition for "moderation" since different readers might have very different and limited understandings of that word. Most people would not have the emotional strength or moral certitude to meet Aristotle's definition of "moderation" or "mean." In *Ethica Nicomachea*, Aristotle (384-322 B.C.) considers "truth telling" to be the mean between "boastfulness" and "mock modesty;" "ready wit" to be the mean between "buffoonery" and "boorishness;" and "cour-age" to be the mean between "rashness" and "cowardice."

Usually abstract words become the most complex and impor-tant subjects for writers. Since abstractions have many word lives, defining an abstract word can take part of or suck up all of the space of an entire essay. Words represent reality, and reality is always richer than it seems to be; so discussing an abstract word becomes a complex exploration. There are different strate-gies for exploring an abstract word, each approach providing one panel that hinges to the others, all ultimately shaping the meaning of a word. Strong writers use as many approaches as they have space to build a strong defense of the word's worth. Those approaches include language reference resourcing, thesauroscoping, quote sandwiching, stress testing, exemplify-ing, and netting.

Language Referencing.

Avoid the impulse to begin a Talking Words essay with a stock introduction such as "Webster's defines this word as . . ." In-stead, cliché-bust by ruling out the obvious, expected definitions of the word. Following through with negation, or explaining what a word is not immediately vaporizes preconceived notions of a word, clearing a path in the reader's head for a fresh look at a writer's definition. In the introduction to her essay "Noble Com-panions," Gail Godwin cliché-busts a pat definition of what a "friend" is:

> The dutiful first answer seems programmed into us by our mea-ger expectations: 'A friend is one who will be there in times of trouble.' But I believe this is a skin-deep answer to describe skin-deep friends.

By quickly ruling out the overused, there-for-us-when-we-need-them notion of friendship, Godwin opens her essay to previously unexplored possibilities of the nature of friendship. Therefore, unlook up words in a standard desk dictionary and steer clear of standard definitions which will yield a pointless Talking Words essay.

Other language reference resources like the *Oxford English Dictionary* (OED), or a book of etymology, move back in time, stripping words to their stems, revealing insight into the original meanings of a word that may have been forgotten, lost over time, or changed through select usage. The prize blood hound is the *Oxford English Dictionary* or OED, a multi-volume dictionary which marks a word's inception and then continues to sniff out the history of each word's changing meaning over years or centuries. After working against the cliche definition, Gail Godwin uses interesting historical information found in the *OED* to make an important point about the word "friend":

> I seek (and occasionally find) friends with whom it is possible to drag out all the old, outrageously *aspiring* costumes and rehearse together for the Great Roles; persons whose qualities groom me and train me up for love. It is for these people that I reserve the glowing hours, too good not to share. It is the existence of these people that reminds me that the words "friend" and ""free" grew out of each other. (OE freo, not in bondage, noble, glad; OE freo, to love; OE freond, friend).

By showing the linguistic link between the words "free" and "friend," Godwin discovers a forgotten dimension of the word "friend" and can then build a personal concept of "noble" friendship that lives in her relationships, but has been lost through ubiquitous usage of the word. Another type of dictionary, *The Enlarged Devil's Dictionary* by Ambrose Bierce, fuels new definitions by cutting to the cynical aspects of abstract concepts. Examples:

> DICTIONARY, n. A malevolent literary device for cramping the growth of a language and making it hard and inelastic. The dictionary, however, is a most useful work." "HISTORY, n. An account mostly false, of events mostly unimportant, which are brought about by rulers mostly knaves, and soldiers mostly fools." "HAPPINESS, n. An agreeable sensation arising from contemplating the misery of another.

Language reference resources also ignite ideas by reminding writers of important subtleties within a word.   In his essay "A Dance for Your Life in the Marriage Zone," Michael Ventura describes a violent fight with his wife and then considers the word "forgive" by breaking the word into bits and then studying the original meaning of each part:

> Pause at the word: "for-give." "for-to-give." Forgiveness is such a gift that "give" lives in the word. Christianist tradition has tried to make it a meek and passive word, turn the other cheek. But the word contains the active word "give,' which reveals its truth: it involves the act of taking something of yours and handing to another, so that from now on it is theirs. Nothing passive about it.

Ventura cliché busts our tired assumptions about forgiveness which render the word as a passive and meaningless act; he then regifts by applying a more sincere and active wrapper to the word.

Thesauroscoping.

All abstractions should be looked up in a thesaurus which provides both synonyms (words that have similar meanings to your abstraction) and antonyms (words which mean the opposite). Both the synonyms and antonyms can be used to generate Talking Words panels. Synonyms for words are often used as careless replacements of the abstraction you are defining. Take advantage of the fine distinctions in meaning by comparing and contrasting an abstraction to its synonyms. These differences yield good philosophical fodder.

Sometimes synonyms come to light in unexpected places. William Least Heat Moon's *Blue Highways* is the account of the author's travels along the back roads of America. While driving the blue highways, Heat Moon considers the meaning of many words. Often, the strangers Heat Moon meets provide the writer with important word distinctions. After Heat Moon explains to one man, Cal, whom he meets in a roadside diner, that he was fired from his job, the stranger thesauroscopes Heat Moon:

> I notice that you use the word *work* and *job* interchangeably. Oughten to do that. A job's what you force yourself to pay attention to for money. With work, you don't have to force yourself. There are a lot of jobs in this country, and that's good because they keep people occupied. That's why they're called 'occupations.'

Not only does Cal make an interesting distinction between job and work, but he also brings in a new synonym, "occupation," for comparison and contrast. A thesaurus is like a case-load of Cals.

A good thesaurus will also provide antonyms for abstractions. In a interview with Nicholson Baker for National Public Radio, literary host Michael Silverblatt points out that often the best Talking Words essays are those where the writer demonstrates that a particular "word means itself and its opposite." Silverblatt's comments are in reaction to Baker's essay "Rarity" in which Baker collects so many examples of rare things that he demonstrates the paradox of rarity—that rare things are found everywhere. Antonyms, therefore, may reveal meanings closer to the word's reality than the word's synonyms.

In a doll-house-buster written for *Salmagundi,* essayist Daniel Harris begins "Cuteness" by proposing that images normally labeled as cute, such as stuffed animals and So Shy Sherry dolls, are actually closely related to the concept of the grotesque, where disturbing deformations actually create the disproportions we find so cuddly. The pitiable, helpless, stubby-bodied, swollen-armed dolls are seductive because they imply a helplessness that arouses our sympathies. Harris lets the definition creep out even further proposing that we impose this notion of cuteness on children because our parental ego needs to perceive them as being more vulnerable and physically maimed than they really are. A corollary to Harris's essay is "On Ugliness as a Basic Injustice" by Francois Giroud, the co-founder of *L'Express* and Bernard Henri Lévy, the philosopher/ playwright. Their discussion defines the paradoxical qualities of ugliness, including its sexual seductiveness.

Quote Sandwiching.
A book of famous quotations surprises by popping out a word's meaning the same way a child's pop-up book turns the two dimensional world into three. A word springs alive in the meaningful context of a well poised quotation, where the quoter notices an unusual, ironic, or sophisticated aspect of an abstraction and carefully articulates its meaning in a well crafted sentence. Many famous quotes come from literature—a novel, drama, poem, or

film, an important speech—and these quotes can help give an example of meaning. Pithy one-liners defining abstractions make old sayings, nursery rhymes, adages, clichés, lines from movies, television shows, songs, advertisement jingles, a public sign or billboard, or even a bit from a stand up comedian memorable and you can make further use of them. Be sure to always cite where you received the example and give the writer credit.

The ability to smoothly integrate and present a quotable line into a Talking Words panel is an art form. A whole paragraph can be built around a great quotation if the writer remembers to sandwich the quoted material between his or her own lead in and follow up. A quote which has been successfully introduced to provide an intelligent response aids in the digestion of an abstract word. Don't just rely on a great quote from an important writer to jaw out a definition of an abstraction; rather, use another's idea to generate your own insights about the word.

For instance, in his essay "Why We Travel," Pico Iyer rides on a famous philosopher's idea to define reasons for sojourn:

> So at heart, travel is just a quick way of keeping our minds mobile and awake. As Santayana wrote: "There is wisdom in turning as often as possible from the familiar to the unfamiliar: It keeps us nimble; it kills prejudice and it fosters humor." Romantic poets inaugurated an era of travel because they were the great apostles of open eyes. Buddhist monks are often vagabonds in part because they believe in wakefulness.

Iyer hitchhikes on the philosopher's idea-bus, and then uses Santayana's words as an expressway for his own definition trip. By creating a quote sandwich—having good lead-in and follow-up—the two writers collaborate towards a common destination: Santayana's own comments detour Iyer into making a new connection—Travel is synonymous with wakefulness.

Often, a great quote ends a paragraph, the quote actually forming a transition for a new Talking Words panel, which Gary refers to as an open-face quote sandwich. Iyer, in his essay on travel, gorges on the open-face quote sandwiches. Here is a taste:

> And we travel, in essence, to become young fools again—to slow time down, get taken in and fall in love once more. The beauty of this whole process was perhaps best described, before people even took to frequent flying, by George Santayana

in his lapidary essay, "The Philosophy of Travel." "We need sometimes . . . to escape into open solitudes, into timelessness, into the moral holiday of running some pure hazard, in order to sharpen the edge of life, to taste hardship, and to be compelled to work desperately for a moment at no matter what."

I like that stress on work, since never more than on the road are we shown how proportional our blessings are to the difficulty that precedes them, and I like the stress on a holiday that's "moral," since we fall into our ethical habits as easily as into our beds at night.

When quotes are used to end paragraphs they leave the reader with an empty stomach unless they are used as a transitional appetizer for creating a response to the quote that opens the following paragraph.

Stress Testing.

Another way to explore the meaning of a word is to subject it to different social pressures; then observe if the word performs differently. There are many social stresses that determine what gets squeezed out of a word: age, economics, ethnicity, education, geography, gender. Consider gender. Many abstract concepts have different connotations when applied to or used by either sex. If a writer were defining "sexy," the essayist would want to show any differences in how sexiness is defined by women and men. In her essay "Waiting," Irish author Edna O'Brien claims that while women wait for love,

men wait for the promotion, they wait for the kill, they wait for the prize, and one has only to watch the antics in Parliament or in the Senate to see with what libido each is waiting for his moment to rise and strike a blow that will vanquish his opponent . . . . Men wait for women, too, once they have decided this one is the one, but they wait more busily and so little atoms of dread are likely to be diffused and tossed up and down so that they scatter.

Ethnic pressure is another stress test. In her essay "The Meaning of a Word," Gloria Naylor shows how the word "nigger" has different implications depending on the ethnicity, age and sex of the person using the word. The same differences appear when testing a word by the generation using it. Words such as "peace," "loyalty" and "honor" meant very different things to the World War II generation then to the Viet Nam War generation. Just when you cannot think of another social group with which to stress test, Vicki Hearne looks at the meaning of words from a dog-happy point of view, and by doing this in "What's Wrong with Animal Rights" for *Harper's Magazine*, she gives new meaning to definitions of "happiness" and "rights" while challenging our sentimental attitudes toward animals.

Exemplifying.

Both *anecdotes* and *analogies* can clarify the meaning of a word or concept by providing sophisticated forms of examples. The anecdote, or short narrative, can be a truthful, experienced epi-sode or an invented one, as long as it feeds real-life interest in the word. In "On Being Black," W.E.B. Du Bois, a writer for the NAACP, skillfully uses anecdotes to define the abstract concept of "black" in the early part of the twentieth century. Du Bois responds to his white, maybe fictional, friend's remark "I should think you would like to travel," with a page long narrative on what blackness means in terms of Jim Crow— black only waiting rooms and Jim Crow railroad cars. The narrative starts with de-tails of how buying a ticket is a torture, involving airless waiting rooms with horrible seating, waiting until tickets are sold at the other window to whites, the confusing and ignorant behavior of the agent who overcharges. Du Bois' anecdote then gives the details of the journey in the car where "the plush is caked with dirt," "impertinent white" newsboys hound people to buy "worth-less, if not vulgar, books," conductors reserve information only for whites, and "As for toilet rooms—don't!"

Another way to develop an original point about a word is by draw-ing an analogy, making a comparison between the abstraction and a specific situation which is less abstract, thereby making the abstraction more concrete. When an analogy makes a con-cept less clear by making an inapt parallel, the analogy is called a *false analogy*. Strong analogies are extended similes that Press truth (see the Press section of the Thought unit) to intensify ele-ments that create similarities or subtle differences with the ab-straction.

In "On Being Black and Middle Class" Shelby Steele contrasts DuBois's definition of being an African-American through Steele's use of apt analogies. Like Du Bois, Steele offers personal anec-dotes to clarify the abstractions "black" and "middle class," which then lead the writer to a new abstract concept, being in a "double-bind"— for Steele the bind is the "trap" of being *both* black and middle class. In order to articulate his moment of epiphany when he finally identified his double bind, Steele uses an analogy which compares his awakening to another type of realization about a different kind of double bind: "It was like the suddenly sharp vision one has at the end of a burdensome marriage when all the long-repressed incompatibilities come undeniably to light." Steele effectively draws in those readers who have no experience being bound by conflicts of class and race by comparing his specific conflict to what may be a more universally familiar bind—the realization of being incompatible with one's current partner.

Netting.
(Review Netting in the Flow section of the Style unit.) Flow techniques, such as Netting, band together all of the Talking Words techniques to premier a word orchestra with a surround sound of meaning. A student, Jason Luparello, uses a netting to define his chosen abstraction—anxiety:

> Anxiety is trouble, time thinking, nausea subjugated by sleep, study, essays, efforts to emulate, exhaustion, procrastination, abstract imagination, a premonition of a catastrophic twisting of an automobile, traffic, concern, conspiracy of the nervous system, routine repetition, talking to women, the phone, ambiguous space between phone calls, a walk down a hall to confront old friends, a figment, frantic completion minutes before a due date, the subsequent date, no today, dismay, dizziness, and yet Carl Jung states, "Neurosis is a substitute for legitimate suffering."

Luparello makes use of the concepts of sizing, specificity and juxtaposition to create a rhythmic flow of associations which defines by creating a gestalt of anxiety. The quintessential Netting defining an abstraction is composed of as many associations to the word with which the writer can make connections.

Workout.
Choose a word that has special significance in your life, a word that infuriates you, a word you have been victimized by, a taboo or dirty word, an abstract label that invites simplistic thinking such as "step-mother" or "hero," a word that is often misused, or overused such as "fantasy" or "hate." Subject your word to at least three of the Talking Word strategies; then begin to draft para-

graphs with each one. After you have composed several rough paragraphs or panels, begin to arrange them into the most effective order. Often essayists will start with the language referencing as a way of opening up new possibilities for the word, but other times an anecdote creates more immediate interest in the word. You decide. For a final paragraph, Netting helps the reader to imagine the varied usages of the word spreading into the world; other times discussion of the word in a famous quote gives the word final stick. Each strategy can be used more than once in an essay. Strategies which define abstract terms can also be used as part of any careful argument or persuasive essay.

Blood Flow

Encircling a large reality that is more prevalent or omnipresent than the reader suspects presents its own defining problems. For instance, in his book *Memesis, the Representation of Reality in Western Literature,* Eric Auerbach explains that the Hebrew writers made God in the Old Testament more omnipresent than the Greek gods simply by never having God meet in council with other gods to reveal His motives, by not letting the reader know where He has been between episodes, and by not giving God physical attributes, something Michelangelo did for every Sunday school student much later. By being nowhere in particular, God came to be everywhere.

More worldly omnipresent phenomena can be placed in time and space: more people are addicted to items than just drugs than we ever can calculate; more families are dysfunctional in more diverse ways than people want to know; and many people are creative in more ways than we normally give credit. A writer communicating the prevalence of a particular subject has the challenge of dramatizing its magnitude so that the reader obtains a realistic sense of how overwhelming or all-encompassing that reality actually has become. A strong writer knows that for most people these realities flow undetected, hidden below the skin of life's normal hustle and bustle. There are three techniques to describe and define an omnipresent reality for the reader without mitigating its prevalence.

Fact Spraying.

One essential technique is to bombard the reader with an endless, unrelenting stream of facts—dates, times, locations, numbers, people, foods, product names, parts, economic groups, professions, case studies, contexts—any details that will flow a consistent layer of reality over the piece of writing. For example, in her book *Distant Mirror: The Calamitous 14th Century*, historian Barbara Tuchman defines the overwhelming force of destruction created by the bubonic or black plague by racing us from one place to another, one time to another, one death count to another, so that we are forced to watch the disease reproduce and flow over the map of Europe. There is no pause; there are hardly any transitions. A typical entry mentions that

> By January 1348 the plague penetrated France via Marseille, and North Africa via Tunis. Shipborne along coasts and navigable rivers, it spread westward from Marseille through the ports of Languedoc to Spain and northward up the Rhone to Avignon, where it arrived in March. . . . In Paris, where the plague lasted through 1349, the reported death rate was 800 a day, in Pisa 500, in Vienna 500-600. The total death in Paris numbered 50,000 or half the population.

The map fills and over-spills. Many essays that define the prevalence of a reality shift from one spray of related items to another, each one forming a paragraph worth of material. For instance, in other parts of the essay, Tuchman shifts to sprays describing physical maladies or theological solutions. All of these topics define the magnitude of the disease.

Outside Viewing.

Creating a knowledgeable persona, or imagining a person who has expectations of what should exist, but then does not find that existence, is a second method for defining an omnipresent reality. The writer uses this person's shock in listing what "should be" to imply the prevalence of "what is not." When using this technique, it is important for the writer to define some attributes of this outside-looking-in person. For instance, if your topic for a Blood Flow essay is the prevalence of western people's propensity to be pack-rats, the outsider you create would be someone who is the opposite, "believing in health standards, ingenuity, traveling light on the planet."

John Gliedman and William Roth use this Martian point of view in their book, *The Unexpected Minority*, which defines the permeating prejudice towards the physically disabled. In this essay, the "Martian" is an imaginary person from an advanced industrial society who "genuinely respects the needs and humanity of handicapped people." This person is constantly put in situations where expectations are not met, thereby dramatizing the prevalence of a disappointing or unbelievable reality.

Gliedman's and Roth's persona would "take for granted that a market of millions of children and tens of millions of adults would not be ignored," and so would expect to find cheap automobiles that could be driven by paraplegics, simple gadgets for domestic use, researching of prosthetic devices with the same enthusiasm poured into space industry research. The "Martian" expects to see disabled people in books, television shows, cartoons, advertisements, factories, resorts, political action committees, and in school rooms in the role of teacher or principal. He does not. The reader then is forced to view and concede to wide-ranging evidence that what should be true everywhere is not true anywhere. For this method, it is important for the writer to repeat phrases such as "take for granted that. . . ," "expect to find. . . ," and "is shocked to learn that. . ."

Baffling.

The reader also becomes more aware of the scope of a given reality when constantly reminded of baffling details, ones that scalpel complacency and the comfort of a narrow vision. Normalcy supports narrowness; the baffling prepares the reader for expansion. For example, aside from fact spraying, Tuchman shows wherever the black plague touches, our normal expectations are also blackened, so that the actual symptoms of the plague seem unnatural, removed from the realm of normal pestilences: "everything that issued from the body—breath, sweat,

132

blood from the buboes and lungs, bloody urine, and blood-black-ened excrement—smelled foul." Such abnormalities creep in throughout the entire chapter: bodies of relatives are left outside for dogs to drag away, women give last rites as priests quickly die off, children and parents abandon each other, and villagers dance in merriment hoping their own ludicrous reaction will fight off the absurd disease. All these details serve to confuse the normal expectations we hold about disease and tooth-pick our eyes for a wider ranging horror than we expect.

Gliedman and Roth baffle our expectations by demonstrating how able-bodied people's minds perversely twist when confronted with the disabled world. For example, the mind of a normal eye-sighted human makes fantastic, irrational assumptions when viewing an older male with an eye patch, immediately assuming this to be a person with a dark past and "a capability for just enough brutal-ity to add a trace of virile unpredictability," but viewing a seven-year-old girl with one evokes fear and pity. We insist that famous disabled people—Franklin Roosevelt, John Kennedy, Elizabeth Barrett Browning, Alexander the Great, Beethoven, Edison, Freud—are not thought of as people who succeeded despite their handicap, but people who overcame it, as if it was not an essen-tial part of who they were. By constantly demonstrating how we have bizarre ideas about the disabled, the writers help us under-stand that "to grow up handicapped in America is to grow up in a society that, because of its misreading of the significance of dis-ability, is never entirely human in the way it treats the person within." This idea is firmly established as a wider ranging reality than the reader could have ever imagined by baffling us with all our baffling reactions to disabilities.

Scope.

Blood Flow strategy courses through more essays than one might assume. For example, defining natural cycles almost requires Blood Flow. "To the Potter's Field" by Edward Conlon is a stun-ning, almost mystical account in *The New Yorker* that spooks the reader with endless facts about the numbers of homeless people who are buried in New York each year, how their burials take place, the people who bury them, and where the homeless dead come from. More refreshing cycles are captured in *Pilgrim at Tinker Creek*, one of Annie Dillard's hypnotic and exhausting flashes of the surprising growth networks and miracles-made-from-the-taken-for-granted that occur in nature. Her flow does not allow the reader's mind to stop buzzing.

Omnipresent subtleties need Blood Flow to sharpen their realities. Trickling flow streams are defined in "Rarity," a chapter in *The Size of Thoughts* by Nicholson Baker, who proves how many rare things surround us to which we are normally oblivious. Baker Blood Flows by bombarding us with the details of model airplanes, the intricacies of movie projectors, the magic of reading aloud, the quirks of punctuation, the complexities of filthy slang, the mind as lumber. The entire world opens up as an unusual gift that is both scientific and metaphoric all at once. Even more subtle is an outline of the variety of sighs and sigh-motivation throughout the world by Bernard Cooper in "The Fine Art of Sighing" in *Paris Review* which describes various kinds of sighs throughout the world and the reasons for them, Cooper's scope taking the reader's breath away.

Some Blood Flows create nervousness and alarm. "A Woman's Work" for *Harper's Magazine* by Louise Erdrich is a dense, metaphorical immersion into the trials and states of mind created by parenthood, especially motherhood: "It is uncomfortably close to self-erasure, and in the face of it, one's fat ambitions, desperation, private icons and urges fall away into a dreamlike *before*." "Forgetting" in David Ehrenfeld's *Beginning Again: People and Nature in the New Millennium* is especially alarming, swamping the reader with frightening instances where we assume knowledge to be cumulative, but in fact "the more advances we make, the more we forget." He cites disappearing earthworm experts, the absence of anyone who knows "at what point in animal evolution was the porphyrin molecule (such as hemoglobin) first adopted for use specifically as an oxygen carrier," and graduate students who do not even know that comparative biochemistry classes once existed to teach such material.

Workout.
Write a Blood Flow about an attitude or philosophy or condition that permeates a larger social strata, geographical area, or time span than most people realize. Topics might include attitudes about food, sex, chemical abuse, or health; perspectives shared

by custodial staffs, teachers, advertisers; natural phenomena such as flies, earthquakes, oxygenators; abuses such as those perpetuated on waitresses, older people, and secretaries. Before you compose, make a big list from your observations and maybe do some library research to beef up your examples.

Be sure to cover as many sub-categories as possible. If you are writing an essay on the prevalence of Americans as pack rats, include paragraphs on people's desks, garages, pockets ad purses, closets and attics, as well as bookshelves and notebooks. You need to examine the unexpected nooks and cracks where no one usually looks—religious rituals, social networks, and people's cluttered minds. Use at least two of the devices listed above and the Flow techniques discussed in the Style unit. Blood Flow works by being unrelenting, with quick transitions, if any at all, and never slowing down for readers to catch their breadth.

Animation

Science book and documentary film writers who define wildlife and scientific events often clip the wings of their own fresh, nothing-taken-for-granted wonderment because they fear losing their "scientific objectivity." The epitome of this self-clip takes the form of blanched identification manuals, jargon-flooded reference books, and textbooks filled with drained prose. The assumption made by these writers is that language is "objective" when it has the cliché terseness and flatness of mathematics, a debatable assumption in itself based on novice, cliché ideas about math. The other assumption is that treating all details objectively means treating all details with equal importance, one blending into the other, as opposed to prioritizing, emphasizing and dramatizing the key defining details.

A case in point is Roger Peterson's bird-manual description from *A Field Guide to Birds*: He describes a bird that

> runs on the ground (tracks show 2 toes forward, 2 aft.) Large, slender, streaked; with a long white-tipped tail, shaggy crest, strong legs. White crescent on open wing." (Song, 6-8 dovelike coo's descending in pitch)

The reader would have field trouble matching this description to the actual bird because so many of this bird's characteristics are shared with other birds. Peterson avoids using any organizational strategy or style technique to help the reader absorb and picture the unique reality of this bird. Instead the reader's consciousness sinks into a swamp of information bits. There are three techniques Peterson could have used to make this bird fly: Using a riddle introduction, building problem-solution paragraphs, and using the style principles of flow, pause and fusion.

Riddle Introductions.

The formula for creating a riddle introduction starts by isolating the most dominant and unique details of an animal or insect, putting aside detailed explanations and minor or less unusual details shared with other birds. Next, the dominant and unique details are presented in short, compound sentences (sentences that combine with a connecting word such as "and"), written usually from a third person point of view (he, she, it, they), sometimes in first person (I, we). This style creates a riddle-like rhythm that showcases crucial details without a lot of clutter. Lastly, the writer does not reveal the bird's name until the end of this introductory paragraph. By withholding the bird's name, the opening details attain a life of their own that firmly presses into the reader's mind, still uncluttered by the self-satisfaction of knowing this name without first having to pay close attention to details.

Another bird writer, George Hollister in *National Wildlife* magazine, uses the riddle introduction to describe the same bird as Peterson:

> He's half tail and half feet. The rest of him is head and beak. When he runs, he moves on blurring wheels. He can turn on a dime and leave change. He doesn't need to fly because he can run faster. He kicks dirt in a snake's face, and then eats the snake.

What is it? At the end (even though we might have guessed) we are told: A Roadrunner. If the reader goes no further, this introduction dramatizes the most crucial defining details needed to identify the bird. Imagine textbooks where all definitions of machines, body organs, historical figures, political structures, diseases, psychological disorders, scientific instruments, and other complicated objects or events, opened with a riddle introduction. We would remember more essential details. Consider student writer Alicia Eddy's riddle introduction for "The Kidneys":

> They take a lot of shit, but are tough regulators. They work for bananas to make you strong, but if treated badly, they can kill you.

Riddles are memorable. If textbooks used this strategy, we could all pass biology tests without having to cram the night before the exam.

To craft your introduction, make a list of the most unique and predominant details of the subject you are describing, but do not include any details that are shared by many others within the group to which your subject belongs. For instance, if you are describing an engineering project, there would be nothing unique about mentioning that it took years to develop. What project does not? However, by being more specific—maybe the project took fifty years to develop—you will have a detail worth including in the introduction.

Start composing the introduction by arranging the details into short, compound sentences in first person or third person. The end result should create a riddle-like rhythm that helps showcase the most defining information:

> He smells . . . but smells like . . ." "He will always . . . but will never . . ." "Sometimes he looks . . . and always looks . . ." "He tolerates . . . however he enjoys. . ."

Notice that these sample compound sentence formats suggest interesting juxtapositions, such as paradoxes, or ironies. For instance, "He can smell microscopic-size food, but you can smell him from fifty feet away." Remember, the purpose of the introduction is to load the most crucial material into a short amount of space (usually one third of a page double-spaced, typed) so that if the reader goes no further, he or she still takes away crucial, memorable information. Mention your subject only at the end of this introductory paragraph. The principles of specificity and juxtaposition discussed under Netting in the Style unit are important to building your introduction, even though the riddle will not not be shaped by long, flowing lists.

Problem-Solution paragraphs.

After the introduction, the body paragraphs of the essay must organize material so that the reader is first involved in a seemingly impossible problem, usually a survival issue, that a particular animal or insect solves through special physical features and behavioral adaptations. Only after the problem has been sufficiently dramatized does the science writer deliver nature's clever solution. Too often, science writers do the opposite, immediately starting new paragraphs by listing interesting or amazing abilities of the animal, such as bizarre mating maneuvers, impossible feeding habits, or genius engineering skills, *before* dramatizing, or even mentioning at all, the problem the animal overcomes by its unique ability. A textbook which employs the less effective solution-followed-by problem organizational format is about as memorable as a stand-up comedy routine where the comedian delivers the punch line before telling the joke.

Science writers forget to use the problem-solution paragraph effectively because they are no longer astonished by the problems they take for granted. Familiarity can mind-zap the most learned. If problem-solution strategy were consistently applied to everything we need to learn, we believe educational systems would become super-conductors. Does anyone really appreciate trigonometry, a wondrous mathematical invention, before being immersed in an engineering problem that requires it as a solution? Do young students really appreciate the United States's political structure based on a checks-and-balance system unless they first view or read about the terror that exists when that system is absent? Does anyone remember how a general won a battle without first experiencing the pressure of that battle's importance and how deadly the obstacles looked before the battle? Too much of what we learn has to do with memorizing unique facts, or solutions, and their problems are either blitzed or ignored.

Permanent learning occurs when the reader helps solve a problem, not when he or she memorizes a solution. Hollister builds his problem-solution paragraphs by first describing, with threatening details, the roadrunner's hot environment and hyperactivity, both conditions which would seem to dehydrate the bird. Only when the reader's mouth dries, does Hollister offer the solution: The roadrunner's ability to locate shade and to feed on reptiles of high water content. Often a solution like feeding on reptiles, gives way to another intriguing problem worthy of dramatization. Hollister annunciates how difficult it would be for a bird without teeth to digest a long snake before revealing the roadrunner's reliance on digestive juices to gradually burn the oversized food little by little. Other writers would simply rely on a checklist of easy solutions—the roadrunner eats animals of high water content to keep from dehydrating and uses its digestive juices to digest large snakes—assuming the reader will find these solutions fascinating despite the fact that these special abilities are dismembered from the theater of the problem.

Trouble Making.

For the body of your paper, often you will need to imagine the problem your subject must overcome, either by doing more research, by knowing the limitations of other related items, or by imagining the problems human beings would have trying to overcome a similar problem. What would it take for us to catch a hoofed animal that runs over fifty miles an hour or to filter microscopic impurities from liquid substance that had unusual properties? These questions help generate material that introduces and dramatizes specific problems in the first half of the paragraph; the ingenious solution is reserved as a punch line in the last half of the paragraph. One student, Melinda Myers, combines several uniquely ostrich solutions, each a response to an environmental difficulty the bird must overcome, into a single problem-solution paragraph:

> The ostrich prefers the soft grasses of lush watered regions, but has adapted to desert conditions in order to survive. The desert sand gets hot enough to cook a chicken, and the terrain of the brush isn't exactly like silk on the skin. Imagine running on stickers, rocks and other sharp objects with bare feet. Well, lucky for the ostrich, he has built-in cushions to protect his soles—a thick layer of padding on the bottom of his feet. When the ostrich must run the marathon, the jogging bird would likely have its bony chest pierced, poked and prodded by twigs, brush, and the limbs of small trees. No problem. The ostrich is protected by a thick breast bone and sternum. Remember how it feels to kneel in church for any length of time? Well if you had knee pads like the ostrich, you could walk on your knees.

The ostrich, like all animals, insects, plants, has unique physical attributes and habits which evolved as responses to survival-of-the-species issues: How the animal gets sustenance; how the animal defends itself against predators and the environment; how the animal procreates and rears, feeds and protects its young. Your essay should address at least four or five problem-solutions.

Farther Afield.

Rather then ending your research paper on a problem-solution paragraph, use the conclusion for extraneous facts, for de-bunking a myth or commonly held belief about the animal or insect which you learned through your research was not true. In fact, many field biologist begin studies based on trying to prove or disprove an hypothesis about an animal. Also, you could include any symbolic, literary, philosophical or metaphorical associations your animal carries. One student writer, Jennifer Hanna, when researching the sloth, used some extraneous facts to formulate this philosophical concluding paragraph:

> A theory exists that the sloth's habitual slowness is mainly due to his psychological hereditary make-up. For example, the three-toed sloth has nine vertebrae and could easily swing his head around very quickly to have a look to his side. But does he? Uh-uh. The three toed sloth, regardless of his situation, takes his time and very slowly turns his head. . . . When these facts are considered together with the sloth's pacifistic nature and tolerance of other smaller species living on or near him, his religion, if he were to ascribe to one, would without a doubt be Buddhism. The sloth is well on his way to release from the cycle of life and death, or *samsara*, by his almost complete detachment to everything. His every move is deliberate and planned, yet a few of his activities have no apparent explanation, as if he were a Zen master attempting to teach his students about the purity of non-being.

Objective Style.

In Hollister's introductory riddle, he is not afraid to exaggerate with statements such as "half tail and half feet." Some writers would argue that this is not "objective," but seen in a flash, this is exactly what the roadrunner looks like. Fossilizing a roadrunner into "long white tail, shaggy crest," as Peterson does, makes the roadrunner unidentifiable and is perhaps a less accurate depiction of the overall visual image the bird presents. Later, in the body of the piece, Hollister also avoids bird manualrrhea by using freighting sentences to realistically capture the smoothness and interrelated actions of roadrunner: "He dashes in circles around a coiled snake, stops within striking distance, shuffles his feet, swishes his tail in the dirt and stirs up a blinding cloud of dust."

The issue of inventive style over "objective" blandness to capture scientific reality is especially clear when comparing Norman Mailer's passages describing the Apollo landing on the moon in his book *Of a Fire on the Moon* to *Journey to Tranquility* by Hugo Young, Bryan Silcock, and Peter Dunn. Listening to the actual audio exchange between Control, Eagle, and Houston moments before landing on the moon is exciting even without understanding the pelting, technical data the three are radioing to each other. The sentences are terse, with constant requests for readings on alarms. As soon as an outside writer decides to be helpful and comment on this exchange, interrupting its original tenseness with explanation, the original danger and excitement of the rapid fire urgency is threatened by the writer's neutering-needs to sound "objective." For instance, Young, Silcock, and Dunn write,

> Apollo II was past the point any previous flight had reached, plunging into the most dangerous and unpredictable twelve minutes of the mission. Houston and Eagle exchanged terse, bullet-like packages of technical data as the seconds ticked away.

These sentences do not create the urgent tone that made either the voyage or exchange sound as gut-wrenching as it really was. These writers tell the reader that the mission was dangerous rather than kiln-fire a description with a style that clear-glazes the event with danger and excitement.

Mailer uses Flow, Pause, and Fusion to blaze the voyage into a believable danger and real commitment:

> Boxed in their bulky pressure-suits, tied in and swaddled like Eskimo children in baskets, all move bulky, always in fear of rapping a bank of switches with the insensitive surface of their suits — "You're so clumsy and there's so much force required to move inside the suit," Aldrin had said, "That everything is WHAM! I could bump right into you and maybe I wouldn't even know it"— constrained in vision, they began their powered descent. The motors of the descent stage were fired. Once again

they braked. Once again the reduction of their speed began to bring them down from high velocity to low. Now they came below the orbital parameter of fifty thousand feet. They were committed. They would land, or they would crash, or they would abort and return to Columbia, but they could not try it again.

To believe that a bland style is an "objective" one is a subjective decision based on cultural assumptions that Mailer proves are not true. Whether the reader feels alienated by science lingo or not, the only way to access and understand scientific phenomena is through fusion or metaphor and analogy. On your final rewrite, be sure to employ Flow, Pause, and Fusion to bring alive the reality of everything in the body of your piece. Remember, this is always an important part of writing anything, but it is typically absent in the bland-makes-it-objective style found in many of your sources.

Scope.

Although Glynis uses animals and insects for this Animation essay, Gary suggests many topics: political systems, a complex machine, organ or system in the body, or even the process used by a specific artist. Artistic expressions are final solutions to a slew of philosophical and aesthetic problems. *Skyscraper* is a documentary film of the problem-solution nature of creative enterprises, a six-part PBS production that documents dozens of unimaginable designing, contracting, and constructing problems in building a New York skyscraper, each problem described in detail, leaving the viewer wondering how such a project could ever advance; then each one is expertly solved with architectural talent, diplomacy, and construction finesse.

In an even more subtle Animation article entitled "Comics and Catastrophe" in *The New Republic*, Adam Gopnik carefully analyzes Art Spiegelman's cartoon stripped novel, *Maus,* a recounting of Spiegelman's Holocaust-surviving father's exploits in Poland trying to escape the Nazis. Gopnik wants to dismiss those who see the comic book treatment of events surrounding the Holocaust as trivializing the event, and who instead want the Jewish holocaust to be depicted in an elevated style associated with religious art. In essence, Gopnik refutes those who desire a loftier visual solution for depicting the Holocaust events. Gopnik follows the Animation strategy to argue Spiegelman's solution, first dramatizing the problems Spiegelman had to solve and then his solution.

One problem he imagines Spiegelman had was to underscore how people can become as "helpless and doomed as mice fleeing cats—but they still think that they are people, with the normal human capacity for devising schemes and making bargains." Gopnik argues that Spiegelman wanted to, "give dignity to the sufferers without suggesting that their suffering had any 'meaning' in a sense that in some way ennobled the sufferers." The solution: Spiegelman drew the Jews to look like cartoon mice and Germans as cartoon cats. A second problem—Spiegelman had a subject too horrible to be depicted realistically. Gopnik points to a thirteenth-century Ashkenazi Jewish cartoon from the "Bird's Head Haggadah," a medieval image of Jews with bird heads celebrating Passover because artists of the time would have seen the celebration as a subject too holy to be depicted realistically. Gopnik argues Spiegelman used a cartoon solution for a similar reason: he had a subject too horrible to be depicted realistically, "the ultimate profanity, that must somehow be shown without being shown."

Workout.
Combine your own experiences with internet and library research to build an Animation paper. Begin by researching an animal or insect. We have our students organize information on note cards. On one side of the card write down unique features of the animal. For instance in her research on the opossum, Glynis found out that this marsupial is able to roll its ears shut like a Venetian blind when sleeping. On the other side of the card should be the problem that is solved by the unique feature. Finding the solution in an encyclopedia is not so easy since most information is presented in an *un*Animation format. Often you must glean the problem by doing more research. It is recommended that you consult at least three sources for this paper. The opossums ability to close its ears solves a couple of possible problems: protects against insect invasion (opossums are notoriously filthy and attract lots of flies, flees, and gnats); protects against noise pollution (opossums have very sensitive hearing and are nocturnal and sleep during the day.)

When you research material, realize that it will most often be written in a manner that does not take the Animation techniques above into account. You will need to rewrite using all the above techniques. Include any source material that is well written and informative in your own paper and expand it, but be sure to give the source credit through proper work-cited documentation. (See Note Taking and Work Citing in the Research section of the Critical Thinking & Research unit and Quote Sandwiches in Talking Words.)

LAYERING:
Ways to Divide

 Sliced Pie

 Double Exposure

Thirteen Ways

At times, an essayist works with an especially multifaceted, complicated, chunky subject whose depth and breadth squirt in every direction as the writer tries to contain it. The essayist then needs to fracture this chunkaplex into more manageable pieces without losing its richness. One traditional way to do manage an amorphous subject is by inventing new cookie cutters that classify items in fresh ways as suggested below under Sliced Pie. Sliced Pie allows for a very systematic layering of reality. More complex mosaic structures, which allow the writer to mix different voices and styles into a single piece of writing involve Double Exposures and Thirteen Ways. These mosaic strategies are more rarely used, surprisingly, given the current fascination with deconstruction— viewing reality with a multiple-perspective eye— which has permeated graduate departments in the humanities.

Sliced Pie

By temporarily slicing a complex subject into serving pieces, the writer gives the reader new insights into complex or chaotic subjects. For instance, Edward Hoagland, in his essay "Heaven and Nature," takes on the messy, unpleasant subject of suicide. Hoagland divides the dark, empty-void of suicide with a mold which orders his insights into a fruitful Sliced Pie:

> Many suicides inflict outrageous trauma, burning permanent injuries in the minds of their children, though they may have joked beforehand only of "taking a dive." And sometimes the gesture has a peevish or cowardly aspect, or seems to have been senselessly shortsighted as far as an outside observer can tell. There are desperate suicides and crafty suicides, people who do it to cause others trouble and people who do it to save others trouble, deranged exhibitionists who yell from a building ledge and close-mouthed secretive souls who swim out into the ocean's anonymity.

Most of us would prefer not to think about why people take their own lives; instead we generalize suicide into one big, avoidable topic. Hoagland dissolves this anxiety with reassuring slices that exemplify how the mess really breaks into understandable, clearly defined reasons for suicide. To bake a successful Sliced Pie you will need labeling, C&Cing (compare and contrast), and paralleling.

Labeling

Death also haunts Erik Himmelsbach, another writer to make use of the Sliced Pie form. After the loss of his mother to cancer, he attempts to make sense of his own estranged relationships with the three men in his and his mother's life, a biological father and two step-fathers. The most successful Sliced Pie essays make careful use of labeling (a technique which causes writer anxiety, since labeling is associated with racism, sexism, and other aspects of stereotyping). In order to separate each dad, Himmelsbach gives them all creative labels—Biodad, Adoptodad, and Fauxdad. The labels achieve two important goals: Labels help organize the material so that a reader does not confuse dads; the labels also capture an essential quality of each dad, the label itself becoming a mini-thesis, centering the reader for upcoming support. For instance, by labeling his real father as "Biodad," Himmelsbach characterizes his relationship with his "real" father as limited to an unclose relationship based on DNA.

C&Cing.

Although each of Himmelsbach's would-be role models shared the common bond of being incapable of intimate bonding with Erik, in order to clarify his life with them, he compares and contrasts the three dads to each other. (See Resemblance and Evaluation claims in the Critical Thinking & Research unit.) Note that Hoagland could not identify the many types of motivations a person might have for "buying the farm" if he did not find the subtle distinctions uncovered by comparing and contrasting different suicides. C&Cing is a key analytical skill for all Sliced Pie writers. Pressing different types against each other also serves to provide effective transitions for moving smoothly from type to type. For instance, after Himmelsbach gives information about his real father, whom he calls "Biodad," the writer then launches into providing details about his relationship to his mom's second husband, referred to by the writer as "Adoptodad." Himmelsbach uses a point of contrast between the two dads to create a transition from one dad type to another:

> Whereas Biodad couldn't care less about fatherhood in the conventional sense, Adoptodad did his damnest to fill the void. He was born to play a dad.

Using a distinction as a transition wires together the different types while adroitly illustrating one of the cuts that slices the dad pie.

Paralleling

The material discovered through C&Cing obtains clarity when written about with parallel structure. In other words, the reader can better follow the differences between groups if the same categories of characteristics, discussed in the same order, are written about within each group. The raucous-flavored pie wedges of Matt Groening's *Life in Hell* slices up types of boyfriends, girlfriends and relationships and carefully parallels all the information. Groening characterizes all his subjects by their advantages, disadvantages, common forms of address, and dialogue.

147

Groening is sure to provide the same list of attributes for each different type, paralleling all the information being classified. So, while the dialogue of the girlfriend labeled Old Yeller says,

> You goddamned spineless good-for-nothing drag-ass, no-talent son of a bitch!!! Can't you see you're making me miserable??

Another type of girlfriend, labeled Woman from Mars moans, "I believe this interpretive dance will explain how I feel about our relationship." The "Advantages" and "Drawbacks" of Big Foot boyfriend are that he "Can tote bales; is easily fooled" but that he "Can break you in half; sweats like a pig." In contrast, The Ace of Hearts boyfriend has the advantage of being "Perpetually aroused" and the drawback of being "Perpetually aroused."

Scope.

Sliced Pie can also be used as a playground for irreverence or lighter subjects. In its "Shouts and Murmurs" section, *The New Yorker* magazine published a short satiric piece by Betsy Berne called the "Tired Chronicles," a classification of different types of tired people where "the down-trodden poor, who don't have time to discuss the intricacies of fatigue" were immediately excluded. Instead, Berne ironically focuses on upper middle-class types: tired married people with kids; tired single people who work somewhat outside the home and those who work exclusively at home; the international, jet-set tired group. Berne's Sliced Pie makes fun of those lucky people, herself included, who lead comfortable, financially secure, even exciting lives, and who receive a perverse enjoyment from the luxury of complaining about fatigue. The Sliced Pie mode allows Berne to register a complaint about people who complain, an uncorking of the middle class, while keeping her satire in a controlled format.

A pie filled with darker humor in a not-for-classroom crust, is used in "Foreigners Around the World" from *The National Lampoon*, written by P.J. O'Rourke. This attack on bigoted worldviews works by dividing all people, from Africans to Swiss, into twenty-one ethnic groups, then making fun of stereotypic prejudices about all of them by using an intentionally bigoted, offensive point of view, exaggerating racial characteristics, so-called good points, proper forms of address, and anecdotes illustrating character. Although satiric, this piece will choke the humorless and politically correct. A sincere, antidote to politically correct-ness is "Mother Tongue" by Amy Tan, published in *Threepenny Review*. Tan's essay is really an anti-Sliced Pie tract where Tan criticizes classification strategies, revealing the problem with try-ing to make assumptions based on careless classifications.

One of the most helpful Sliced Pies from the world of psychology is "Malignant Aggression: Necrophilia," a section in The *Anatomy of Human Destructiveness* by Erich Fromm, who divides the socio-psychological world into necrophilia and biophilia. In its extreme form, necrophilia is characterized by a desire to sexually abuse corpses, but Fromm sees this physical perverseness as a metaphor for any tendency to transform something that is alive into something stale, including to solve problems with force; to focus on sickness and failure; to react with indifference towards favorable change and others' enthusiasm; to maintain an obsessed attachment with the past, material things, and regulations; to re-spond to humor with self-consciousness, rather than with spon-taneity. Biophilia is the opposite: preference for the new over the certain, molding through love and reason, and believing that good-ness is a reverence for life.

Psychology and sports mix in "Psychiatric Study of Professional Football" in *Saturday Review World* by Arnold Mandel, a psy-chologist hired by the San Diego Charger football team, who no-ticed that offensive players, suited to choreographed offensive plans, had neat lockers; defensive players, suited to wrecking those plans, had messy lockers. Mandel noticed other personal-ity traits compatible for the large variety of talents called for by the different positions on both squads. For instance, someone who had toughness more akin to sacrificial stubbornness rather than explosiveness, could best meet the requirements for play-ing a middle offensive linemen. Mandel then used each of his carefully analyzed and classified football positions as metaphors: His mother having the qualities of an offensive lineman and Woody Allen having the despair and vanity of a wide receiver.

Workout.
Get ready to use Slice Pie with a group of human beings. Do field work and begin taking notes at a place where you work, hang out, or visit often. In choosing a subject, stay clear of selecting

polarized groupings such as good students versus bad students or coffee drinkers versus tea drinkers. Distinctions between stark opposites here are too obvious and do not warrant an essay. Better subjects would be different types of business students or different types of breakfast eaters, seemingly homogeneous groups which allow the the writer to be more revealing by highlighting subtle distinctions. Try to identify at least four or five sub-categories or types. Begin with the type you know the most about and list all their defining characteristics—physical traits, examples of behavior, typical language usage, purchases, favorite dishes—include anything that might be relevant to making telling distinctions with comparable items in other groups.

When listing traits for the other types, consider parallel details. Glynis wrote a Sliced Pie on coffee drinkers that considered each sub-group's type of coffee drinks, use of cream and sugar, frequency of drinking, the drinkers' appearances, their profession, their dialogue, whether the coffee was to-go or enjoyed tableside. You never know which details will best help define your groups, and sometimes after the first draft you will need to combine two groups because of their similarities, or conversely, pinch a new sub-group off of one you already created.

Once your groups are detailed, come up with interesting labels for each type. It may be helpful to review the chapter on Recyclables, Melted-together Words, and Line-ups in the Style unit, the last two usually functioning as adjectives describing nouns. Using Recyclables, Glynis relabeled her Sliced Pie on Coffee Drinkers as Mud Guzzlers, mud being a slang word for coffee and guzzler being a synonym for drinker. In her draft, Glynis identified a type of coffee drinker, the serious coffee drinker, whom she relabels as the hyper-mud-o-phile, borrowing Greek and Latin to help underscore that group's dominating characteristic.

Introductions and conclusions should be done last. The best Sliced Pie essays are those that not only carefully classify, but which also make a point or give a reason why they are identifying different types. Hoagland thinks about reasons to commit suicide because he is aging, depressed, and is frightened that he is giving suicide consideration. Himmelsbach reviews his relationships with his various fathers because his mother's death makes him realize that she filled the dad role. Your own introduction can be personal or a general observation but avoid trite openings such as "There are many different types, each with their own characteristics." Also avoid summary conclusions such as, "There are many different types of coffee drinkers, but as you can see they all love coffee." Rather, try a Mandel á la mode conclusion for your Sliced Pie (see Mandel's essay on football above), extending the slices by turning them into metaphorical labels for people you know, celebrities, or historical figures. In any case, gourmet torte slices without ice cream are better than corn-bread-crumb endings.

Double Exposure

Looking at old family photos gives us an eerie feeling because we are reminded of the dual nature of any reality. There is the reality of the photograph: Parents holding their infant at a baptism; a thirteen year old swallowing manhood at his Bar Mitzvah; a high school graduate waving her diploma; newlyweds shading their eyes at the Colosseum in Rome. The viewer sees the costumes, smiles, setting, and other visual clues that help remind everyone of the event. Then there is the hidden reality of the day, the psychological drama hidden from the camera lens: parents embarrassed that their infant urine-soaked the priest; the Bar Mitzvah boy recovering from throwing up a pastrami sandwich at his reception; the graduate's turmoil over her boyfriend going away to a different college; the couple's inability to conceive a child on their Roman holiday.

Aside from the obvious dual nature between the physical, conscious world and the psychological, subconscious world, there are many other dual realities. For instance, a doctor looking at a body notices its mechanical and chemical anatomy and discovers unseen disease and sickness invading that body. However, an artist looking at a body notices shapes, shadows, lines, and colors that might be exaggerated to satirize human vanity. Neither the doctor's nor the artist's view is more valid or "real" than the other; neither interpretation is right or wrong, nor part of a more positive or negative endeavor. Working in tandem, the two views represent a more rounded view. Capturing this dual reality in a written piece is an exciting challenge for a writer. Following are three basic kinds of splitting.

Personality Splitting.

For Judy Ruiz, the double layered perspective of her essay "Oranges and Sweet Sister Boy" allows her to write about her mental illness in a format which mirrors her sometimes disjointed view of reality. Ruiz, who suffers from paranoid schizophrenia, struggles with her own identity while also trying to come to terms with the fact that her brother, who is undergoing a sex change operation, is trying to physically change his identity. Ruiz splits these concerns between two distinctly styled paragraphs which alternate throughout the essay since, as the writer notes, "sometimes dreams get mixed up with not-dreams." In the first version, Ruiz reasons her way through her crisis using a lucid narrative style where events unfold in real time: "I am sleeping, hard, when the telephone rings. It's my brother and he's calling to say he is now my sister." Although the information in the first version is highly personal and extraordinary, the tone remains clear and the style rational.

Ruiz's first version is juxtaposed by another style text which is distinguished from the first through the use of a smaller font. In this second version, Ruiz replaces her more rational prose with memories, dreams, and random thoughts which are communicated through a style which uses incomplete sentences ("My Mother. My father."), shifting circumstances (the conception in Dallas at the same time she is a passing girl), surreal details ("false teeth slipping down"), and symbolic references ("the Creators"):

> My mother. My father. I am conceived near Dallas in the dark while a child passes, a young girl who knows and doesn't know,

who witnesses, in glimpses, the creation of the universe, who feels an odd hurt as her own mother, fat and empty, snores with her mouth open, her false teeth slipping down, snores and snores just two seats behind the Creators.

This second version allows Ruiz to convey disturbing thoughts and past events that would lose their gnarled timbre in a more traditional prose style. Yet, the reader can only unknot and interpret the ideas and images in the second version by relying on clues communicated in the first version. In Ruiz's essay, the two versions operate together to help the writer decode her hidden thoughts and troubling memories. Ruiz's use of the Double Exposure helps to underscore her divided feelings over her brother becoming her sister. This ambiguity is reflected in Ruiz's conclusion: "Something in me says no to all this, and that this surgery business is the ultimate betrayal of the self. And yet, I want my brother to be happy." Ruiz's Double Exposure reminds her reader that often we deal with serious difficulties through a complicated blend of our reason and intuition.

Academic Splitting.

In her article "Boobs in Toyland," published in *The Village Voice*, Gwen Blair is sensitive to the dual nature of reality when she writes her article on the Barbie Doll. On the one hand, Blair nods to the historical, economic, and sociological view of the Barbie phenomenon. Most of the body of Blair's essay is an academic account and analysis of the history and development of the famous doll: We learn that since its inception, one plastic doll has been produced for every female in the United States and Canada; that Ruth Handler invented Barbie after watching her own daughter, named Barbie, play with adult fashion dolls; that Handler teamed with her husband who was a plastics expert to fashion a mature-figured doll, pooling all their savings to run commercials on the 1950's Mickey Mouse show, and that sales reach over $7 billion dollars a year.

Yet Blair knows that there is another Barbie reality, one having to do with her owner's secret, private fantasies. Blair includes the private reality of Barbie ownership by intersecting the more academic reality with testimonies and confessions of young women who played with Barbie as young girls. In these italicized versions, we get shocking testimonies that would never surface in an academic paper. From Delores, 29, artist:

> *I never really liked Barbie. I thought she was snippy and bitchy and when she sat down all she could do was stick her legs straight out. Still, she was so much better than my mother. . .*

Just after the primary text's reasoned voice mentions that "Barbie also served as a focus for her owner's insecurities, frustrations, and fears," Blair makes another intersection with confessions from Paula, 23, a secretary:

> *I resented that Barbie always looked just right, no matter what I did to her, and I was always a mess. And it was so irritating to look at those blank bumps that were her breasts. There was nothing to identify with. First I drew in nipples. Then I bashed them on my night side table.*

When the primary text coolly points out that Barbie and her male counterpart, Ken, also "provided a certain outlet for her owner's sexual curiosity," another double exposure gets to the bottom line:

> *I wasn't sure who was on top and who was on the bottom, so instead Ken and Barbie had sex flying through the air. Once I used Ken to masturbate, but then I felt guilty. I was afraid he'd remember.*

The two realities, one academic, the other intimate, each distinct in style and the type of information given, complement one another to create a whole, balanced picture.

Academic splitting can also have a more scientific exposure. One of the most effective examples is a deadly Double Exposure called "The Day the Bomb Went Off: an Imaginary Event," by Erwin Knoll and Theodore Postol, written in 1978 when nuclear obliteration seemed eminent. Both exposures are written with objectivity, but one version imagines the flesh-and-blood effects of a twenty-megaton nuclear bomb explosion on specific neighborhoods in the Chicago area; the second, italicized version coldly explains the scientific facts. The contrast is chilling.

Humor Splitting.
Double Exposures can also be humorous, such as in "Gender Gap: It's in the Genes," in *The Los Angeles Times*, by Beth Ann Krier and Jeannine Stein. The primary exposure discusses the differences between the attitudes of men and women shoppers, including their purposes and methodology, while a second reality

is represented by different stand-up routines from well known comics. "Anguilo's Republic," from *New England Monthly* and compiled by Robert Bertsche, is a compilation of quotes by the Boston mob boss, Gennaro Anguilo, recorded by the FBI. The quotes are Double Exposed with quick, cliché, classical headings used by great thinkers from antiquity and the Age of Reason. The contrast, between these wisdom-flags and Anguilo's gutter remarks, is a killer: "On The Meaning Of Time"—"Time marches on! Time waits for no one. I got the f——— hole burning in my f—— brain!" or "On Prudence"—"When a guy knocks ya down, never get up unless he's gonna kill ya."

"The Killing Game" first published in *Esquire* by Joy Williams Double-Exposes the verbal style of hunting magazines, represented in italics, with Williams' own anti-hunting sarcasm which gives the hunters' entries a context that turns the statements into self-damnation. For instance,

> The animal becomes the property of the hunter by its death. Alive, the beast belongs only to itself. This is unacceptable to the hunter. *He's yours ... He's mine ... I decided to ... I decided not to ... I debated shooting it, then I decided to let it live ...*"

Without Williams's comments, the reader might easily ignore the egotistical possessiveness inherent in the hunters' lines. To create the second, italicized exposure, Williams strings together several examples from different sports articles that all make abrupt use of use first person "I" and possessive pronouns ("yours," "mine") to put emphasis on the hunter's ego's, his pride, as well as verbs that underscore the hunters' fascination with control ('decided," "debated"). Later she uses her first exposure to imply that hunters' use the hunt to sublimate their sex drive:

> They use sex lures ...*The big buck raised its nose to the air, curled back its lips, and tested the scent of the doe's urine. I held my breath, fought back the shivers, and jerked off a shot.*"

Workout.
Pick any subject to write on such as an important political event, a classroom experience, a scientific discovery, a business transaction, an architectural creation, or a parent. Pick a subject that you know exists in two realms of reality, one an official version and the other a more intimate version, one more literal and the other more spiritual, one more scientific and one more flesh-and

blood, or one more serious and one more humorous. Both versions must be informative, well supported by details, and underscored with an appropriate, consistent style. This is not a pro and con strategy or intelligent view versus stupid view tic-tac-toe. Both versions must be equally credible and meaningful.

Do not use any transitions when you cut back and forth, but do place the parts of both versions that seem to have related material close to each other. One exposure should be double spaced and one either single spaced or written in italics or both. Move from version one to version two, and back to version one, at least once per page or else there will not be enough of a Double Exposure effect. On the other hand, do not cut back and forth more than twice per page— from version one to version two, back to version one and two—or else the piece usually becomes too complicated to read. Many students find it easier to write two papers and then splice them together into one.

Thirteen Ways

"Thirteen Ways of Looking at a Blackbird" is a poem by the well-known American poet and insurance executive, Wallace Stevens. The poem looks at blackbirds in thirteen different ways, through thirteen very short stanzas, written in thirteen different styles to capture a more complete picture on what blackbirds signify than would be possible with a poem written from one perspective, in one voice, through one style. In Stevens's poem, one stanza has a prophetic tone that makes the bird a reminder of down-to-earth, feminine intuition as opposed to masculine, idealistic illusions:

> O thin men of Haddam
> Why do you imagine golden birds?
> Do you not see how the blackbird

Walks around the feet
Of the women about you?

Another verse seems more like a haiku depicting the bird as a lively observant force countering vast, static forces in the world:

Among twenty snowy mountains
The only moving thing
Was the eye of the blackbird.

Another one of the thirteen verses is in a folk tale format to dramatize the bird as a figment of a threatened imagination:

He rode over Connecticut
In a glass coach
Once, a fear pierced him,
In that he mistook
The shadow of his equipage
For blackbirds.

And still another verse is written like a mathematical equation where the bird completes a trinity that includes the abstract forces that bind two people, "A man and a woman and a blackbird/ Are one."

Egyptian Realism.

Energizing the truth through as many shifts in focus and styles as Steven's poem may seem unconventional but the concept is nothing new in the visual arts. Art historian E.H. Gombrich argues that ancient Egyptian artists worried much more about completeness than smooth transitions, not painting what could be seen at a given moment from a single point of view, but rather painting all important angles at once. For instance, one can more completely see the totality of a human's eye, its circumference and shape, from a frontal view; the other facial features, arms, and leg movements are more vivid from a profile angle; so for accuracy's sake, the Egyptians combined frontal and profile views. According to Gombrich, the Egyptians were not concerned with creating illusions more comfortable to the eye, but with ensuring accurate identification of a person so the gods could make correct soul-identification after the depicted person died.

Many art critics see modern cubism as this same attempt to transcend the illusion of visual perspective which is limited to a single point of view, possible only at a single point in time, by incorporating several angles of view from different times—from the top,

157

front, back, or sides—all in one view at one time. In the twentieth century, hundreds of modern writers and painters such as Cezanne, Chagall, Picasso, Faulkner, Joyce, Woolf, Barthelme, even architects such as Frank Gehry, splinter the assumption that a work of art should be primarily judged on its ability to create one-point-perspective verisimilitude.

There are other strong justifications for advocating Egyptian-realism thought. "Making the Eye a Better Witness" by Edwin Chen in the *The Los Angeles Times* covers the work of UCLA psychologists who discovered that eyewitness accounts of crimes become much more accurate when witnesses are asked to not just describe what happened, but to describe their own frame of mind at the time, reconstruct the crime in a variety of time sequences other than from only beginning to end, and to recreate the incident from the criminal's perspective as well as their own. In short, witnesses most accurately interpret reality by creating a Thirteen Ways, eye-witness portfolio. "World View" by Barry Starvo, also for *The Los Angeles Times*, demonstrates that it is impossible to depict the globe accurately in a two dimensional map. He reviews six versions of the globe popular at different times, including Buckminster Fuller's fold-out map, and explains how each inevitably exaggerates different visual qualities with different political implications, all visualizing some aspects of reality and none ever totally encircling it completely. The maps taken together create a topographical Thirteen Ways.

Fragmenting.
Thirteen Ways works in essay writing when the writer needs to capture a subject from several angles. The most important concept for creating a Thirteen Ways essay is to perceive it from as many different angles as you can. Thirteen Ways does not try to develop two angles as completely as Double Exposure; however, the variety and number of fragments allows for more far-ranging perspectives, voices, and tones than Double Exposures. Each fragment can range from one word to several paragraphs and also can be argumentative, defining, narrative, satirical, in fact, involve any of the styles and organizational strategies listed in this book. This fragmentation nourishes any multi-faceted, complex subject.

For instance, Peter Blaunder wrote an article entitled "New York Style" for *New York* magazine by compiling seventy-nine stanza-like viewpoints on New York style, effectively Egyptianizing the reality of the city in a manner impossible to accomplish in a more unified, easy-on-the-mind's-eye essay. The jolting diverse points of views, articulated through disparate styles without smooth transitions, reminds the reader that the complexity of New York style can only be captured through radical shifts of perspectives. For instance, some entries are very simple, such as Isaac Bashevis Singer's one word entry, "RUSH." Other entries are more metaphorical such as John Chancelor's: "The avenues in my neighborhood are Pride, Covetousness, and Lust; the cross streets are Anger, Gluttony, Envy, and Sloth. I live over on Sloth, and the style on our street is to avoid the other thoroughfares."

New York style is an enormous subject, but no matter how narrow the focus, you can splinter the subject into innumerable fragments. *The 100th Boyfriend* is a compilation by Bridget Daly and Janet Skeels that includes one hundred viewpoints in different voices on boyfriends. One boyfriend entry is written as a ten line catalog of attributes including,

> Joe polished the bottoms of the Revere ware pans once a month
>
> . . .
>
> Joe thought I looked good in shorts as long as I didn't walk too fast
>
> . . .
>
> Joe was the kind of man you take home to your parents and leave there.

In another anecdotal version a women, looking for common denominators in boyfriends, is finally shocked to discover that it "was bad eyesight," while another entry, laden with metaphors, includes replaying the tape machine to listen to the boyfriend's voice, "sucking on those vowels," but there are ninety-seven others to go before the concept of "boyfriend" is complete.

So that the reader expects such variety, we find that it is best to number each fragment down the center of the page. The following are the beginning entries of a composite made by students on the subject of money, one stanza-paragraph employing a quick netting, the other an extended metaphor like Chancelor's above:

1

Money is—
Groceries to the housewife
Drugs to the junkie
Stamps to the stamp-collector
A word-processor to the writer
Contributions to the philanthropic
Diet Pills to the obese
Nothing to the transcendentalist

2

Start with a man and add a touch of ambition. Let stand until lonely and then thaw out woman and introduce at low heat. Mix both into limited amounts of responsibility and finally marry. Put both at work at medium heat, allow both to buy material things, get raises, buy a new house as a tax write off. Turn up heat and bake both until worn out and then introduce small amounts of alcohol until both are well marinated. On high heat, sear both until bitter. Separate and divide assets. Serve on corporate plates among greenbacks.

3

People love to manipulate one another to get more money. My mother and step father told me they would pay for me to go to college but when the time came they told me to take out a student loan which they would pay back later. Years later I found out that my divorced father and my grandmother were also sending my mother money to help me go to college but she never made this clear and it was a long time before I even knew to thank them: I wasn't even sure what to thank them for—Helping my mother out?

Paradoxing.

One of the keys to writing a good Thirteen Ways is to not only juxtapose different styles and events between the paragraph stanzas, but within each stanza as well. These sections enrich the subject by creating fragments within the fragments. In the New York essay, Blaunder often focuses on bizarre juxtapositions and paradoxes such as Annie Flanders who said,

Tuxedos in the daytime and sunglasses at night. Earning off the books and learning on the job. Being invited to a party you can't get into and getting into a party you weren't invited to. A pair of worn jeans and a $900 belt. A limo to the airport and a budget flight to Rome. Downtown luring uptown and uptown luring downtown. Dressing white in winter and dressing black in summer. Not caring and caring desperately. Makeup on boys and crew cuts on girls. Nine to five P.M. and nine to five A.M. New York.

In contrast to this hustle, some juxtapositions are touching images of cultural integration. James Morton, Dean of St. John the Divine, remembers a forty foot Christmas tree with unusual decorations:

> 2,000 origami paper cranes folded by New York school children as part of a tradition started in Hiroshima by an eleven-year-old girl who was dying from radiation and made the first such cranes on her deathbed.

Sketchbook with Voices by Eric Fischl, with Jerry Saltz, was reprinted in *Harper's Magazine* at the time of Fischl's retrospective at The Whitney Museum. This compilation captures the essence of contemporary art by including an exercise or admonition from different artists on each page of the sketchbook. Many of these entries have paradoxical advice: Chuck Close says, "Make a painting in which every part of the painting is of equal importance," while Cindy Sherman demands, "Do your own work, but use someone else's clothes," and Jennifer Bartlett reveals the psychological, "In the morning make long lists of things to do. In the afternoon write down whose ideas they were."

Vignetting.

To give Thirteen Ways some flesh and blood, it should include a few entries that are anecdotes, very short exemplifying stories, happening simultaneously. (See the discussion of anecdotes in Talking Words under the Encircling unit.) For instance, some of Blaunder's sections, like Steven's glass coach stanza above in "Thirteen Ways of Looking at a Blackbird," are mini-drama's. Consider David Mamet's on New York style:

> I was down in the village recently on a very rainy day when a cab pulled up at a light. A young man and a woman started to get out with their baby as the light turned green, and a second car pulled up behind them. The man in the second car got out and started yelling, 'Are you out of your fucking mind? Are you out of your fucking mind?' That is New York style.

A similar Thirteen Ways of a city, more focused on political tension than style, is entitled "Jerusalem — Fall 1990" by Aaron Back in *Tikkun: A Bimonthly Jewish Critique of Politics, Culture & Society* discovered in *Harper's Magazine*. The piece was written two months after the Iraqi invasion of Kuwait. It is built of various vignettes that describe the wide ranging reactions of the author and people to one another in various types of encounters after three Israelis were stabbed to death by Palestinians revenging Palestinians killed earlier on the Temple Mount. One vignette describes a landlady who shows sincere personal concern at one moment and raises rent fifty percent the next; in another vignette a Lamaze class is filled with talk of calming babies while one friend argues that blowing up houses to punish people is no worse than losing a house through foreclosure in the United States.

Scope.

Other tastes of Thirteen Ways essays are often centered on creative choice and its implications. Both Margaret Atwood's "Women's Novels" in *Likely Stories: A Postmodern Sampler* and "Not-Knowing" by Donald Barthelme, use multiple entries to capture all the angles that develop a fictional work. Taking the commercial aspects of creativity into consideration, syndicated columnist Art Buchwald, in "And Just What Is a Newspaper Editor," describes the editor from his own point of view, then the reporter's point of view, then the publisher's, and finally the syndicated columnist's, who, of course, sees the editor as "forthright, brave, intelligent, and honorable, . . . a credit to his profession and race" for choosing the piece in the first place. Buchwald's essay has Thirteen-Ways spirit, but stays in one humorous voice. Camille Paglia's "The Diana Cult" for *The New Republic* does not shift styles in each section of the essay, but is fractured into different "archetypal" perspectives, regarding England's Princess Diana as Cinderella, the betrayed wife, the princess in the tower, the mater dolorosa, the pagan goddess, the Hollywood queen, the beautiful boy. (Paglia's essay was written several years before Diana's tragic death).

Workout.

Pick a subject that you feel is so large and complicated that it would be more honest to write about it through jolting, multiple angles than through a smoothly transitioned, single-perspective essay. Possibilities include a complex work of artistic merit, a city, a person, money, education, a philosophical viewpoint.

You should have a minimum of eight ways of looking at your subject, numbered down the middle of the pages in order to prepare your reader for the dramatic shifts between entries. Some angles may be heavily metaphoric and others academic; some very short and others more developed; some focused on a specific detail and others making insightful generalities; some mini-dramas and others analytic; some humorous and others very serious; some spiritual and others down-to-earth. Remember that any of the other stylistic and organizational patterns discussed in this book can give you ideas on how to think and write one of your paragraph stanzas.

Be sure that each of your paragraph stanzas works well by itself. Sometimes students include filler entries that are shallow, written from a narrow person's point of view, or lacking in specifics and careful style. Some of the samples above are compilations which made the writer's job easier. You can also get ideas from other people, but you must think they are legitimate. Mold and shape them so they are distinct and communicate clearly, and accept them as your own. Every entry must fill in a crucial angle.

BURSTING:
Ways to Disarm

 Devil's Advice

Mocking with Media

Trojan Horse

Sincerely Yours

Disarming an opposing view-point by revealing its absurdity, popping its fantasies, or highlighting its hypocrisy, presents special challenges. An essayist needs to argue with conviction but without sounding overwrought. If the essayist's unbridled passion becomes overwhelming, there is the risk of committing critical thinking fallacies. For instance, being enraged breeds the *ad hominem* fallacy, attacking the opponent's personal attributes rather than the details of the opponent's position. On the other hand, approaching a charged issue with a gutted attitude and a flat voice suffocates the sincere conviction necessary to disarm a point of view already barricaded with its own use of fallacies.

Satire, parody, metaphorical instructions, and intimate recounts are often overlooked as some of the most effective devices for enabling the essayist to passionately argue a case without running the risk of overindulging the emotions. These strategies demand control and so burst an opponent's position by indirectly making the same points covered in a straightforward argument. However, the points carry more weight because these strategies jerk the reader's eyes open. Since hitting the strategy's ironic note requires concentration and careful modulation of voice, running amuck is avoided, and there is little risk of letting emotions roam too freely.

We have found that in order to burst successfully, writers must work within a clearly defined format which can support a combination of passion, sarcasm, and wit. Devil's Advice, Mocking with Media, and the more subtle uses of Trojan Horse and Sincerely Yours, provide hardware which can accommodate the weight of a charged tone. In order to argue effectively, you will find it helpful to review the Scrub section under the Style unit since a target's language is usually swollen with euphemism, and pricking it can always be a part of bringing the opponent down to reality.

Devil's Advice

Strong proposals rely on some or all of the five basic methods for putting together an argumentative piece: supporting with facts and statistics, citing authorities, offering examples, answering objections by the opposition, predicting consequences. Sometimes, when relying on these methods alone, we find ourselves unintentionally "preaching to the congregation," our argument reaching only the ears of those who already favor our position. No matter how well a position is argued, it is very difficult to get the opposition's attention: facts and statistics bore, and skeptics know they can be manipulated; authorities can be fatted with self-interest; predictions can appear to be guess work or empty threats; the opposition can always claim to be misunderstood. Most of all, an opponent's self-righteousness is formidable armor against any rational argument. Devil's Advice penetrates this protection.

Ironic Agreement.
First of all, Devil's Advice seduces the opponent by appearing to be agreeable. However, this agreement is ironic. Since the es-

sayist is creating a proposal that he or she does not truly believe in, Devil's Advice is tongue-in-cheek humor. The tongue-in-cheek praise and advice advocated by the ironic proposal confuses the opponent, puts the opponent off guard, and raises the spirits of readers victimized by the opponent's self-importance.

For instance, if you believe the state should impose automobile seat belt laws, then you pretend to agree with those who are against those laws: You argue that not only is it your right not to wear seat belts, but new laws should require people to take their seat belts out of their cars immediately. If you are sickened by spousal abuse, then take the side of abusers and argue that husbands and wives should take boxing lessons and solve problems by using violence. In 1729 Jonathan Swift published "A Modest Proposal," one of the iciest pieces of Devil's Advice ever written. In actuality, Swift intended to create sympathy for the oppressed, hungry, Irish Catholic peasants, and focus anger on wealthy, bigoted, English absentee landlords and the English aristocrats whose government silently let the Irish bleed. Therefore, he pretended to be on the side of those English landlords who think of the Irish as less than human. Swift develops what he knows are hidden and not-so-hidden hatreds for the Irish, formalizing those hatreds into a proposal so raw and grim that no one would want to claim support for them.

Exaggerated Proposal.
Devil's Advice slices through an opponent's argument by humorously exaggerating the opposition's hidden motives and illogic into an overblown, formal proposal, bringing the negative aspects of the argument into an intense light. Swift does this by offering a logical proposal for a "fair, cheap, and easy method" to deal with the "prodigious number of children" in Ireland. In the "modest," logical tone of a benevolent social planner, Swift's persona proposes a plan whereby Irish children instead of "wanting food and raiment for the rest of their lives . . . shall on the contrary contribute to the feeding, and partly to the clothing, of many thousands."

As with all strong proposals, first the writer must outline all the benefits of the plan. For example, Swift points out that his plan would also prevent voluntary abortions, a sacrifice "which would move tears and pity in the most savage and inhuman breast." Secondly, the writer crunches numbers: Swift makes a careful analysis of how much it costs to raise a child to the first year, and does careful, realistic calculations on how many Irish women are "breeders." Finally, Swift gets to the bottom line which he hopes "will not be liable to the least objection":

> I have been assured by a very knowing American of my ac-
> quaintance in London, that a young healthy child well nursed is
> at a year old a most delicious, nourishing, and wholesome food,
> whether stewed, roasted, baked, or boiled; and I make no doubt
> that it will equally serve in a fricassee or a ragout.

Also, like all good proposal arguments, the plan elaborates on results: "a child will make two dishes at an entertainment for friends"; "the fore or hind quarter will make a reasonable dish. . . boiled on the fourth day"; infant's flesh will be in season all year long, but especially in March because "there are more children born in Roman Catholic countries about nine months after Lent"; the carcass may be skinned to make "admirable gloves for ladies, and summer boots for fine gentlemen;" and finally, although it would help to replace the abuses of deer hunting, allowing adolescents into the meat supply would not be recommended since boys would be a tough chew and girls would not be far from becoming breeders themselves. Another bonus: "men would become as fond of their wives during the time of their pregnancy as they were now of their mares in foal, their cows in calf, or sows when they are ready to farrow."

Minimized Horrors.

In order for Devil's advice to be successful, the writer must keep showing the horrors of the proposal to clue the reader on how outrageous the proposal is but then minimize those horrors by acting as if the horrors are an advantage in order to keep in the spirit of the proposal. If you were writing a proposal that advocated racial bigotry, it would be important to bring out all the horrors of racial bigotry, lest a racial bigot think you share their point of view, but then quickly try to minimize those horrors to bring the reader back to the straight-faced realism of the plan. For instance, you might write: "We need to block economic opportunities for minority groups, (This phrase is part of the exaggerated plan.) and hope that when those groups are out of the economic picture the racial group to which you belong is not next on the chopping block. (This second phrase that is a negation of the plan strikes horror in the bigoted reader). If that happened, you are least a believer in true democracy." (This last sentence minimizes the horror and brings the reader back to the plan.) In the seat belt law example above you would follow with grotesque results, but with an excuse: "If we take seat belts off of children, sure there will be some kids thrown out the front window and run over, but remember, the world is over-populated."

The horrors of mistreating the Irish are always front stage in Swift's essay in his reference to killing and eating babies. That is too horrible even for English that hate the Irish. In fact, the grotesqueness of Swift's essay dominates any discussion about the Irish so strongly that people who wished to voice any anti-Irish opinions would hesitate, knowing they risked getting some of Swift's essay splattered all over themselves. The horrors are always minimized by the advantages of the plan. Near the end of the essay, Swift cleverly suggests horror through agreement. He asks anyone who thinks he has a better proposal to first ask the miserable Irish if they do not agree whether they would have been better off sold as food at a year old since he is sure the answer is "yes." Finally, lest anyone think Swift's persona has a personal interest in the plan, he points out that he does not have his own "children by which I can propose to get a single penny."

Scope.

In a slightly different use of the strategy called "No Wonder They Call Me a Bitch," Ann Hodgman, a contributing editor to *Spy* magazine, describes spending "the better part of a week eating dog food" in order to verify dog food advertising claims. She turns on the skillet, cooks up Gaines-burgers, samples "a piece of red extrusion," the patty "leaking rivulets of red dye." After lining up seven flavors of Milk-Bone Flavor Snacks on the floor in order to make gourmet decisions about which to eat, she realizes,

> Unless my dog's palate is a lot more sensitive than mine — and considering that she steals dirty diapers out of the trash and eats them, I'm loath to think it is—she doesn't detect any more difference in the seven flavors than I did when I tried them.

Hodgman writes gut-punching Devil's Advice by actually describing herself carrying out her outrageous proposal.

Mark Twain in his "Advice to Youth," an address to students, smokes out their hidden corruptions through an outrageous proposal to learn good lie telling since "many a young person has injured himself permanently through a single clumsy and ill-finished lie, the result of carelessness born of incomplete training." Twain's "advice" includes details on how to manipulate parents and become good conformists.

It is difficult to find contemporary pure tastes of Devil's Advice, and we hope students will revive this classic satiric form. A good example is "Miracle Drug" by student Gregory Bedford, who gives Devil's Advice restoring the benefits of cocaine, including "increased awareness of financial matters, heightened creativity, and sharpened social skills." Financial advantages include developing very prudent spending habits to keep up with the cost of cocaine, which means trimming non-essentials such as "food, medicine, and hygiene products" since coke's numbing effects "will hide from the body any symptoms of approaching illness" and nose-numbness makes soap and deodorant irrelevant.

Workout.

First you need to pick a target: a politician, an employer or teacher, an organization or institution, a relative or friend who has betrayed you. Then you need to sniff out and make a list of all the target's immoral, hidden motives and the illogic of its not-so-hidden positions. You need facts about your opponent, so you may need to do some research.

Now you are ready for the rough draft. Instead of arguing against these stupidities, first exaggerate them by making the opponent's wishes even more extreme or outlandish, smoking out what your opponent could never admit to even to himself. Now, "support" these horrors. Support them by formalizing them into a well developed proposal and by standing on your opponent's soap box, not your own. Allow the absurd to be show-cased. Keep a cool, steady voice, and without flinching, propose embarrassing desires and illogical solutions. Write as if you expect praise rather than contempt, but of course what you offer is worthy of contempt. Remember to consider all the components of a well argued proposal outlined above in the first sentence of Devil's Advice. The juxtaposition of your outrageous proposal, packaged in the competent, traditional components of a business or persuasive essay proposal, will create a tongue-in-cheek satiric essay. What you praise or advise will be too outlandish for anyone to accuse you of really believing. Anyone who does, deserves to be confused.

Remember to minimize the horrors. Even though the essay is agreeing with an outrageous version of the opponent's position, some extremists could still find the proposal acceptable. You must sneak in enough negatives to make sure readers find your proposal unacceptable. One way to sneak these in is to mention the downside of your proposals, but either act as if they are of minor importance, or give outlandish reasons why they are beneficial.

Cool Down.
Review the Scrub section under Style. Consider inflating parts of your proposal by creating euphemisms or terminology for various steps, stages, items, or actions. In other words, try using euphemism as a way of making your proposal more official.

Mocking with Media

Mocking with Media is a strategy that allows the writer to simultaneously burst both cliché arguments as well as the writer's simplistic faith in formulaic writing. It works by forcing an exaggerated situation into the typical, stereotypic devices of any written form of communication—a local newspaper, business newsletter, personal ad page, legal brief, restaurant criticism, travel book, or any other written format that has become standardized. The subject matter itself gets the wind punched out of it, because it looks more absurd when it is pressed into the cliché restrictions of a specific writing format. Both style and subject magnify each other, rendering each other ridiculous. Mocking with Media is a symbiotic satire.

Human Target.

Gary understood what makes this concept work while studying a piece entitled "God Is Dead in Georgia" by Anthony Towne, written originally for *motive*, a magazine of the United Methodist Church. Some students always think the essay is an attack on religion, but most see it as an attack on God's "massive diminishing influence," on people who see God and the Trinity only in materialistic and political terms. A slew of other mockings on the same subject showed up years later in "He's Back!!!" edited by Lewis Lapham for *Harper's Magazine*, all mocking different promotional formats people easily believe in, and again mocking those who assign Jesus political and celebrity worth. A topic reflecting more earthly concerns, a pure taste of Mocking With Media happens in "Coyote v. Acme" by Ian Frazier, for *The New Yorker*, which makes fun of the violent gimmicks in "Road Runner" cartoons by using the medium of legalese.

Target Weight.

The second key principle is to create a situation that is either too monumental or too light weight for the media format in which you are going to write about your human target. When the situation is too monumental, the media format's gimmicks will not be able to hold its weight which will help you make fun of that format as explained below. For instance, in the example above, the death of God would be too monumental for the everyday associations we have with newspapers. Jesus's second coming would be too glorious to be subjected to the public relations formats in the *Harper's* article in which Ron Suskind writes a typical advance memo for Jesus:

> DAY ONE—Theme: Traditional values. In reintroducing You, we don't want to create converts so much as tap existing support. To evoke a yearning for simpler days (from A.D. 1 through Eisenhower), it is important to rely on those oft-recited parables. Of course, they'll need to be reworked (boiled to thirty seconds, max) . . .

Al Franken writes Jesus's monologue for *Saturday Night Live*; Gerry Howard at Norton redoes a dust jacket for *The New Testament*; clothes designer Adele Lutz works out wardrobe notes for official meetings, street gatherings, and stadium dates; and Phyllis Robinson mocks storyboard formats for a one-minute television commercial announcing Jesus's arrival.

On the other hand, the Coyote's ill fate in the *New Yorker* essay mentioned above is too light weight for the importance we assign to legal briefs, helping to make the briefs seem absurd. Another example of using light weight fill is a discussion of a Taco Bell television commercial featuring country music singer Willie Nelson which is thinly spread into a deconstruction literary theory. In "Deconstructing Willie: The Taco as Imperialist Symbol" written for *Texas Monthly* and later picked up by the *Utne Reader*, Stephen Harrigan mocks the jargonesque literary analysis that chokes English department graduate courses. The literary theory eye-balls the commercial's deep significance, such as the taco becoming a symbol of "rapacious imperialism," since in the empty shell "we see the sad defeat of the maize culture that once flourished in the American Eden."

Style Target.

Mocking with Media is always a twofold attack, first undercutting a philosophical point of view and then ripping a standardized writing format and its style. The key to successful satiric mimicking is to compile a list of all the typical stylistic and organizational devices (including sentence structure, word choice, subtopics, and points of view) that have turned that format into a formula so it is no longer a sincere, articulate form. The satiric writer makes sure to use everything in this list. If you have weighted correctly as described above, the stress of your topic will also help tear open the format's fabric.

For example, in "God Is Dead in Georgia," Towne hits all the techniques used in typical local newspapers: First he squeezes as many credentials as possible into a freighting sentence:

> God, creator of the universe, principal deity of the world's Jews, ultimate reality of Christians, and most eminent of all divinities, died late yesterday during major surgery undertaken to correct a massive diminishing influence.

Towne uses the journalism technique of including trivial details with what are at best secondary people, here including a long list of famous theologians and their universities as the assisting "unsuccessful" surgeons. He pokes fun at newspaper's tendency to narrow on the most cliché public relations responses:

> The Pope, in Rome, said, in part: 'We are deeply distressed for we have suffered an incalculable loss. The contributions of God to the Church cannot be measured, and it is difficult to imagine how we shall proceed without Him.'

Also the reader finds typical newspaper avoidance of intelligent public response and coverage of only the most worn out, non-threatening responses: "'At least he's out of his misery,'" comments a supermarket housewife.

Towne uses legal, flank-protecting language typical of newspapers' concern to avoid responsibility for positions and sources, such as there being "unconfirmed" reports that Jesus, "sometimes" called the Christ, "reputed" son of God, will assume the authority, "if not" the title, of the deceased God, and that "the case is complicated by the fact that Jesus, although he died," was resurrected "so may have not died at all." Finally Towne includes diversions attending to other parts of the newspaper and "human interest" notations to turn serious, complex notions into souvenir-shop items and financial concerns. For instance, the stock market drops sharply until traders get wind that Jesus, "see 'Man in the News,' p. 36, col.4 — who survives, plans to assume a larger role in the management of the universe." The newspaper promises an upcoming "24-page full-color supplement with many photographs reviewing God's long reign," and requests "pertinent letters, photographs, visions and the like" from the readership.

In the "Coyote v. Acme" essay targeting human fascination with the violent ploys of animated cartoons, Frazier uses all the devices and language of legal briefs by having Wile E. Coyote go after Acme Company, defendant for "personal injuries, for loss of business income, and mental suffering" due to "gross negligence" of products purchased from Acme to catch prey. Premature detonation of one product results in several disfigurements to Mr. Coyote including "severe singeing of the hair on the head, neck, and muzzle" as well as ear fracture, "causing the ear to dangle" with a "creaking sound."

173

Scope.

Some Mocking with Media can even be unintentional. "The Right Jail" by an anonymous author for *M:The Civilized Man* was published by the editors of *Harper's Magazine*, who saw its unintentional humor. This is a guide to minimum-security federal prisons used for wealthy or celebrity white-collar convicts that inadvertently mocks both travel books and the comforts of these prisons. Prisons are starred, with Allenwood getting four stars since "Accommodations" are superior, "Cuisine" excellent with a "variety of choices at every meal, salad and fruit bar at lunch and dinner, kosher and vegetarian meals . . . 'Work' decent, producing oak and walnut desks for government officials of GS-15 rank. . . 'Ambience and amenities' include a full law library, computers, tennis courts." Then there is one star Maxwell. No vegetarian meals here.

In the world of art, "Fabrizio's: Criticism and Response" by Woody Allen, in *The New Yorker*, mocks the style of literary reviews, particularly restaurant reviews, as well as people's need to find exaggerated importance in everyday life:

> One lovely touch at Fabrizio's is Spinelli's Boneless Chicken Parmigana. The title is ironic, for he has filled the chicken with extra bones, as if to say life must not be ingested too quickly or without caution . . . One is reminded at once of Webern, who seems to crop up all the time in Spinelli's cooking.

What could be a mocking of trivial research papers, and definitely of American gullibility, happens in "A Neglected Anniversary (The Bathtub Hoax)" by H. L. Mencken included in his *The Bathtub Hoax & Other Blasts and Bravos*. It is a faked, but well "researched," history of the bathtub including "facts" such as "the first American bathtub was installed and dedicated so recently as December 20, 1842 . . ." Some Cincinnatians resist the tub at first, the bathtub being "an epicurean and obnoxious toy from England, designed to corrupt the democratic simplicity of the republic." The medical profession worries about "zymotic diseases." Mencken later admitted researching the real history of the tub would be a "dreadful job."

A great contemporary equivalent of this is a whole museum in Los Angeles called The Museum of Jurassic Technology which spoofs museum presentation prose, not to mention the nature of museum exhibits themselves. For instance, while looking at an exhibit of geometric drawings and instruments used by Geoffrey Sonnabend to refine his theory of forgetting, the viewer picks up the exhibit phone and listens to a history which makes fun of the inventor as artistic dreamer, science's reliance on simplistic visual models, and euphemism:

> . . . Geoffrey attended a recital of Romantic lieder by the well known vocalist, Madelena Delani. After the recital, Geoffrey returned to his room, but (according to his own accounts) feeling listless, went out again to walk about the grounds. During what proved to be a sleepless night, Geoffrey conceived of the intersection of the plane and cone which was to become the basic model for the structure of the mechanism for forgetting which is the crux of his three volume work—"Obliscence: Theories of Forgetting and the Problem of Matter.

Workout.

To begin you need a social target and a medium/media target. First decide what political, social, economic, or philosophical position you want to render ridiculous. Make a list of items or positions that you want to cover about this target. Next decide on a language format you would like to target. We have had students go after public television pledge break formats, letters offering insurance and credit card deals, musicals, legal briefs, travel books and articles, scholarly journal writing. After choosing a target and medium, make a list of at least ten of the organizational and stylistic devices used by this target. If you pick a certain type of newspaper article, the list we have already discussed with regards to Towne's article above may suffice.

Now the two targets must be brought together. First create an outlandish event. For instance, if Towne had wished to attack the clichéd, simplistic attitudes men and women hold for one another, then the headline for the article would be "Men and Women Divide the Earth," or if attacking environmental negligence, the headline might read "Scientists Announce the End of the Sun Is Tomorrow." Use the outlandish situation to explore all the related issues and details of your target. You must write using all ten of the devices listed which are characteristic of the communications device you also wish to unravel.

Trojan Horse

Although we are usually willing to listen to advisory instructions for practical matters like baking a devil's food cake, growing hybrid tea roses, organizing an overstocked closet, saddling a stallion, or building firm abdominal muscles, when it comes to more personal matters—sexual technique, intimate love, personal hygiene, social etiquette, and morality—we become resistant to advice, no matter how helpful. One way to sneak through the gates of obstinacy is to ride inside a Trojan horse—metaphorically camouflaging serious philosophical guidance behind seemingly practical, innocuous advice. Because the target-reader believes the advice or information to be about something non-personal, this reader lets down his or her guard, allowing the advisor to surprise the reader by hiding in sub-textural instructions and then delivering counsel about sensitive issues. Trojan Horse depends on four devices: Instructing, Grabbing, Ripening, and Fusing.

Instructing.
W. S. Merwin, wants to address the fragility of relationships, particularly the unimaginably difficult task of rebuilding an intimate relationship once there has been a devastating rift. While many of us would prefer to hold on to our forgive-and-forget mentality and approach the rebuilding with a false sense of clean-slate optimism, the wise essayist opens our eyes to the truth: Relationship reconstruction is tough, fragile, almost impossible work. Borrowing from the "How To" genre known as the process essay, Merwin climbs into his Trojan Horse with a hypothetical set of instructions entitled "Unchopping a Tree." The incredible task suggested by the title immediately smoke signals the reader that the how-tos given in Merwin's essay have more than literal value. The instructions— about the meticulousness, riskiness involved in and compromise necessary for putting a tree back together after it has been chopped to pieces—parallel what it takes when repairing an emotionally damaged personal relationship.

The process starts with "you" taking the "leaves, the small twigs, and the nests that have been shaken, ripped, or broken off by the fall; these must be gathered and attached once again to their respective places." The instructions include warnings that give the process a metaphorical dimension: ". . . much depends upon the size, age, shape, and species of the tree." Even after giving the instructions, Merwin intimates that the results are still tenuous and that this whole painstaking process will not necessarily last:

> Finally the moment arrives when the last sustaining piece [of the scaffold] is removed and the tree stands again on its own . . . as though its weight for a moment stood on your heart. How long will it stand there now? What more can you do?

Merwin's final considerations hint to the reader that the directions given in the essay could be applied to a more philosophical arena—making reparations to something which has sustained non-physical damage.

Grabbing.

While the literal directions cloak the more philosophical meaning of the Trojan Horse essay, the use of second person, imperative voice helps to build an in-your-face relationship between Merwin and his reader. (See "Second person" in the Opt section of the Style unit.) The reader's analytical powers will be provoked by the philosophical analogy suggested by the surface text, but the writer's imperative, second-person voice, with the implied "you" to make a demand, insures that the reader cannot escape from this odd job. The imperative voice disarms the reader because he or she is being told to do something, to act instead of passively observing something. The distance between advisor, receiver, and the task to be performed is minimized. The subtlety of the writer's hidden message is balanced by the pugnacity of the imperative voice. Merwin begins with a toned down command: "Start with the leaves, the small twigs, and the nests that have been shaken ripped, or broken off by the fall;" Merwin's continues with enjoiners: ". . . watch for a leaf or a twig to be snapped off yet again . . . listen for the nuts to shift." The active verbs which are packaged as coaxing commands nudge the target into an active reading of the instructions.

Ripening.

In *The Size of Thoughts*, Nicholson Baker includes a recipe for hot chocolate sauce to put on ice cream, but fills out a typical recipe with sensory details and suggestions for a cooking attitude which are normally left out of literal recipes:

> Entertain yourself by breaking the ingot of chocolate into its two halves and pushing the halves and the subsiding chunk of butter around with the tip of the butter knife. Then a b a n d o n the butter knife and switch to a spoon. . .Stir idly. . . you'll be able to brandish the whole solidified disk of chocolate merely by lifting the spoon. It looks like a metal detector.

Merwin uses sensory details which are usually left out of just-the-facts directions to move his reader beyond the realm of the literal process and into the metaphor. "Unchopping a Tree" is loaded with suggestive words which seem slightly out of place for the ostensible task but which serve both the surface and the subtext of the essay: "When all is ready the splintered trunk is lowered onto the splinters of the stump. This, one might say is only the skeleton of the resurrection." While these instructions are good advice for someone who is literally unchopping a tree, words like "skeleton" and "resurrection" help establish a sub-textual dimension to the process. In addition to these ripe nouns, Merwin also sprays his directions with ambiguous statements, which, once the metaphor has been planted, can aptly apply to both the literal process and the subterranean advice:

> Now the tackle must be put into place, or the scaffolding, depending on the surroundings and the dimensions of the tree. It is ticklish work. Almost always it involves, in itself, further damage to the area, which will have to be corrected later. But as you've heard, it can't be helped. And care now is likely to save you considerable trouble later.

Merwin supplements his process with ironic appraisals such as "ticklish work," and kindly gossip such as, "But as you've heard," phrases which not only hint at helpful attitudes the worker should maintain, but which keep forcing the target-reader beyond the typical, practical process essay. The avuncular tone of Merwin's instructions, a voice which may seem slightly out of place for a literal set of instructions, also reminds the reader that there is figurative advice being given. The reader can sense the Trojan Horse.

Fusing.

Student writer Kristin Showalter's Trojan Horse essay gives advice on how to control a mate. Since controlling others is a sinister endeavor, Showalter needs to clandestinely suggest ways to achieve this comical goal. She uses many of the above techniques employed by Merwin, but Showalter adds Break-ups and Line-ups (see the Fusion section in the Style unit), which metaphorically transport the reader from how-to-prepare-a-horse facts to how-to-control-your-mate realities:

> At this point, all the careful contact will distract the horse, but be cautious. You will feel <u>your</u> <u>spurs</u> at your own heart when you notice the horse's muscle mass, the gleam of the velvet coat, the rich brown hue of his eyes. Now you must fasten the <u>strap of the love bridle</u> under the horse's jaw. You are ready to lead the horse to the hitching post. Gently wrap the <u>reins of commitment</u> over the post so if the equine spooks, he will not be aggravated by the <u>love reins</u> tightening on the <u>ego post</u>. He will feel free to step away even if it's not too far. Don't worry. It's the horse's illusion.

The Break-ups and Line-ups work in conjunction with the ripening techniques ("all the careful contact will distract," "You will feel," "your own heart," "It's the horse's illusion") and the use of the grabbing imperative voice to build a prize Trojan Horse.

Scope.

In another essay, "How to Get Out of a Locked Trunk" from *Harper's Magazine*, writer Philip Weiss Trojan Horses himself. On the surface of the essay, Weiss appears to be working out a puzzle—getting out of a locked trunk. Weiss rationalizes his obsession with a claim:

> Every culture comes up with tests of a person's ability to get out of a sticky situation. The English plant mazes. Tropical resorts market those straw finger-grabbers that tighten their grip the harder you pull on them, and Viennese intellectuals gave us the concept of childhood sexuality—figure it out or remain neurotic for life.

The writer's musings about other "sticky situations" which begins first with puzzles and then moves to a psychological type of maze, hints that the essayist's fear of being locked in a trunk might be a metaphor for a psychological locked trunk of sorts, which the reader soon understands is Weiss's impending marriage.

In his process narrative, Weiss chronicles all the advice and tips he receives from "experts" on the subject of escaping from a locked trunk: Representatives from *Car and Driver*, Automotive Locksmiths in New York City, The Center for Auto Safety and the Motor Vehicle Manufacturing Association, and finally from Phillip's friend's father, Emmett, a retired mechanic. Weiss joins his subtext to his surface by showering his search for locked trunk information with mentions of wedding plans and references to his fiancé. The author works out premarital anxiety as he learns methods for escaping from a locked trunk, seemingly without the narrator overtly acknowledging his fear and without realizing that he is his own Trojan Horse target. Instead of using an imperative voice which would have directed the implicit advice to others, Weiss opts to use the first person narrative so his Trojan Horse's locked trunk becomes a vehicle for giving himself advice.

Workout.

English teachers call instruction essays process papers, but you will take the genre to a more interesting level. You will disarm a group or person that holds simplistic attitudes—about relationships, education, financial success, morality, business ethics, religion, raising children—by giving that group or person Trojan Horsed instructions seemingly about how to do something mundane and unrelated. Or like Showalter, use your Trojan Horse as a cover for delivering secret or sinister advice which must be kept hidden below the surface of the text.

First you will need some instructions that have metaphorical possibility: chopping a tree, making a cake, creating a legal process, a recipe for homemade Tamales, step-by-step instructions for doing your own divorce. You will borrow the format, and even some of the content of one of these sets of instructions, but you will need to change the material using the instructing, grabbing, ripening, and fusing techniques above so that the instructions hint at advice you want to carry beyond the target-reader's walls.

In choosing your instructions you might not have an idea how the process could be used as a metaphor, but sometimes, the metaphor begins to emerge as you translate the directions into the imperative voice. If, for instance, you are using instructions for programming some sort of telephone answering device, then maybe the philosophical advice has something to do with figurative communication. If your directions are for rewiring a lamp, then consider how "light" could be used as a metaphor for "enlightenment." Instructions for an abdominal workout routine which tout the benefit of working stomach muscles to strengthen the back, might be analogized to having more backbone in the figurative sense—being strong when friends or co-workers try to take advantage of you. Other possibilities for a subtext can evolve if, like Merwin, a writer considers "un" doing a process or set of instructions: unmaking a cake, unlearning to swim, uncleaning an attic, unpreparing a will.

Create discrepancy between your text and sub-text. For instance, in a book which shows how to prepare your own will, step four outlines instructions for community property ownership problems:

> If **a** significant amount of your property came from a personal injury settlement and you and your spouse disagree as to how it should be left, you will want to check the specifics of your state's law.

Pretend that you have decided to use this format and subject as a metaphor which disarms simple-minded views on how people learn. You call the essay "Transferring Your Knowledge to Your Lover." When you are at the place in your instructions where the above advice could occur, you might write the following:

> If a significant amount of your knowledge came from suffering and you and your parents disagree as to how to leave it with others, you want to check with Shakespeare's *King Lear.*"

Remember to choose a sub-textual topic which is not practical and comes from a completely different arena then the surface topic. If you have a surface of practical instructions like baking a cake, and you use these directions to metaphorically suggest how to make lump-less gravy, you are not creating a Trojan Horse.

Once the directions are in a prose or essay form, keep going back over your piece looking for verbs and nouns which can be replaced with a Break-Up metaphor or modified noun with a a Line-up Adjective. Look at all your verbs. Edit as many to-be verbs (is, am, are, was, were) as possible and then replace those active verbs with a body part verb where appropriate. Break-ups and Line-ups will allow you to suggest your metaphorical process or advice. In addition to Break-ups and Line-ups, which act as elevators bringing the reader from the surface of the text into the basement, a Trojan Horse will also make use of ambiguous instructions, or directions that cut both ways and go with the surface directions and the subtext. Choose suggestive nouns which jar the reader out of literal readings. We have noted that students who practice the Trojan Horse form become more careful readers of literature, sensitive to subtext.

Sincerely Yours

One of the most sincere and potent ways of disarming is to write a letter. Most English classes teach how to write business letters, turning missives into a business suit with a tie. Form letters are shred material, disappointing because letter writing comes with an expectation of being more personal: Unlike books and essays, letters are hidden in envelopes, to be opened only by the addressee. When not dressed up, most people think of letters as slobs at the beach: show-off post cards with simplistic, having-a-great-time and five-second thoughts scrawled on the back. The best letters, including the best business letters, will always be those that are carefully thought out and directed to a small group of people or to a particular person. These letters can burst illusions because they are intimate.

Even when we accept that letters are supposed to be intimate, most people rely more on barfing their feelings into the envelope rather than building a careful, persuasive case, well supported by details. One of the most famous letters ever written was writer Franz Kafka's 1919 letter to his father. In the beginning he mentions one of the advantages of using letters to disarm:

> Dear Father: You asked me recently why I maintain that I am afraid of you. As usual, I was unable to think of any answer to your question, partly for the very reason that I am afraid of you, and partly because any explanation of the grounds for this fear would mean going into far more details than I could even approximately keep in mind while talking.

The letter continues for sixty pages, outlining evidence of Kafka's father's hypocrisy, egocentrism, smugness, control strategies, arrogance, and strategies for belittlement.

Facting.

The first part of a good letter which will deal with any of the kinds of personal injustices Kafka wants to cover must outline and describe the facts or evidence of this injustice. When upset or angry, letter writers too often ignore these facts, their minds racing to a furious telling off before recreating justification for such a final judgment. This makes it easy for the reader to dismiss the letter. The writer needs to chronicle past events in a dispassionate tone so that the reader is forced to admit to what happened. This is also helpful for any uninvolved readers who need to be brought up to date. (Often it is important to send copies of letters to others to find out where they stand and also to put pressure on the initial addressee who may be motivated to listen because he or she is worried about what others think.) Furthermore, by outlining the facts dispassionately, objectively, you are leaving the recipient some space for disagreement with what happened, if there is any.

One of the best developed letters we have seen was published in *Harper's Magazine* by the famous Hollywood script writer Joe Eszterhaus and written to Michael Ovitz, then the head of the most powerful Hollywood talent source, Creative Arts Agency (later one of the top executives at Disney.) Ovitz had threatened Eszterhaus with having his foot soldiers "blow [Esterhaus's] brains out" all because Eszterhaus wanted his old friend and first agent, Guy McElwaine, to be his agent, and Ovitz felt threatened because Eszterhaus brought in about $1.25 million a screenplay. Without any anger in Eszterhaus's voice, the first part of the letter carefully outline's Ovitz's threats, including one threat Eszterhaus received through Ovitz's "lieutenant", Rand Holston: "Mike's going to put you into the fucking ground."

Interpreting.

After clearly recounting what happened, the second part of the letter must explain what was wrong with what happened. Too many writers assume that once the facts are presented that their significance is self evident. Not so. Even if the reader cannot deny what is described in the first part of the letter, he or she will either rationalize, minimize, revise, or deny any harm done by the injustice of the events. Therefore it is extremely important for the writer, still in a very rational voice, to explain the effect of the recipient's actions, not only for the writer's clarity and other parties involved, but for the reader-perpetuator. For instance, a dishonest manager not only hurts customers or employees, but also him or herself in terms of the energy wasted trying to cover up lies, having employees waste time defending themselves against becoming scapegoats and directing hostility towards the manager, and never being at peace in the work place.

The second part of the letter to Ovitz explains what Eszterhaus believes is wrong with Ovitz's comments—how it is cliché gangster movie blackmail, what the role of agents should be, how clients are not agent's possessions. Eszterhaus also explains the pain to his family, including discussions and a decision to stay in an older house, putting an expensive home they had just purchased up for sale because Ovitz's threats made Eszterhaus' financial future so uncertain.

Cussing.

At this point, Esterhaus's letter is fairly long, well developed, calm and detailed. Only at the very end does Joe Eszterhaus tell Ovitz off:

> So do whatever you want to do, Mike, and fuck you. I have my family and I have my old imperfect manual typewriter, and they have always been the things I've treasured the most.

If Eszterhaus had said "fuck you" at the beginning, the letter would have been tossed, not only by Ovitz, but by everyone else, including the Writers Guild of America, who came to Eszterhaus's rescue and backed Ovitz down. By the end of the well documented letter, third party readers begin to whisper "fuck you" to Ovitz too, so that when Eszterhaus says it, we applaud.

In contrast, a letter from D. C. Dumbass in Westminster, California to the editor of *Thrasher* , a monthly magazine about skate boarding, starts "All right, call me a dumbfuck, but I just found out the other day that Washington, D.C., isn't in the state of Washington." Here the profanity comes at the beginning, but it is self-deprecating, directed only at the writer himself; so in this context the profanity seems acceptable. This letter is short and ends with an angry denunciation of everyone for never educating him, but it stays funny and sincere so we take his complaint seriously and feel society has been properly disarmed for a Geography education glitch. The decision to use profanity in any letter or essay should be considered by the context.

Styling.

Writers become so satisfied once they get organized and pour their guts out that they often forget that letters need the advantages of good style that effective essays have. Style is key to how well a letter bursts with its sincerity. In an extreme example, Bob Millington in *The Age,* a Melbourne, Australia newspaper mixes styles in "An Open Letter to M. Jacques Chirac." The letter, discovered by *Harper's Magazine,* is addressed to French president Chirac when he announced France would resume its nuclear testing program by staging more explosions in the South Pacific near Australia. What makes the letter especially disarming is that it mixes French and English to create a sarcastic tone that also chop-livers French language purity. The letter starts, "Je suis a bit fromaged off avec votre decision to blow up La Pacifique avec les Frog bombes nuclears," and ends with,

> Reconsider, mon ami. Otherwise in les hotels et estaminets de l'Australie le curse anciens d'Angleterre — 'Damnation to the French'—will be heard un autre temps. Votre chums don't want that.

Usually though, tightening examples with Freighting, getting detailed interpretations with Telescoping, emphasizing with Pause, and sparking connections and brightening exactness with Fusion give a letter the proper voice, pace, and interest.

Workout.

Write a letter to someone to whom you have something very important to say, but one in which what you have to say involves a truth that would be so devastating to the receiver that you prob-

185

ably could never really send the letter. The letter could be to anyone personally important to you: a family member, an employer or employee, a lover, a friend, someone dead or alive, a teacher or coach. To truly test your control with an emotionally charged issue, it is important that the letter is about an injustice that you witnessed first hand and that the letter would have serious fallout for you if you sent it. Once you have actually written the letter, you may decide that you really should send the letter after all, or more likely, you will decide to burn it. Letter writing need not always result in a sendoff. A letter writer confronts a recipient with the same emotional intensity whether the would-be recipient actually receives the letter or not; yet the writer's deep, inner feelings are released and clarified in the letter writing process whether the letter is sent or not.

Follow Eszterhaus's procedure described above: First, withhold any judgment or anger while you carefully outline the injustice in complete detail. Your just-the-facts tone will make it so that your target cannot deny what happened. In the second part of the letter, explain what was wrong with the unjust action. Many will admit to doing what they are accused of if their actions and words are carefully documented in the first part of the letter, but still the recipient will fail to see what was wrong with what was done or will rationalize his or her actions away. Do not let your target out. Make the injustice clear, explaining how it is both hurtful to others and the recipient's self. Wait until the end to suggest your present position and make sure any telling-off is commensurate with the crime. Always assume someone else will be reading the letter; you want them to follow your line of thinking and come to the same conclusion you have come to. Be sure to rewrite your letter with style.

3
CRITICAL THOUGHT
&
RESEARCH

PEEL
FILTER
PRESS

Cracking Humpty Dumpty

Style makes up the tools by which writers capture and give strength to details, whereas deciding which details to consider in the first place and what to think and write them, forms another immense dimension of writing. Whatever an essayist writes about—a business proposal or legalities; a work of visual, performing, gourmet or literary art; histories or political events; science or engineering; virtually anything—the essayist must first become a *thinker* who discovers a truth, and then a writer who articulates that truth to a reader who previously had not perceived it. For the thinker-essayist, being open to discovery and being honest about findings takes intellectual endurance and emotional strength. In fact, many people, afraid to explore, simply lock in their preexisting ideas as ultimate truths. They turn their back on writing as discovery.

In any argument, three processes are essential: Peel offers some ways to open details to discover their worth; Filter demonstrates how to articulate the connections between a detail and its worth; Press explains some ways to check and further explore that worth through research and an awareness of critical thinking fallacies.

PEEL:
Seeking Meaning

 Inductive Analysis

 Deductive Analysis

● *Claims*

"Nay, it is. I know not 'seems'" is one of Hamlet's knife-like lines in Shakespeare's famous drama *Hamlet, Prince of Denmark.* In the play, through both reason and intuition, Hamlet tries desperately to cut through the appearance of what *seems* to be true, to what *is* true. Hamlet's struggle is every good writer's struggle. If truths were transparent, most of the need to write would disappear: everyone would agree on which economic and business venture to follow, works of artistic merit would be immediately understood, legal issues would move quickly to conclusions, personal feelings and intentions would never result in discord, and history would never leave mysteries. Real life is more complex. People who try to simplify reality by ignoring complexity and ambiguity, do not become strong writers.

Inductive Analysis

Trying to consider any experience in its entirety, whether it be a relationship, business merger, literary film, political candidate, or a technological device, increases the risk of ignoring crucial details that might change the experience's meaning or worth. Gulping down a whole, multi-faceted experience in one bite tempts the essayist to desperately swallow undigested, simplified conclusions about its truth. To prevent being confused by "seems," dazzled by surface deceptions, or overwhelmed by real complexities, a critical thinker needs to peel the examined experience or item apart, isolating its details; then the thinker should carefully consider the value of each detail on its own terms, separated from the whole. These are the first steps in an inductive analysis.

Inductive thinking is a way of thinking that demands withholding any judgment, or hunch (also called an *hypothesis*), or assumption (also called *warrant*), except for one particular assumption— that it is possible to derive a general conclusion from an ample number of particular examples. Logicians call this assumption a *generalization warrant.* By not avoiding important details, and by examining each detail's implications, the inductive thinker creates a conclusion that will bring all those implications together. The final conclusion, which usually moves from particular details to a general idea, is also known as a *thesis.*

When implications begin to contradict each other, as so often happens in examining the arts, the essayist has a more difficult time making the conclusion inclusive. Sometimes this means the conclusion evolves into a more general statement; other times the conclusion becomes a more complex thesis using *ambiguity* (a statement that is not cloudy, but intentionally uses rich, suggestive language to convey more than one meaning, such as to say that the images in a surreal painting "buckle" to imply both coming apart and coming together), or *paradox* (a statement that seems contradictory or absurd but which is well founded such as Paul in Corinthians saying "For when I am weak, then I am strong"), or *irony* (a statement that means the opposite of what is said, or in a larger sense, that describes the incongruity of two realities such as a story being about "beauty that is grotesque inside.") Making a thesis inclusive requires a fired imagination. Inductive thinking has the power to yield original and insightful opinions because the conclusion is gradually discovered at the end of a journey. However, in logicians' terms the inductively arrived at thesis is "probable," not "certain," because of the potential to gather unobserved details with new implications. For example, the number of details of plot, character, setting, light, color, and composition in a film can play endless games of peek-a-boo, where some details are missed on first viewing. (See *Gathering* below.)

After arriving at this thesis, when the writer finally starts building an essay to express it, the thesis can be either implied or stated throughout the entire piece, or stated only once at the beginning, end, or in the middle of the piece. Most English composition instructors require students to state the thesis in the introductory paragraph. However, in a sampling of essays from the yearly *Best American Essays*, the thesis statements will be found in a variety of places or implied and never directly stated.

Gathering.

Details or facts can be illusive. In observing any situation, whether it be a personal, legal, political, verbal, visual or any other experience, details play peek-a-boo. We observe them; then we lose them. The mind can consider only so many at one glance. When we observe a person, political situation, painting, novel, absolutely anything, and then try to form an opinion about this situation, our minds—always easily distracted—begin to wander: Did I really notice certain details? Do those details matter? We tell our writing students it is normal to panic when experiencing a play by Shakespeare, a painting by Salvador Dali, or scientific and legal discoveries because of the overwhelming complexity of this *primary source*. (Primary sources are the ones you are directly observing while *secondary sources* are materials that are helpful in understanding the primary source. As a writer, you are creating a secondary source.) It is virtually impossible to begin writing without first focusing on details, writing each one down so that it is isolated from the others, and considering the detail's implication without reference to the other details. This listing of details gives our minds room to fully concentrate and observe new details without fear of forgetting or losing information and without being distracted by the complex maze that makes up the whole.

Juicing.

Collecting details is only the first part of discovering truth. Every detail has literal, *denotative* significance as well as implied, *conno-*

tative meaning. Often it is tempting to believe that life and its various subjects are simple and that details have only literal significance or surface meaning. For instance, some people look at a garden and are aware of "green plants," nothing else. Literally, a garden is not much else. Others look at the same garden and think "peaceful respite from work" because their minds quickly, almost subconsciously, break plants into their elements—green, shade, oxygen, freshness—and think about the positive implications of these elements. On further reflection, these viewers may even refine those implications further, taking into consideration aspects of the garden's design that forces the eye to wander between plants before coming to places of rest. This might in turn lead to implications having to do with life journeys, the worth of existence, and one's place in the universe.

You can get through life without being so aware. However, strong essayists know that all details have meaning and that the more details considered, the more meaning becomes refined. When confronted by a picture of a baby taking a bath, a person of the Western world may see the image as representing cleanliness, since babies and water are both details which imply rejuvenation. But as the anthropologist Edward Hall points out in his article, "The Anthropology of Manner," women in India are visibly offended when shown such an image. These women take one more detail into consideration and think about its implications: The water is still, not moving. They wonder "how could people bathe a child in stagnant water?" Writing should raise an audience's awareness and that means showing readers new details and their new implications.

Scope.

Garrett Mattingly's "Curtain Raiser," an historical account from *The Armada*, is a special lesson in details and implications because he dramatizes the worth of an event about an historical figure who herself dramatizes the implications of an event's details. The figure is Mary Queen of Scots and the event is her own beheading. She turns her own death chop into an artistic drama because she knows that the treatment of the details of her trial can establish her as a martyr instead of a criminal. She designs and paints the day of her own execution by arranging every detail: Wearing the red garments associated with martyrdom in paintings; resting one hand on her escorting officer's sleeve; raising her crucifixion high and praying for forgiveness over the sentencing voices of her executioners; and pinning her kerchief to her auburn wig so that after the "dull chunk of the axe" when the executioner raises her now beheaded face to the cry of "Long live the queen!" both kerchief and wig come off in his hand, allowing her head, with "shrunken and withered and gray" stubble on a shiny skull, to pull off and roll on the platform, a shriveled humiliation that finalizes her thesis: She and her cause are not to be seen as criminal but are to be pitied.

Deductive Analysis

Unlike inductive thinkers, deductive thinkers start with an established truth to examine a particular experience. Logicians call this truth a warrant (also called a major premise.) The thinker then observes an example and if it can be articulated to support the warrant, the thinker by necessity connects the example and the warrant to make a claim. In the syllogism—"All men are mortal. Socrates is a man. Socrates is mortal."—"All men are mortal" is the warrant (or major premise); "Socrates is a man" is the supporting example (or minor premise); "Socrates is mortal" is the claim, (which can also be referred to as the conclusion or thesis). In logicians' terms, if the connection between the warrant and example is strong, the truth of the warrant will make a deductive claim "certain," not merely "probable."

Deductive thinking is useful to essay writing in the humanities so long as the warrant is thought of as a hypothetical truth or procedural assumption and not an absolute, all-men-are-mortal truth. Hypothetical truths might include Kant's theory of morality, a definition of neoclassical art, Jung's ideas of the collective unconscious, the authority of sacred art, principles for developing characters in a novel. Deductive thinking can be applied by using one of these hypothetical truths, gathering details from a particular experience (such as a written document, painting, gourmet meal, business deal), and then articulating the connection between those details and this warrant. Using a hypothesis to analyze is the opposite of inductive analysis where the writer avoids a start-up assumption.

Since deductive thinking cannot advance beyond its major and minor premise, deductive thinking is not as likely to nurture original thought as inductive thinking. However, it does encourage helpful connections with preexisting ideas whereby insights can be gleaned that before were hidden in the premises. For instance, deductive reasoning helps decide the extent to which a work of art conforms to a preexisting definition of an artistic movement; a business deal is supported by past business practices; a personal relationship matches a psychological concept for a healthy relationship; a legal precedent supports a legal case. Sometimes the humanities tend to overemphasize deductive thought—students are taught definitions of intellectual movements, aesthetic concepts, or philosophical theories and asked to explain how a poem, painting, or case study harmonizes with these preconceptions. These warrants quickly set the focus of an argument and so can stymie the evolution of an unexpected thesis. Originality dissipates.

English teachers tend to think that an essay is deductive if the thesis is at the beginning and inductive if the essay uses the thesis as a conclusion. A thesis can occur anywhere in either an inductive or deductive essay—introduction, body, conclusion—and the thesis or warrants can even be implied instead of directly stated. The placement of the thesis does not determine whether it was arrived through inductive or deductive analysis: Induction and deduction describe the initial thinking that goes into an essay and not its final, formal organization. Finally realize that some parts of an essay can be thought through inductively, other deductively.

Gathering.
If you wish to do deductive analysis, you will need to read about different theories or concepts that you feel would help you better

understand your primary material. Before analyzing your primary subject matter (poem, business deal, current event, painting, restaurant), wear this hypothesis like a pair of sun glasses, screening in only those details with implications of your primary material that validate this hypothesis. Unlike a biased cooked head (see Eclipse below), the deductive thinker accepts the concept with academic, rather than a personal, commitment, and considers the hypothesis to be a tentative, vulnerable, start-up truth. This allows the writer to vanish the hypothesis if it cannot be supported or proves to be unhelpful in understanding the subject matter being analyzed.

Kinks.

An established theory or hypothesis usually has matured through others' inductive thinking. In other words, a past thinker harvested implications of details and gradually discovered the hypothesis that the present essayist is now using as a start-up truth. However, there is never a full guarantee that the hypothesis evolved in the past through careful, inductive thinking or if it did, the details or circumstances that were used to form the hypothesis may have changed. In any case, the start-up truth is always vulnerable because the analyzed details and implications may not smoothly or realistically relate to the hypothesis. In this case, a good deductive thinker will start over with a new thesis to try to validate the primary material's details; a poor deductive thinker might start milling material to conform to the thesis, which will eventually sap any essay's credibility based on that thesis.

When writers analyze someone else's endeavors, they often try to use the creator's intentions as a starting hypothesis. What people intend and what they finally create—a business proposal, a work of art, a legal case, a relationship, a novel, a student's paper—are often two different things. Final creations are the yield of intentions but also of intuition, unconscious reactions, accidents that are capitalized upon, accidents that are not capitalized upon, and misunderstandings. This means that anything to be analyzed has its own life, essence, worth, or truth and its creator is always left behind. To judge the worth of anything solely by someone's intentions is called the *intentional fallacy*.

Enthymeme Testing.

Created by Philosopher Stephen Toulmin for an argumentation model, enthymemes are miniature deductive arguments that are useful for testing a thesis statement which was reached through inductive or deductive thinking. Enthymemes are made up of a claim followed immediately by the reason(s) supporting the claim, usually connected by the word "because" or "since." For instance, the claim "Students should study films such as *sex, lies, and videotapes* and *Manhattan*" can use the word "since" or "because" to connect the claim to its reason, "students need to learn about complex love relationships." Since the reasons supporting your thesis or claim may be scattered throughout your introduction, or even throughout your entire essay, the act of creating an enthymeme forces you to validate the existence of supporting reasons(s) and confirm that the claim and reasons are clearly expressed.

The enthymeme also allows you to better consider the strength of your thesis. By defining the claim and support, you can more easily locate your *hidden assumption* (also called a *warrant* or *minor premise*). Your argument is only as strong as this assumption, and when the enthymeme helps you perceive it more clearly, you may need to devote part of your essay to making a case for the assumption, and if you cannot, then you need to rethink your thesis. For instance, in the claim above there are at least two hidden assumptions: that students need to understand the nature of love's dilemmas and that the two films present complex views about love. A strong essay addresses these concerns. In the enthymeme "Henry James's character Daisy Miller can be considered an innocent American girl because her outer behavior is in harmony with her true feelings," it is easy to see two assumptions: First, that outer behavior usually reflects people's true feelings; second, that innocence can be defined as having one's outer behaviors in harmony with one's true feelings. Would you be able to defend these hidden assumptions? We dare you.

You may use an enthymeme to test your thesis and then decide it is actually effective enough to use as an opening statement in your essay. Many English teachers require students to have an enthymeme before they start working through details and implications, in which case the enthymeme is tantamount to thinking deductively and excludes inductive discovery.

Scope.

In a deductive analysis, an essayist could start with an hypothesis established by feminists and use it to evaluate Shakespeare; or borrow a theory of English romantic poets to grasp a popular ecology-themed movie; or employ the surrealistic painters' manifesto to evaluate a greeting card; unfile a presidential economic policy to interpret a bill passed by Congress; apply a work by Emmanuel Kant to evaluate a Protestant moral stance; use a conclusion made by any essayist in a college anthology to understand another writer in the anthology. In each case, the first work provides the start-up truth which screens in the details and implications from the primary source to validate that truth.

A great short essay, which is the result of a deductive analysis, is "Baseball Smadhi: A Meditation of the National Ritual" by Peter Gardella, first published in *Touchstone,* the Manhattanville College daily newspaper. The essay uses a mandala, "a design that aids meditation by drawing attention from its borders toward its center" as the thesis or hypothesis for understanding the game of baseball. Every aspect of the game is analyzed in terms of the mandala, including the pitcher's mound, "marking the center of a square," to returning home as completing the "cycle of life," to Jungian associations of three, to Martin Buber's definition of religious ritual being outside of time since "whether ten minutes or half an hour has passed has no more relevance to a baseball game than to a Mass." By filtering the dynamics of baseball through the lens of the mandala, Gardella spiritualizes this quintessential American sport and gives insight into baseball's hidden appeal.

Claim Cast

Now that you have inductively or deductively gathered all your details with their implications, you can better sculpt the thesis that pulls those implications together if you know what kind of *claim* you are making. (A claim is just another word—along with hypothesis, conclusion, and major premise—which means thesis. Academia can be term tiresome.) There are five major types of claims: resemblance, evaluation, causal, proposal, and definition claims. They can be used separately but many essays chain several claims together for reinforcement.

C&C Prep.

Compare & Contrast can be the scaffolding for all five claims but is crucial to the resemblance claim (which argues whether something is the same or not the same as something else) and the evaluation claim (which goes a step further and argues why one of the items is better or worse than the other). C&C generates ideas and details even if it is disassembled after the rough draft. Here is why C&C is so important:

Having a good friend brings with it the following experience—The friend appeals to us because of a combination of strengths, maybe moral and psychological or intellectual and emotional. As we get to know more about any of these qualities, we become more aware of the friend's strengths and weaknesses. However, nothing brings these attributes and weaknesses more quickly into sharp focus than comparing and contrasting them to similar ones in another person. When we do this, positive and negative attributes we took for granted in the first friend intensify for one of two reasons: because they are confirmed as plausible by seeing them again in a second person, or because they are contradicted by what we see in the second person.

For instance, the first friend may seem appealing because he or she always offers unconditional support for whatever we do. We enjoy this and take it for granted that friendship requires this attribute. Later we meet a second friend who believes that friend-ship is not based on unconditional support, this friend congratu-lating us for positive achievements, but also offering helpful criti-cism when we fall short of goals or grow weak taking certain stands. By comparing friends, on just this single issue, a discus-sion takes place in our minds because the contrast calls into ques-tion the worth of unconditional support and, ultimately, the worth of both friendships. Meaningful C&C never simply points out a comparison and contrast of a detail; it always answers this cru-cial question for the reader: Regardless of the apparent similar-ity, how does each particular difference from each source result in a difference in implications? In other words, what difference does each difference make? The answers spawned here could become an essay's primary food source, especially in evaluation claims.

Sometimes C&C can be a quick flash. When unfamiliar details or realities are made clearer by comparing them to more familiar ones, such as comparing the details and functions of a medieval knight's horse to those of a businessman's automobile, the com-parison is called an *analogy*. In analogies, the emphasis is more on similarities than contrasts. (See the Talking Words chapter in the Form unit for more on the function of analogies.) On the micro-stylistic level, metaphors are implied analogies. Metaphors, where the word "like" or "as" are used, such as in "her lips are like red roses," are called *similes* and are directly expressed mini-analogies.

Resemblance Claims.
Although resemblance claims center on the similarities between different items, the ripest ones also point out key subtle differ-ences. An insightful collection of essays which makes use of Compare & Contrast is *For Keeps*, by film critic Pauline Kael, who reviewed movies for over thirty years at *The New Yorker* and was the most influential American film critic of the twenti-eth century. Kael often explored the implications of visual and literary aspects by claiming these film elements resembled paint-ings and other fictions. To capture the inferences of the details in Bob Fosse's film *Cabaret*, an anti-musical about Berlin in 1931, Kael compares and contrasts these details—sometimes directly and sometimes with metaphor—to twentieth-century

painters who depicted the angst and terror of Europe prior to Germany's love affair with Hitler:

> The whory chorus girls displaying the piquant flesh around gar-ters, the Max Beckmann angles and the Edvard Munch hollow are part of the texture, too. . . Though it uses camp material, it carries camp to its ultimate vileness—in the m.c.'s mockery of all things human, including himself. His lewd smirks, like Sally's broad, fatuous, flirtatious grins, are emblems of corruption. *Caba-ret* does not merely suggest Egon Schiele's moribund, erotic figures and the rictus smiles and rotting flesh in the paintings and graphics of artists such as James Ensor and George Grosz but captures the same macabre spirit—and *sustains* it.

Evaluation Claims.

To make an evaluation claim, Kael would claim one artistic ex-pression was better, more effective, funnier, or grimmer than the other. To do this, she would have to kick her resemblance claim up a notch: "Bob Fosse's *Cabaret* is better at capturing the gro-tesque than painters such as Beckmann, Munch, Schiele, Ensor, and Grosz." Note that there must be a basis for evaluating the worth of an item over another—in this example it is "capturing the grotesque." Each element—here that would include details of shape, color, lighting, angles, and facial expressions from Fosse's film and from each of the painters' paintings—must then be measured against an established criterion to rank the value of the work. Sometimes an essayist might establish several criteria for evaluation. For example, part of the essay may explain how one artist is more successful than another at developing ideas that have universal appeal, how an artist has clearer insight into 1930's fascism, or an artist is more insightful about the attraction of decadence.

Evaluation claims flood our intellectual lives: arguing that one architectural design is more of a problem solver for an office than another; that one business deal has more promise than another; that one historical figure has more leadership qualities or fragilities than another; one automobile is a more efficient pur-chase than another; that one political platform has a more hu-manitarian position than another; one short story better merges the spiritual with the grotesque than another.

An offshoot of the evaluation claim is *refutation*, where details and implications are gathered not as support for your own claim, but as support against another's claims. Refutation uses C&C thinking because you, the writer, refute another thinker by comparing and contrasting point for point all the major details and implications made by that writer to your own details and implications, using your support to defuse the other writer by showing what is strong in your position. Even when you are not arguing against something already articulated, a good essay can be written by anticipating the details and implications your opposition might possibly use against you. By comparing and contrasting these with your details and implications, you rebar your essay while crumbling away the opposition's footing before they get started.

Causal Claims.

This claim (sometimes called a cause and effect claim) argues whether something causes something else or whether something is the result of something else. If you change the previous claim —"Students should study films such as *sex, lies, and videotapes* and *Manhattan* because students need to learn about complex love relationships" to "When students study films such as *sex, lies, and videotapes* and *Manhattan* they better understand complex love relationships"— you create a cause and effect claim. This second claim argues that studying the films causes students to have a specific understanding. Causal claims appeal to our need to predict results: children's behavior causes parents to react to them a specific way; a parent's behavior causes children to feel guilty; a particular political agenda leads to social reforms; a play dramatizes a character's reasons for losing faith; a new approach to writing causes students to care more about the way they express themselves; exposure to Italian cuisine makes for better California cuisine; going to medical school ruins an intern's health; a holy-war philosophy inevitably leads to a terror.

Proposal Claims.

This claim argues whether something should or should not be implemented. For instance, the example above under the enthymeme test is a proposal claim: "College students should study films such as *sex, lies, and videotapes* and *Manhattan* in order to learn about complex love relationships." This claim proposes a plan of action for a college film literature course and gives a supporting reason. Note that if the word "should" was changed to "will," then part of the proposal claim would suggest a causal relationship between teaching those films and what would happen as a result. A causal claim is often an essential aspect of a proposal claim because proposals usually spotlight the effects of taking or not taking a specific action.

The claim or thesis could also be written like this: "Students should study films such as *sex, lies, and videotapes* and *Manhattan* instead of films like *Gone with the Wind* and *The English Patient* because students need to learn about complex love relationships, not sentimental ones." This is still a proposal claim but now it includes an evaluation claim because the writer uses a criterion for judging the two sets of films (complexity that is not sentimental) and claims the first two films meet this standard better than the second two. Usually, strong proposal arguments bolt on an evaluation claim in order to strengthen itself over alternative plans. (Note that these last two examples are built upon hidden assumptions such as "complex relationships are more important than sentimental ones." The essayist must defend these assumptions as well.)

Definition Claims.
This claim argues that something is or means something else. Again the claim "Students should study films such as *sex, lies, and videotapes* and *Manhattan* because students need to learn about complex love relationships" could be changed and turned into a definition claim if worded "The films *sex, lies, and videotapes* and *Manhattan* are films about complex love relationships." Note that in all the above claims somewhere in the essay the writer would have to define what "complex relationships" means. Several definitions claims can flash throughout any of the above essays where the the worth of the essay's terms and key items need to be defended. (See Talking Words in the Form section.)

A deductive analysis craves definition claims because these arguments start with a concept and then argue how details from a primary source fit the definition of that concept. For instance, one might deductively analyze the film *Manhattan* by first hypothesizing it is "a romantic comedy," or "an expression of

Spinoza's philosophy," or "a dramatization of man's existential angst." The writer would define one or more of these terms and then explain what aspects of the film support each definition. An inductive analysis would yield a definition claim for *Manhattan* that could not be defined ahead of time and would probably be unique to this film.

Workout.

Write an inductive analysis about a primary source such as a short story, a famous painting, an economic policy, an historical event, a building, a collection of sociological case studies—anything that seems unique, ambiguous, complicated or deceptively simple. You should write about something you can observe directly, not through others: an actual document or report; a painting (perhaps photo-copied); photographs, charts, blueprints; descriptions of events (not editorials); interviews, a short story or poem. The topic may depend on your ability to decipher the formal details that are important for observing a particular subject. For instance, analyzing a fiction writer requires careful study of that writer's organization, style, dialogue, setting, use of character; a painting requires observation of the title, colors, textures, composition, lighting, shape, as well as details of subject; an historical event means looking into documents, letters, eyewitness accounts, memoirs of participants. For now avoid secondary sources which include critical evaluations by other writers on or related to the primary sources.

Begin by writing notes listing all important details, and then opposite each one, jot down your thoughts about each detail's implications or significance. These notes will take hours of time. After you gradually discover and finally articulate this general truth, you will use it as your paper's thesis. The whole paper must be devoted to explaining how all your details and their implications support this thesis. You will find this thesis in different places in different essays, although writing and critical thinking teachers usually prefer that claims be organized with an introduction stating the claim followed by paragraphs that support the claim. However, any of the strategies from the Form section could be used to organize an argument essay. For instance, Double Exposures could be used for a resemblance claim; Strip Tease could be used for an evaluation claim; Animation, Flashback, and Sincerely Yours could be used for a cause and effect claim; Raising the Dead, Trojan Horse, and Devil's Advice could be used to make a proposal claim; Talking Words, Blood Flow, and Thirteen Ways could be used to make a definition claim.

If you are going to do research, this analysis may later serve as a first part of a larger, researched paper or may be integrated with researched material. If you do a Deductive Analysis, then you will need to research a theory, concept, or philosophy and then support this thesis with details from your primary source. Again, this deductive analysis and research may generate an entire paper or serve as only part of a larger paper.

FILTER:
Expressing Thought

 Verb connection

 Metaphoric connection

_____ *Structural connection*
.....

Whether you write an inductive or a deductive analysis, as you approach the final revision stages, you will need to use style to connect all the details in the argument to their implications and to the thesis. These links must be carefully modulated. This takes finesse. Sometimes the bond is forceful and clear cut; other times the bridge is subtle. Creating this connective membrane involves making direct, metaphoric, and structural connections between details and implications.

Verb Connection

An appropriate verb cleanly and directly grafts details to ideas or implications. The essayist first must decide how definitively or vigorously the two should fuse. For instance, sometimes details *strongly suggest* ideas: rain <u>symbolizes</u> growth; a crown of thorns <u>alludes</u> to Jesus; a long sentence describing the actions of an automobile <u>represents</u> the car's movements; colors <u>signify</u> emotions, spiritual importance, or moods; a hedge of plants <u>exhibits</u> order and control. Other times details <u>reinforce</u> ideas that have been established earlier in the essay: light entering a chapel or window in a painting <u>emphasizes</u> the motif of unexpected hope; an unselfish action <u>validates</u> a person's love for someone else; metal furniture <u>underscores</u> the utilitarian mood of a room; the use of a specific word <u>sharpens</u> a writer's sarcastic perspective on a political situation.

Sometimes a detail can only <u>subtly suggest</u> an idea: dark clouds <u>hint</u> at worse times to come; a legal precedent <u>implies</u> that a law should be overturned; a low dining room ceiling <u>suggests</u> the protection of a primitive cave. Other times details *dramatically create* ideas: her decision to throw out the textbook <u>propagates</u> several creative thoughts about who she is; in a painting, the yellow sparkles of paint on the nude's body <u>unseals</u> her inno-cence; the husband's rejection of his wife <u>reveals</u> his cynical view of love. Still other times details define the limits of implica-tions: the architect's use of hard edges <u>restricts</u> the occupant's awareness of nature as being chaotic, while the use of a long, narrow window <u>closes off</u> the occupants to the vastness of na-ture; a B flat in a particular tune <u>confines</u> one's joy; the business's bottom line <u>focuses</u> on efficiency.

In every case, the verb helps connect the details on the left side of the sentence with the implications, suggestions, or meanings on the right side of the sentence. Use your thesaurus to find the verb that mostly accurately captures the strength of the connec-tion between every detail and its meaning. If you have a difficult time finding connective verbal tissue, it may be because you have not first carefully, inductively analyzed the most important impli-cations of the detail.

Metaphoric Connection

Inherent Qualities.
Since metaphors always carry a compressed load of associations, they effectively suggest the worth of any details onto which they are fused. (Review the Fusion section under the Style unit.) For instance, before art critic Peter Schjeldahl wrote his essay on cement titled "Hard Truths about Concrete" he first made a list of details or observations about concrete: it spreads quickly and then stops all of a sudden; it can conform to any mold but the mold must be tight, made with laborious care; it is not as supple and flexible as wood, clay, even plastic once it sets; it is impossible to change its form once it has hardened. In order to discuss the implications of these details—in this case to suggest that concrete is idiosyncratic, uniquely feisty, and taken for granted—Schjeldahl fuses all the physical attributes of concrete to metaphors. In his essay, he uses Line-ups and Break-ups which are associated with animate objects to describe cement, a metaphor technique often referred to as *personification.*

Schjeldahl describes unhardened concrete as "Promiscuous, doing what anyone wants if the person is strong enough to hold it, concrete is the slut, gigolo of materials." Later he writes,

> Once it has set, what a difference! Concrete becomes adamant, fanatical, a Puritan, a rock, Robespierre. It declares like no other material the inevitability, the immortality— the divinity—of the shape it comprises, be the shape a glopped heap on the ground or a concert hall, ridiculous or sublime.

The personified Line-ups such as "promiscuous," "adamant," "fanatical;" the possessive Break-ups taken from parts of prostitution such as "slut, gigolo of materials;" the metaphorical analogies such as "a Puritan, a rock, Robespierre," the Break-Up verb "declares," all connect concrete's physical attributes to an implied idea of concrete's worth. The metaphors give concrete a specific, unique presence that can no longer be taken for granted: a presence that is more active than the reader could have imag-

207

ined. By capturing this active presence, metaphor establishes and supports the implied thesis of the essay. Using figurative language, a direct expression of the thesis might read, "Concrete is a paradox, having both a fanatical and promiscuous soul, but a soul of a 'pitiless idiot' that 'will never notice' a viewer's derision."

Comparative Qualities.

Metaphors also sharpen arguments, such as resemblance claims mentioned above, that are dependent on Compare & Contrast. For instance, one might compare F. Scott Fitzgerald's 1925 novel *The Great Gatsby* to Terrence Malick's 1973 film *Badlands*, two works of American Literature. The novel and the film have many points of comparison: Both works use narrators—Nick Carraway and Holly—who serve double duty as participants in the dramatic events they recount; both works feature an enigmatic character, Jay Gatsby and Kit Carruthers, who pursue strange dreams; both Malick and Fitzgerald use the American landscape—the Wasteland of post WWI New York and the Badlands of North Dakota—as metaphors for the dramatic events which take place in these venues. As the differences and similarities between the two works are listed and analyzed, an argument becomes quickly overrun with sentences hammering points of comparison and contrast. A writer who compares Gatsby to Kit will need to use qualifying phrases within the argument essay—that is, clauses which express the defining qualities of each subject. Without using metaphors, one might write:

> Whereas Gatsby's pursuit of his dream, that of being reunited with his lost love Daisy, is a carefully devised plan, Kit's fulfillment of his dream, obtaining the identity of a notorious outlaw, is not the result of any particular resolve. Gatsby is an obsessive schemer; Kit is an opportunist. Gatsby undervalues the role of fate and forgets to consider those factors which are out of his control and which ultimately keep him from realizing his well-planned but ill-fated dream. On the other hand, Kit relies solely on the random hand of fate to deliver him from anonymity. He acts impulsively by whim and fancy, killing people without malice or motivation, but always fooling himself into believing that he is in total control by inventing convoluted rationalizations well after the crime has been committed.

The qualifying information helps to keep the defining characteristics of Jay Gatsby and Kit Carruthers separate and clear for the reader. These modifying phrases also set up important points of comparison and contrast for the argument.

However, too many of these modifying clauses make an argument tedious, interrupting the flow, and creating a plodding pace which is antithetical to the rhythm of persuasion. Modifying phrases also eat up space that could be used for more details and implications. To remedy both problems, modifying clauses can be edited with the use of Fusion—especially Line-ups created with Melted-together words (see the Pause section in the Style unit) and Break-up verbs. Both Fusion techniques give arguments condensed, subliminal reinforcement by squeezing a whole phrase worth of details into every part of the argument.

Whatever items are being compared or contrasted—famous buildings, politicians, classrooms, short stories—use details and images from the subject to create metaphors. When comparing and contrasting elements from two works of fiction (characters, plot, style, setting, theme or point of view) the metaphors should come from the details of both works. Many writers tend to use the details to create similes as a way of delineating one subject from another. In comparing Gatsby and Kit in the works above, a writer, borrowing the details of their physical descriptions to help reveal similarities and differences in their personalities, might write:

> Gatsby's personality is like a silk shirt, smooth and elegant, as contrasted to Kit's persona which is like a Levi jacket, durable and tough.

While the point of contrast is now infused with metaphor, the similes take up space, break the persuasive flow, and another sentence will still be needed to explain the significance of these metaphorically described characteristics. The problem of cumbersome similes is solved by tailoring those same simple details of clothing into an informative Melted-together Line-up:

> Gatsby's silk-shirt demeanor whispers a mysterious past, just as Kit's Levi-jacket behavior aids and abets his tough, serial killer image.

This transformation from simile to Line-up metaphor creates new space, allowing room for new comparative claims, details, and implications. It also creates a more forceful connection between an idea about each character and a crucial detail that supports that idea.

Aside from using single details of a novel, play, speech, poem, or other primary sources, pithy lines and quotes can be transformed into Melted-together Line-ups to create metaphors. For example, in *Badlands*, Holly, Kit's girlfriend and the narrator of the film, reports that while she and Kit are on their multi-state homicidal tour, Kit accuses her of "just being along for the ride." The absurdity of Kit's observation might be amplified and compared to an absurd comment made by Gatsby. Gatsby declares to Nick, his best friend and the narrator of the novel: "Can't repeat the past? Of course, you can." These famous and revealing quotes can be converted into powerful Melted-together words, solidifying points of comparison:

> Kit's just-being-along-for-the-ride accusations and Gatsby's can't-repeat-the-past?-Of-course-you-can assertions underscore these two idealists' diminishing sense of a reality which looms over their strange dreams.

The Melted-together words help to keep the comparison of individual details distinct, yet the form creates a parallel structure which allows a reader to more easily access and contemplate the similarities of those details.

Details from both works can also provide a list for Break-up verbs. An exploration of the similarities and differences of the two narrators Nick, from *The Great Gatsby* and Holly, from *Badlands,* might use the details and imagery from certain scenes as sources for creating Break-ups verbs. In one darkly ironic scene in *Badlands*, just before he and Holly begin life on the run, Kit insists that Holly retrieve her school books from her locker so that she doesn't fall behind on her studies during their killing spree. In an important scene in *The Great Gatsby*, Nick, at Gatsby's request, hosts a disastrous tea, where Gatsby contrives to reunite with Daisy for the first time since the lovers' separation five years earlier. Student Pennie Crane uses the schoolyard and tea party imagery as metaphors, for describing Holly and Nick as narrators:

> Holly, using a naive, sit-at-the-back-of-the-classroom tone, narrates her life with Kit. Holly desktops her experiences, literally recounting events but lockering any emotions or judgments. As she dime-store-romances her narration, Holly reveals her immature priorities, cliché notions of love, trite view of loyalty, and her total lack of a moral center. Nick's language requires more mental homework than Holly's. Each of Nick's passages

causes a did-he-really-say-what-I-think-he-said? reaction from the reader. Unlike Holly, Nick cannot completely sugar his true emotions. He teaspoons his careful and elaborate criticisms, pretending to reserve judgments, hoping to avoid spilling the smallest spot of moral indignation, until the very end of the novel, when Nick forgets etiquette: He finally replaces the small sips of light judgments with big gulps of censure and outrage.

Again, the metaphors, Break-ups working in tandem with Line-ups, allow a reader to quickly see the distinctions between the two narrators and are reminded of important supporting details. (After making these careful distinctions Pennie will want to provide details, probably in the form of quotes to illustrate and support her assertions about Nick and Holly.)

Finally, note that the use of flow to bring sufficient numbers of details together helps build a context so that the metaphors are more easily interpreted. Writers should avoid metaphors that make arguments more convoluted, usually ones breaking from the mood and imagery of the subject being discussed. Detail-reminding Fusion that uncovers previously buried implications is a powerful argumentative tool.

Structural Connection

Adding Punch.

When details and their implications are brought together with Flow techniques discussed in the Style section, arguments fuse into a powerful force. When crucial details are spread out and away from the thesis, the thesis fades; when they are pulled together with Flow techniques, they not only strengthen one another, they move in closer to the thesis statement or other general ideas used throughout the essay. Consider the following stylistically unfiltered student example:

I think that the J writer of Genesis is probably trying to depict a world that is ruled by corruption. God empowers Abraham, one of the patriarchs of future generations. When Abraham is in the land of two different rulers, that of the Pharaoh and that of Abimelech, he tells his wife Sarah to pretend like she is his sister. By doing this, Abraham is able to protect himself from rulers who might need to kill him if they think the only way to have her is to get rid of her husband. Abraham comes out ahead by the scheme, receiving gifts from the rulers, but God punishes them because they innocently have adulterous sex with Abraham's wife. Later on in Genesis, two angels visit Lot and the men of Sodom. Both young and old think they are good looking angelic dudes and want to rape them. However, Lot wants to befriend the angels, they are holy guests after all, so to take the heat off, he offers his two virgin daughters to the men of Sodom and God does not intervene with punishment. What kind of sick, greedy world is this? Then later, Jacob, who is a person of "guile," and his scheming mother Rebecca, trick Esau and steal the blessing all with God not intervening in the least. In fact, Jacob becomes one of the next important patriarchs. I think that the J writer is telling stories that suggest the world as a place full of deception and greed and furthermore, these a r e the attributes that make for powerful rulers, because these men end up being on "God's side."

By not using the Flow techniques of the Style section to tighten, the student's point is lost. The student is making a controversial point regarding the satiric nature of Genesis and writing with flab not only confuses the argument but encourages people who disagree to want to cut into the fat and take the whole piece apart. When the passage is rewritten with Flow, everything essential above can be said in less words, pulling details and implications closer together to each other and the thesis. The argument becomes more muscular and more difficult to attack.

In Genesis, the J writer depicts God supporting a trilogy of injustices: He super-charges Abraham, a patriarch who schemes to protect his flanks by calling his wife his sister, thereby setting up the Pharaoh and Abimelech to innocently "go into her" thus earning this duo a one-two punch from God; He blinks while Lot tosses his virgin daughters to sodomizers in order to curry favor with angels; God launders a blessing that was stolen through a scheme devised by Rebecca and Jacob, the brother of "guile," —all inequities which immerse the reader in a world where empowerment is on the side of cowardice, deception, and greed.

Implying Meaning.

The actual structure of a sentence—both its word order and its use of punctuation—has the magical capacity to suggest how the details in a sentence should be perceived and so indirectly suggests what the details imply. Structure tells us how to read a sentence: which details to flow together; which material to give pause and stress. Structure creates a meaningful voice.

As discussed under Pause in the Style unit, the Very Short Sentence can suggest many meanings depending on its context, including creating crankiness (as in the Didion example), anticipation (as in the Angell examples), or sarcasm (as in the Williams example). Long, flowing sentences have just as much potential to create meaning. Consider again some of the sentences used to show scope in the Flow section of the Style unit such as Norman Mailer's sentence from *Of a Fire on the Moon* in the Freighting section. The structure of the paragraph-long sentence tells us that the details have the importance of variables in an algebraic equation, whereby a change in one detail affects every other one discussed in the sentence.

For instance, the fact that the craft is "going from weightlessness to one-sixth gravity" is affected by every other detail given in surrounding phrases, such as being "flown for the first time in the rapidly changing field of gravity of the moon" and "one-sixth gravity had never been experienced before in anything but the crudest simulations," and these elements are in turn hinged onto and altered by all other phrases in the sentence such as "the weight of the vehicle reducing drastically as the fuel was consumed" which implies that there is an interplay between the changing field of gravity and weight as fuel is consumed. Therefore, the writer does not need to state overtly that each detail is dependent on every other one: the structural flow of all the Lem details into one sentence declares dependence.

Packaging these information loads into shorter sentences would suggest a different meaning because each load would be disconnected by the reader's voice, requiring the reader to perceive the elements as independent from each other:

> It was the first time the lem had been flown in the rapidly changing field of gravity of the moon. Of course, one-sixth gravity

had never been experienced before in anything be the crudest simulations. Now the astronauts would experience going from weightlessness to one-sixth gravity. The actual weight of the lem would continue to be effected by how much fuel was consumed and that in turn would change the effect of gravity on the lem.

The uses of length and structure to connote meaning are endless. So much relies on what subject or content enters the structure. For instance, the following image from Flannery O'Connor's story "Greenleaf" is about the "steady rhythmic chewing" of a bull which Mrs. May hears in her sleep and reminds her of "some patient god" who has "come down to woo her." Her thoughts are filtered through a sentence that uses length, exaggerated by several breath-catching compounds, to describe an insatiable bull and to underscore Mrs. May's obsession, paranoia, desperation, and sexual yearning:

> She had been aware that whatever it was had been eating as long as she had had the place and had eaten everything from the beginning of her fence line up to the house and now was eating the house and calmly with the same steady rhythm would continue through the house, eating her and the boys, and then on, eating everything but the Greenleaf's, on and on, eating everything until nothing was left but the Greenleaf's on a little island all their own in the middle of what had been her place.

On the other hand, Jamaica Kincaid, in "On Seeing England for the First Time," uses length to run together diverse motifs from the English novels she was forced to choke down while growing up as an Antiquan in an English colony. By running these motifs together, not allowing them the importance of their own sentence, Kincaid reduces each one to an inconsequential tick on a list, creating a sarcastic flow that hisses at the details' superficiality:

> And having troubling thoughts at twilight, a good time to have troubling thoughts, apparently; and servants who stole and left in the middle of a crisis, who were born with a limp or some other kind of deformity, not nourished properly in their mother's womb (the last part I figured out for myself; the point was, oh to have an untrustworthy servant); and wonderful cobbled streets onto which solid front doors opened; and people whose eyes were blue and who had fair skins and who smelled only of lavender, or sometimes sweet pea or primrose.

Analyzing Style.
One final point about style, both in terms of structure and word choice. The microcosm of style is a rich topic for an inductive analysis in itself and whenever you write about anything—a business report, an article in a magazine, a book, a memoir—you should consider the implications of style because it reveals so much about what the writer's true perspective. For example, "Long Sentence" by Michael Kinsley in *The New Republic* is a two page inductive analysis of every topic, word, and grammatical choice in one crucial, long sentence made by 1996 presidential hopeful Reverend Pat Robertson, defending himself against accusations of being anti-Semitic. In part of the sentence, Robertson says we must ensure that the trend is "not for the elimination of the Jews." Responding to Robertson's call for caution through a style that combines a negative "not" with a horrifying situation, Kinsley replies, "Does Robertson think that anti-Semitism consists of wishing for the 'elimination' of the Jews? This is setting the bar awfully high."

Inductive analysis of written Forms, such as those discussed in the last unit, are also intriguing. Poetry includes an array of language forms and *Poetic Meter and Poetic Form* by Paul Fussel, Jr. remains one of the best books to clearly explain the implications of different metrical variations and stanzaic forms. For example, Fussel explains how the sonnet form allows a writer to exploit the principle of imbalance: the Petrarchan sonnet forces the poet to combine sexual build up and release with a rhyming pattern and length that allows a "relatively expansive and formal meditative process," whereas the twelve-line problem development and two line solution couplet of the Shakespearean sonnet invites "images of balloons and pins," a form that encourages "wit, paradox, or even a quick shaft of sophistry, logical cleverness, or outright comedy."

Workout.
Look at your Inductive or Deductive Analysis and decide which sentences should be tightened using the flow techniques to add punch and perhaps suggest meaning. Decide where to use Pause techniques to stress important points, add drama, or tighten. Revise all your verbs by using either the Verb connections or using Metaphoric connections. Decide which phrases, ideas, and de-

tails could be merged more effectively using metaphoric connections. All of this revision will give your critically thought through
essay life. Otherwise add it to the the academic dust pile. If you
are adding research to your argument, you might want to work
through the Press unit below first and return to this Workout.

PRESS:
Testing Thought

 Research

Fallacies

Eclipses

There are essentially three very different ways to test your critical thinking. The most involved is to do research. Research means looking up outside material and using it to argue against, support, and expand your own analysis. Most English teachers prefer their students not to analyze their primary material before going to the library. Why we disagree is explained in "Preconditioning" below. The second is to make sure you have not relied on critical thinking fallacies and the third is to question your personal capabilities.

Research

Most people enjoy researching without knowing they are doing it. A person has a house plant and cannot decide where he should put it to get enough light. This person calls the nursery, talks to a friend who has a similar plant, and maybe consults a book. All the advice from these sources blend or synthesize in the person's brain, resulting in a decision as to where to put the plant. After watching how well the plant does in this new place, the person meshes these observations with the previous synthesis to decide on an even better choice of location. The person has created a research project without knowing it. An even less conscious research synthesis happens when a teenager makes a careful decision about dating a person, the teenager's research consisting of several live interviews and phone calls plus careful "field" observations. Of course, as is the danger with any carefully done research, synthesized material can always be scorched by one's emotions. Often one makes the wrong choice for a date.

Pre-analyzing.

In the academic world, the library is the primary research source. However, be forewarned—enter library waters only after mental conditioning. Whether researching a new refrigerator, tracking critics on a famous painting, or running down economic reports to confirm a business proposal, first inductively analyze all the details of your primary material—the old refrigerator, the painting, or the business proposal—before wading into secondary material. After inductive analysis, the information from your researched, secondary material will mean much more because now your mind can compare and contrast your inductive analysis with the new material you are looking up. Your inductive understanding will help you to *evaluate* your research: It will force you to ask whether the researched information adds to, argues against, or expands your previous inductively arrived at thesis. Without your own analysis to measure research against, your mind can get lost in a sea of material where every current and wave seems overwhelming.

Finding Sources.

Encyclopedias often give very abbreviated information, but they mention many of the subtopics related to your subject which you can then research further in other books and articles. For instance, if you were writing about Abe Lincoln, the encyclopedia would mention documents, political events, and other historical figures you may decide to investigate. Library reference sections are filled with special encyclopedias such as ones on Rock Music, Utopias, Catholic Saints, Sports, Legal Precedents, Film History, or Plants. These resources are informative, but not necessarily critically insightful.

For more insight, look for books on your topic in the computer catalog. When one bites, you do not need to read the whole book. Instead, always look at the Table of Contents or back index to fast forward to the pages on your topic. Look up magazine articles in the *Reader's Guide to Periodical Literature,* now often on a computer. Although some magazines are written to more educated audiences than others, magazines found in the Reader's Guide tend to be written for a larger audience, not specialists. For journals that tantalize specialists, consult special indexes such as the *Art Index* or *Social Science Index.* The articles listed here are very focused but are prone to be jargon-stuffed with technical language. Major world newspapers also have their own indexes.

The larger the library (and some major universities have one or two large main libraries and several specialized libraries) the more you may need help from librarians. They are expert detectives, knowing of encyclopedias and indexes you never could have thought existed. Most libraries also have extensive holdings of video documentaries and films. Use them. The internet provides sources that range from the encyclopedic to the intimate, from the up-to-date to out-right lies. (See below on investigating.) One of the best resources are interviews with experts, researchers, professors, and others directly involved with your topic.

Listing Sources.

Keep a list, called a *working bibliography* or a list of *works cited* of all your sources. Write down everything about the source you will need for the final works cited page. There are many good research how-to books that have proper works cited formats approved by the Modern Language Association which, by the way, often makes changes, so you may want to consult a new edition of their own style handbook for research papers.

In general, books or other whole work items include the author's name, and then the work's title which is underlined, followed by the place of publication, the publisher's name, and the date published. Magazines, newspapers, and other sources not published as whole works are different. The author is listed first but then you write the title of the article or chapter which is put in quotation marks, and next the source title which is underlined or italicized, then the date, and next the page numbers. Note that your second line must be indented five spaces.

The next two items will not show up on your final works cited page but you need them now. First write the library call number next to each source in case you need to go back to it for more notes or to clarify a note you already took. Secondly, write a number or visual code (triangle, circle, running-G) next to each source. Your note cards (described below) from each source will have the same code on them so that you do not spend time re-writing source information every time you make a note card. You will simply look at the code on the card and know what source it came from.

Evaluating Sources.
Often English instructors train writers to use researched matter as their only material to inductively reach a decision, deleting any of their own analysis or inductive evaluation of the primary material. However, never rely on secondary sources simply because they are written by authorities. There are many writers with credentials who are poor writers, lack insight, and most importantly, do not develop their arguments carefully. When you simply use their name and credentials to validate an idea, you are committing a cheat called an *appeal to authority*. Doubt. Be suspicious. Always read critically, making sure other writers have inductively arrived at their opinions by using strong examples connected to implications with clear explanations. If they do not, even if their opinions agree with yours, reject their work and find stronger writers.

Taking Notes.
When taking notes from researched sources, put each idea on a note card rather than on a page of notebook paper. Putting each idea or detail on its own separate card frees you to psychologically shatter that source into information bits which can be more easily rearranged, then shuffled together and synthesized for your own purposes. Also this allows the researcher to separate material from the source's style since many outside sources, although knowledgeable, are not stylistically well written or have a style that will be compatible with your style.

Put three items on each card. First, write only one idea or detail from your source into your own words, unless you want to quote it. Secondly, put the specific page number you took the note from because you will need it to make a parenthetical reference later. Most students think that parenthetical references and footnotes are used only with word for word, direct quotes from the source, but only the quotation marks (" ") signal that. If you use any ideas or details from a secondary source, you must give that writer immediate credit in your paper by mentioning his or her name and and page number. (See Citing Sources below.) In academic papers, citations are for giving credit to another person's idea, regardless of whether it enters your essay in quotes or in your own words. Failing to give credit to another, called *plagiarism*, is tantamount to stealing. Thirdly, write the code or number from your works cited list (see above) to remind you which source the material is from without taking the time to write any other information on every card, not even the author's name.

Evaluating notes.

You have two main options for proceeding at this point. One is to inductively analyze each note, whether it be a fact or an idea, writing down the implications of the note on the back of the card. To do this, you need to follow the procedure explained under "Peel: Seeking Meaning." By working with all the implications of your notes, and following the procedure discussed under "Inductive Analysis" above, you will arrive at an overall thesis for your paper.

The second option, which we highly recommend and outlined above under "Pre-analyzing," is to have done your own inductive analysis of your subject (whether it was visiting a prison or private school, reading a short story, witnessing a trial, viewing an icon) without the help of secondary sources. Now you can evaluate the research you have been doing more effectively. Reading each of your notes, decide which ideas and details support, argue against, or expand the thesis you did before. Make a note about each possibility on the back of every note card. The most important thing though is to consider whether to change, strengthen, or expand your original thesis. Maybe a little of each is in order.

Organizing notes.

Shuffle out and stack your cards in piles according to a specific organization. One organization may be to simply divide the cards according to which can be used to support your thesis, which you will argue against, and which expand on your original analysis. You might organize your paper according to sub topics. For instance, if the paper were about a film director's point of view, you might arrange notes according to different periods of the director's life, or in terms of his use of story line, editing, and photography to underscore his or her point of view, or in terms of what other critics have written, what the director has written, and what actors and production members have said. These are traditional ways to organize. Depending on what argumentative claim you are making, you can employ different organizations from the Form unit.

Drafting, Quoting, & Citing.

Word processors help eliminate the need to make a detailed outline of the paper before rough drafting. Simply pick up the first pile of your organized cards, form smaller piles of subtopics, and start writing the notes into a rough draft. Always immediately combine the researched material with its implication as discussed under "organizing notes." If you need to, review ways to blend quotes into your own prose under Quote Sandwiches in the Talking Words unit under Forms. If you have long quotes of more than four lines, indent ten spaces, block the quote, and do not use quotation marks. Several examples can be seen in this book. Quote sparingly using only what is pithy, rich, or shocking. Useful and supportive information that is not particularly well articulated should always be paraphrased.

Remember though, not only quotes, but any ideas or facts that come from outside sources must be cited, even though they are rewritten in your own words and with your own style. The Modern Language Association has made this process sensible by requiring in-text citations instead of footnotes at the bottom of the page. For instance:

> Even though the Qunitians fought the Quibblians, they managed to produce art that equaled the best art of Hellenistic Greece (Johnson 21).

The page number for this note comes off the writer's note card, and the name Johnson comes from the code on the card that matches up with the writer's Works Cited list of sources. Note that the period goes outside the parenthesis. If the writer had mentioned Johnson in the sentence (Johnson says, that even though. . .) then the writer would only put the number 21 in parenthesis. If you use more than one source by this Johnson, then you will need to include key words of each title in the parentheses so the reader will know which source you are referring to (Johnson, Spoof 21). If you are using more than two Johnson's, then you will need to give their first names each time as well: (H. Johnson, 21). If you use two sources to document an idea, use a semi-colon to separate them: (Johnson, 21; Henchke, 33). Consult a Modern Language Association handbook or research book for ways to document other situations.

Final Drafting.
Rewrite, rewrite, rewrite using style, more style, and more style to make your paper tighter, more lively, smoother, and clearer. Immerse yourself in the Filter section above.

Works Citing.
The final list of sources used in your essay from your working bibliography (created under "listing sources" above) is entitled "Works Cited" and is arranged in alphabetical order, author's last name first. The Works Cited page comes at the end of your essay. If the work does not have an author or editor, list the work alphabetically on the works cited page by the first word in the title but ignore the articles "a," "an," and "the." (If you used Modern Language Association formats when you created the "working" bibliography page above, you will have all the information you need to create the final Works Cited page.)

Workout.
In order to make the paper you wrote under the Peel section richer, subject it to research. Research results in discoveries. First of all, the opinions may refute your claim or the reasons that support your claim. If so, you need to reexamine your details and their implications and hidden assumptions. If you still feel your analysis is more correct, then you will need to synthesize any opinions arguing against you and with your own support, argue

against those secondary sources, showing how they fail to consider important details, implications, or lines of reasoning that you found. On the other hand, some of your research will likely support your thesis. You will use these writers and their details, implications, explanations to support your thesis. A more exciting discovery is when secondary sources neither agree nor disagree with you, but give you information that expands your own argument into areas you had not considered.

Always consider using research to compare and contrast your primary material to other similar material. As discussed under Claim above, this will force you to consider details you previously took for granted. In some cases, there will be so many important comparisons and contrasts that you will need to change your thesis.

Fallacies

Fallacies are ways the human mind intentionally or unintentionally cheat-jumps the gap between a detail and its worth. These are referred to as *logical fallacies,* but we think "ideas that pretend to be logical" more accurately describes these blips in critical thinking. Careful inductive thinking based on sound *exemplification*—using a number of examples, using detailed examples, and using the most representative examples—chokes out most fallacies.

Below are three groups of fallacies: Entries listed in Group I are primarily word-play cheats; group II includes fallacies dependent on short-cutting the steps of an argument; group III contains fallacies that appeal directly to people's emotional and intellectual insecurities. In our literature courses, we often require students to mention which fallacies characters either commit or take action to avoid. To see most of these fallacies playing their cheating best, watch Sidney Lumet's 1957 film *Twelve Angry Men*, a great depiction of a logical-fallacy pressure cooker.

Group I—Word-play cheats.

amoeba vocabula: Using vague expressions, such as "kind of," "sort of," "seems to be," which gobble up accurate descriptions of details or support essential to understanding of an argument: "Flannery O'Connor is sort of a dark humor writer and kind of Catholic in her point of view." Writers often use these waffling phrases when they are unsure of their argument or want to avoid seeming aggressive. Moderate positions can be argued without the distracting use of amoebas. Edit them out.

begging the question: Supporting a claim by offering reasons which essentially repeat the claim in different words, also known as circular logic. For example, to say "Sexually explicit literature is objectionable because it is immoral," begs the question because "immorality" is "objectionable." A word becomes a quick-change artist by appearing two times disguised in different costumes.

equivocation: Using the same word in two different senses without acknowledging the shift so that the reader is manipulated into thinking the word means the same thing both times. For instance, "Students should not be taught critical thinking because there are enough people in the world who are too critical" uses the word "critical" first to refer to careful, analytical thinking and the second time to suggest cantankerous, irrational attitudes. However, the writer is pretending that the stem "critical" means the same thing both times.

euphemism: Substituting a more pleasing or important sounding word for a reality that is not so pleasing or important. This cheating permeates the language world. Read the whole Scrub section in the Style unit for examples and problems associated with euphemism.

Group II—Short-cut cheats.

a priori judgment: reaching a conclusion without sufficient evidence, often referred to as a *hasty generalization*. If a writers states, "poetry is always about love or nature," the person ignores poetry about politics, prison, laborers, and demons. The hasty generalization is an error in thinking which can be considered the mother/father of all fallacies: In avoiding a priori judgments, you avoid many of the other fallacies.

ad ignorantium: arguing that something is valid because it has not been proven wrong. Arguments and claims always have the burden of proof. This fallacy is also known as *shifting the burden of proof.* One cannot claim that "Hamlet's fatal flaw is his inability to take decisive action because no one has been able to come up with other weaknesses." Unless the thinker argues how the inability to take decisive action is Hamlet's fatal flaw, the argument is an unsupported, unsubstantiated, invalid opinion.

fallacy of composition: claiming what is true for one fictional or real life occurrence is also automatically true for others with similar dynamics. For example, just because the color white is a symbol for purity, chastity, and goodness in one novel does not mean that white represents purity, chastity, and goodness in all other works of fiction.

non sequitur: providing irrelevant reasons which do not follow a claim. Usually a statement which contains a non-sequitur has a leap in logic where some thinking steps have been skipped, so that the claim and support do not snap together cleanly: "Jane is a pretty girl because she was born and raised in Georgia."

post hoc propter hoc: assuming a causal relationship between two events based just because the two events happened close in time. Also called the false cause fallacy. "I left the house without a sweater and woke up with a cold the next day, therefore forgetting my sweater caused my cold."

either-or fallacy: Reducing points of view by assuming there are only two positions or conclusions, one of which is usually depicted as unattractive. Also referred to as *false dilemma or fallacy of bifurcation.* Polarized thinking also attempts to erase irony and nuance. An ultimatum usually attempts to create a false dilemma: "The protagonist in the story is either a good guy or bad guy" blocks out the idea that the protagonist may be a complex mixture of both.

misapplied generalization: taking a generally true statement, such as "English teachers allow literature to influence their lives," and assume that it is true about a particular group of teachers. This is the opposite of the fallacy of composition.

slippery slope: claiming that a specific action or inaction will inevitably lead to other less desirable actions without arguing how or why this will happen, such as when someone says "If people do not read moral literature, they are bound to lose their sense of morality." Unless you are unusually clairvoyant or have valid data, it is very difficult to know or prove a hypothetical effect or outcome.

subjectivist fallacy: holding onto one's ideas by hiding behind "it's my opinion" as a way of dismissing other arguments. While we are each entitled to our own opinions, when arguing, regardless of whether the subject is academic or personal, strong critical thinkers must back up their opinions with support.

Group III—Appeal-to-insecurities cheats:
ad hominem: substituting a personal attack for a well supported argument about other issues. For example, the statement, "Woody Allen cannot make moral films because he violated social mores by marrying his ex-girlfriend's adopted daughter who is years younger than him," uses personal material to criticize the worth of someone's ability to make an artistic statement. However, one may legitimately and logically attack someone for their personal beliefs if those beliefs are the issue.

ad misercordium: justifying a position by arousing the reader's sense of pity rather than sense of reason. Arousal of pity can be the justifiable end of an argument, but it is a fallacy when pity is used as a distraction for dealing with other issues. For instance, people would use ad misercordium if they argued that Shakespeare's Iago and Melville's Claggert do not deserve our harsh judgment for their evil motives and actions because they had unfair, unhappy pasts.

affective fallacy: judging the worth of a creative work solely by

227

its emotional results. Whether a film, novel, work of art, or poem scares your pants off, jerks tears out of your eyes, chokes you on your own guilt, or makes you feel virtuous in the face of evil personified is largely irrelevant. This judgment is a fallacy because a film, book, or painting might appeal to one's emotions but present a simple-minded view of reality in order to evoke those emotions. The worth of some works are decided by their ability to dramatize social, moral, and psychological insights—such works might arouse our emotions too, but their worth is not based solely on this arousal. Judging works solely by how they entertain or massage emotions, runs the risk of supporting unimportant, unrealistic, or undeserving positions.

bandwagon: arguing that a position is valid or correct because a number of people share the same belief. Conformity is irrelevant support because what others think can be right or wrong, strong or weak. We all know examples in history where people held terrible, regrettable political, scientific, spiritual, or aesthetic positions in order to conform to the masses.

ego es ibi: assuming the only legitimate judgment of the worth of a work of art is based on its ability to create verisimilitude. Much visual and literary art is unconcerned with depicting "real" life and puts emphasis on exaggeration instead. The surreal paintings of Salvador Dali can not be considered "bad" art just because Dali's imagery does not mimic real life.

irrelevant appeals: claiming something is true based on *authority, faith, common sense,* or *moderation* to substantiate a view of reality. Although these notions deserve consideration, they all have inherent weaknesses: authority can be wrong, mired in self-serving values; faith can be unreliable, seduced by time-worn fantasies; common sense can be simple-minded, ignorant of subtleties; moderation can be weak, restrained in emergencies, and a killer of spontaneity. Thomas Jefferson would have snapped his crow quill if someone had suggested that the Declaration of Independence was an unsound document since it lacked what would have been considered a moderate stance at the time he wrote it.

red herring: diverting the difficult issue at hand to an irrelevant issue that has more emotional appeal or is simpler to argue. Also known as a smoke screen. For instance, instead of exploring a fictional character's more subtle thinking and manipulations, a critic might focus only on dramatic actions, or their absence, and make this the center of interest.

straw person: purposely misinterpreting or mistaking an opponent's argument or claim as a way of making it easier to denigrate or attack that argument. For instance, we could argue that Henry James uses involved, long sentences to carefully depict characters' subtle, complex rationalizations for making decisions. Someone who wanted to denigrate this argument might say we are "only impressed by James's wordiness so fail to see how he is a second rate writer."

tu quo que: justifying an action or position by accusing your opponent of the same thing or something equally reprehensible. "Since the clerk at the grocery store was rude to me, I am justified in stealing some peaches."

well poisoning: dismissing someone's insightful arguments because of their prejudiced, self-interested, or negative motivations. Ideas, claims, and arguments must be analyzed and evaluated on their merits and not on the person's moral track record. This fallacy is similar to ad hominem because someone poisons the well by bringing up an irrelevant, negative attribute of an opponent to distract from the issue at hand.

Eclipses

When the procedures of Peel, Filter and Press outlined above do not seem to be working, start questioning your own mental abilities and attitudes. Understanding implications calls on bringing together sensitivity, life experience, education, and imagination, all bounded by reason. Unfortunately, there are many ways this understanding can be eclipsed. One is having a cooked head, a mind that is already decided or biased; the other by having a raw head, a mind lacking in maturity or intuition.

Cooked Heads:

Cooked heads are thinkers who are hard boiled by assumptions and prejudices, self-eclipses called *unwarranted assumptions*. A made-my-mind-up-before-I-thought-about-it writer is often someone who is a mental sloth; other times someone who is either arrogant or insecure, believing his or her life, culture, philosophy, politics, or god is better than everyone else's and so is threatened by new information that might complicate or change these views. Also, this person tends to judge the worth of unique details by shoving them into familiar, general notions that may be true in other situations, but not about the one at hand, a fallacy known as a *misapplied generalization*. At best, a cooked head rots in cliché.

A version of unwarranted assumption occurs when someone's jealousy for another person is unfounded. No matter what information contradicts the jealous person's suspicions, that information is distorted by the jealous person's passion to gather support for reasons to be jealous. Even a sincerely kind act on the suspected person's part is interpreted as an attempt to cover up misdeeds. Maybe someone's kind acts are really not sincere, but maybe they are meant to flatter; to assume that flattery is always a fingerprint for betrayal would be a misapplied generalization because flattery could simply be a weak attempt to gain emotional approval.

Academic reactions to the Brothers Grimm's fairy tales are often based on unwarranted assumptions. Biased by Disney versions, and before rereading the originals, many people assumed that women played primarily passive roles in the original tales, while sentimentalists, also biased by Disney, were sure that the tales expressed unambiguous allegories of good over evil. When a reading of the original tales revealed that more often than not females were the strong character in the tales (sometimes to good ends; sometimes to evil ends) and that often the reader is left with ambiguous feelings about the nature of good and evil, cooked heads had a hard time accepting the true nature of the tales. They still tend to either dismiss the tales on other grounds, such as objecting to their use of the grotesque, or notice only selected tales that support their point.

José Knighton, a poet and explorer who wrote "Eco-Porn and the Manipulation of Desire" for *Wild Earth* (reprinted in *Harper's Magazine*), demonstrates how we are seduced away from the subtle beauty and essential life forms in nature because our minds are prejudiced by dramatic nature photography. We make the unwarranted assumption that the only environment worth protecting is one that is unique or dramatic. For Knighton, our love affair with dramatic landscape photography reflects this moral sensibility. He points out that our desire for dramatic, light-shadow drenched landscape photography is "like pornography" because "it attempts to seduce the beholder by presenting an image divorced from its actual physical context." Sometimes this photography cheats reality by using special filters but its focus on atypical, monumental land forms separated from the surrounding landscape always caters to our unwarranted assumptions. Knighton concludes that because of our unwarranted assumptions, we glamorize "scenic" spots at the expense of caring for more productive overgrown woods, mosquito-ridden swamps, and seemingly empty plains.

Raw Heads.
Even when an observer of details avoids having a cooked head, being *immature* or having *poor intuition* can choke off the crucial understanding of implications. Lacking certain educational or life experiences, an essayist can be insensitive to the importance of a given detail in art, fiction, case studies, historical events, business deals, personal relationships, anything in life. Immaturity can easily result in taking certain details for granted and dismissing others too quickly. Immaturity can also butcher curiosity, allowing impatience to bruise the complexity of details, or loosen insecurity to kill unfamiliar details. Educators will seldom admit that maturity has so much to do with wiring the thinking process. Insight does not enter the brain on a disc; it comes from mental software already sensitive to special input.

Bad intuition or lack of imagination creates the same problem as immaturity. One of the most dangerous unwarranted assumptions educators can make is that logical thinking has nothing to do with these harder to define elements. While intuitive insights finally need to be tested and thought through logically, intuitive knowledge is based on a culmination of hundreds of past experiences that help live-wire the brain to find clues to understanding the significance of the detail at hand. In his book *Creative Evolution*, Henri Bergson points out that intuition is a type of knowledge that is superior to either instinct or intellect when those elements are forced to work independently from each other.

To complicate matters, some thinkers substitute simple-mindedness for careful consideration of reality and call it intuition. For instance, people often want to excuse bad behavior by claiming that they can intuit an inner goodness in a person who has otherwise run amuck, when actually they do not want to accept who someone really is. In "What You See Is the Real You" from *The New York Times*, Willard Gaylin, a Columbia University professor of psychology, argues that implications of actions reveal who people really are, not the feelings and intentions that lay dormant in their inner selves that are never realized. He asks, "Does it matter if Hitler's heart was in the right place?" He points out that the unconscious life of a man may be an "adjunct to understanding him" but not a substitute for his behavior in describing him. "The inner man is a fantasy . . . It has no standing in the real world which we share with each other."

Aberrations of intuition aside, a strong thinker knows that intuitive feelings can short-cut longer thinking processes to find clues that still need to be tested. Intuitive minds can peel to the truth faster than minds dependent on step-by-step reasoning which slosh through reality and are then easily mud-eyed by quick or subtle changes. Intuition allows thinkers to fast reverse and fast forward to look for clues, using those clues as temporary reference points, exploring new sequences that might reveal a previous detail's missing implications. Sometimes this cross-word puzzling is called *lateral thinking* because the thinker is not *vertical thinking*, which would mean using details and implications as building blocks that must follow each other in a predictable, sequential order such as going from small ideas to the large ones they support. Successful business people, reliable critics, sensitive parents, understanding ministers, conscientious students, creative scientists, and others rely on strong intuition. There is not much academia and books like this can do about that.

Index

ABOUT THE AUTHORS

Gary Hoffman studied architecture at University of California Berkeley before studying English and art at the University of California Los Angeles where he received his Master of Arts, then completed post-graduate work and taught English at the University of Southern California. He has taught writing and literature for over twenty-seven years, as well as studio art for eight of those years, at Orange Coast College. He has also been a freelance landscape designer for over twenty-five years. Glynis Hoffman received her Masters of Arts in English at California State University at Fullerton. Before teaching at Orange Coast College, she was a writing consultant and business correspondent. She has taught writing and literature in the California State University system, at several community colleges, and at the Fashion Institute of Design and Merchandising. Gary and Glynis enjoy cooking, viewing international cinema, visiting architectural sights, gardening, and reading.

ORDERING

Single orders: For less than ten copies of *Adios, Strunk & White,* please have your local or virtual bookstore or library order from their distributor or wholesaler.

Textbook orders: For classroom use, your campus bookstore must order directly from Verve Press (SAN 659-0598):

> Verve Press
> P.O. Box 1997
> Huntington Beach, CA 92647